"Dr. LeMay's research on Millennials was mind blowing. The media executives left her training with a better understanding of best practices and practical advice on how to implement change in their newsrooms on a global scale."

Sonia Tucker, *Former CNN's Chief of Protocol Affairs, and current founder of Global Media Connections*

"For employers, managers and people who need a better understanding of Millennials, Dr. LeMay's book is a must read. There's been so much misinformation about Millennials. It's refreshing to read a book that lays it all out in real terms that everyone can understand."

Don Jurgens, *Managing Director, large financial services company*

"As Millennials become the dominant generation in the workforce, Dr. LeMay's book on Millennials and intergenerational conflict provides a wealth of information and ideas for scholars and practitioners alike."

Stacy Campbell, *Ph.D., Professor of Management, Coles College of Business, Kennesaw State University*

"Dr. LeMay's interpretation of the data she collected sheds new light on a subject that challenges most employers today: How to successfully engage Millennials in the workplace. Her ability to distill the various sources of information into a very readable book is the real value of the work. It is a very effective guide for both executives and trainers alike."

Louis Coroso, *Former Director of Leadership and Management Development for a large financial services company and retired senior U.S. Army officer*

D1431058

Millennials and Conflict in the Workplace

This book unravels the mysteries and confusion surrounding Millennials. They are now the largest group in the labor force and their presence redefines the workplace for many organizations. Many older workers, who struggle to understand Millennials, often define them by stereotypes rather than their actual attributes. The historical and social events that occurred when Millennials were growing up are reviewed, which can result in traits and values specific to this cohort. The research behind this book explores the conflict styles of Millennials compared to Generation Xers and Baby Boomers – the unique strategies they are likely to use to address conflict in the workplace. This book shares the results of interviews and focus groups providing first-hand accounts from Millennials and non-Millennials about their work interactions. And the results from approximately 11,000 test-takers of the Thomas-Kilmann Conflict Mode Instrument provide fascinating findings about generational differences in conflict styles. Millennials grew up with technology at their fingertips and tend to avoid conflict and seek advice from their online support groups. The book will also dig into Millennials' powerful use of social media and how they use it to further their causes. They have a strong desire to know what's happening now and find it difficult to "turn off." This book explores generational differences and finds an increase in unassertive styles in Millennial males. This work shares what Millennials want and value in a workplace and what employers can do to recruit and retain this valuable cohort. Millennials' diversity, political and social engagement, and the implications for the broader society are explored. This research fills an important gap in the research on generational cohorts and conflict management and provides valuable information to scholars and practitioners alike.

Dr. Cynthia Pearce LeMay is a senior-level researcher with over 30 years of executive and consulting experience, focusing on conflict resolution strategies, intergenerational conflict, and the Millennial generation. In the corporate retirement industry, Cynthia last served as Vice President for Principal Financial Group. Prior to Principal Financial, she was a member

of senior management at Northern Trust Retirement Consulting. During her career, she has negotiated billion-dollar agreements, participated in union negotiations, and led a Human Resources department. She has earned lifetime certification as a Senior Professional in Human Resources from the Society for Human Resource Management and is a certified Mediator. Cynthia holds a Ph.D. from Kennesaw State University, USA, where she teaches in the business school while continuing her consulting and training business.

Millennials and Conflict in the Workplace

Understand the Unique Traits of the Now Generation

Cynthia Pearce LeMay

Routledge
Taylor & Francis Group

NEW YORK AND LONDON

Designed cover image: © Getty Images

First published 2023
by Routledge
605 Third Avenue, New York, NY 10158

and by Routledge
4 Park Square, Milton Park, Abingdon, Oxon, OX14 4RN

Routledge is an imprint of the Taylor & Francis Group, an informa business

© 2023 Cynthia Pearce LeMay

The right of Cynthia Pearce LeMay to be identified as
author of this work has been asserted in accordance with
sections 77 and 78 of the Copyright, Designs and Patents
Act 1988.

Library of Congress Cataloging-in-Publication Data
Names: LeMay, Cynthia Pearce, author.
Title: Millennials and conflict in the workplace :
understand the unique traits of the now generation /
Cynthia Pearce LeMay.
Description: New York, NY : Routledge, 2023. |
Includes bibliographical references and index. |
Identifiers: LCCN 2022027728 (print) |
LCCN 2022027729 (ebook) | ISBN 9781032160337 (hardback) |
ISBN 9781032160320 (paperback) | ISBN 9781003246824 (ebook)
Subjects: LCSH: Conflict of generations in the workplace. |
Intergenerational relations. | Young adults—Employment. |
Generation Y—Employment. | Personnel management.
Classification: LCC HF5549.5.C75 L46 2023 (print) |
LCC HF5549.5.C75 (ebook) | DDC 658.30084—dc23/eng/20220616
LC record available at https://lccn.loc.gov/2022027728
LC ebook record available at https://lccn.loc.gov/2022027729

ISBN: 9781032160337 (hbk)
ISBN: 9781032160320 (pbk)
ISBN: 9781003246824 (ebk)

DOI: 10.4324/9781003246824

Typeset in Bembo
by codeMantra

For my mother, June Pearce – you are a trailblazer who showed me anything is possible. Thank you for your unwavering love and support throughout this journey.

Contents

Foreword

Millennials and Conflict in the Workplace: Understand the Unique Traits of the Now Generation is a complete and thorough reading that dismantles many of the negative stereotypes against the largest generational cohort of our times, Millennials. Dr. Cynthia Pearce LeMay's book represents a major contribution to the literature on generations in the workplace and society. It shares insights on the dominant conflict resolution styles of all the generations, including Generation Xers and Baby Boomers, and their impact on voting behavior, attitudes towards diversity, and social media use. The significance of this interdisciplinary research project transcends the field of Conflict Management and impacts the disciplines of Sociology, Psychology, Political Science, and Management.

With its theoretical and methodological rigor, *Millennials and Conflict in the Workplace* stands out from all the other books on Millennials across all disciplines. Grounded on the Thomas-Kilmann theory on conflict resolution style, Dr. LeMay employed an impressive arsenal of methods of investigation to increase the validity and reliability of her study. Using mixed methods, *Millennials and Conflict in the Workplace* is based on longitudinal and same-age quantitative studies with 10,911 participants coupled with interviews and focus groups with approximately 50 participants. The size of this large national sample and impressive triangulation with qualitative methods of investigation elevates *Millennials and Conflict in the Workplace* to the status of essential readings on Millennials. The book is of great value to students, scholars and educators, managers, conflict mediators, counselors, consultants, journalists, social workers, and many other professionals who are managing multigenerational organizations. I hope that you will enjoy this unique scientific study revealing the dynamics of generations in the workplace!

Darina Lepadatu, Ph.D.
President of Georgia Sociological Association

Preface

Having worked in the corporate sector for many years, I noticed how different generational cohorts approached work and, at times, the conflict this created. For my Ph.D. research, my goal was to conduct a rigorous study that would lead to practical recommendations for managers and employees in the workplace. As Millennials are the largest cohort in society and the workplace, and will remain so through 2041, they will have significant impact. They are the 'digital natives,' raised with information at their fingertips and are always in touch with what's happening now. To study Millennials, a mixed methods approach was used combining interviews and focus groups as well as statistical analysis of 11,000 participants. While the focus is on Millennials, other generations are included to provide comparison of generational differences. The results find Millennials are more likely to avoid face-to-face conflict and rely on their online support group for help and advice. There are also fascinating findings about how Millennials differ from other cohorts, particularly males who employ less assertive conflict styles than males from other generational cohorts. This research also looks at the political and social issues of importance to Millennials as they will continue to advocate for change aligned with their values and interests. This diverse, talented, and technologically savvy group will redefine our places of employment and advocate for change addressing issues including racial inequality and climate change. They will favor a larger role for government and programs such as health care for all and paid parental leave. My hope is that this book will clear the fog of confusion surrounding Millennials and help organizations recruit and retain this valuable cohort.

Acknowledgments

I would like to acknowledge and thank the following individuals for their contributions.

Dr. Darina Lepadatu, Ph.D., thank you for your continued encouragement, support, and expertise to steer this research. Your deep knowledge across sociology, business, conflict resolution, and qualitative methods was invaluable.

Dr. Stacy Campbell, Ph.D., your expertise in generational research and research methodologies provided significant suggestions and refinement to this study. Thank you for your continued feedback to strengthen this work.

Dr. Joshua Johnson, Ph.D., thank you for your willingness to field numerous questions about quantitative research and provide suggestions to make this research more robust. Your statistical expertise was instrumental to this study.

Ross P. Williams, MSJ, journalist extraordinaire, many thanks for your valuable contributions and suggestions. This book would not have been complete without input from a talented Millennial.

A special thanks to all those who volunteered their time to participate in this study.

To my family – thank you for your support and encouragement.

Chapter 1

The Millennial Majority

What's in a Name?

Let's step back for a moment to the halcyon days of the 1990s and 2000s, ad executives, journalists, generational researchers, and others tried to come up with a new catchy name for the generation following Generation X. Generation Y seemed like the obvious choice, and that's what the folks at Ad Age (1993) came up with in August of 1993. Generation Y is still sometimes used, but even Ad Age conceded in 2011 that Millennials was a better name, according to USA Today (Horovitz, 2012).

Over on PBS, they tried out "Generation Next" in a 2007 docuseries focusing on the lives of American youths getting started in the world. That name has some pros. It describes what it is referring to, the next generation. It rhymes with Generation X. It brings to mind Star Trek: The Next Generation and all the technological doodads this cohort was sure to use. But as a descriptor, Generation Next went the way of free America Online, CDs, and dial-up internet. Others thought it would be a good idea to name the generation after the major events they lived through such as the 9/11 and some proposed names like the Echo Boomers or Baby Boomlets, in reference to the fact that the generation was large and mainly the progeny of Baby Boomers.

In the end, it was actually two researchers we'll meet in the next chapter, Neil Howe and William Strauss, who are often credited with coining the term Millennial to refer to the generation, and it stuck. Howe told Forbes in 2015 that it was clear in the early 1990s that the generation to come would be different and needed a distinct name, and the oldest members of the generation would be coming of age around the turn of the millennium (Sharf, 2015).

Starting in the 1600s, the word millennium had an apocalyptic connotation related to the 1,000-year period after which Christ would return to earth. It carried the idea of the end of the old world and the birth of a new one and captures the sense of change people felt as the calendar approached the year 2000. It also aptly describes the generation as pioneers

DOI: 10.4324/9781003246824-1

in the new, interconnected world and the radical cultural shifts they have lived through.

As a side note, Gen Z really dodged a bullet when you go back and look at some of the names proposed for their generation. Tossed-out ideas include references to the world of tech, including Generation Wii, named after the once-popular video game console made by Nintendo, and sounding much less favorable than "the Greatest Generation"; iGeneration, after Apple's line of products; Gen Tech; Digital Natives; and the Net Generation. Luckily for them, Generation Z stuck, and the cheeky term Zoomer was a later addition, playing on the Boomers before them. Thus, they were spared the indignity of explaining to their grandchildren what a Nintendo Wii was and why their generation was named after a game where you shake a remote control at a television to make your character hit a tennis ball.

So that's how the two youngest generations got their names, and if, before reading this, you've ever found yourself wanting to know why Millennials are called that, our research shows there is a good chance you are one since Millennials like to know "why."

The Sizable Millennial Cohort

Today, it is more important than ever to understand the Millennial generation as they are the largest cohort in the United States. In 2000, Baby Boomers were the majority numbering 78.3 million strong compared to 76.4 million Millennials, 67.5 million Generation Xers, and 39.3 million individuals from the Silent Generation per the U.S. Census Bureau (2018). It was in 2005 that the large Millennial demographic overtook the previously dominant Baby Boomer generation, reaching 78.8 million in size versus 78.2 million Baby Boomers (U.S. Census Bureau, 2018). By 2020, Millennials significantly increased their size relative to other generations numbering 85.2 million compared to 67.6 million Generation Zs, 70.9 million Generation Xers, 73.5 million Baby Boomers, and 20.6 million from the Silent Generation (U.S. Census Bureau, 2022). The growth of generations in the United States is shown in Figure 1.1.

The size of the generations in the United States in 2020 is shown in Figure 1.2. It is interesting to note that Baby Boomers are still slightly larger than Generation X.

Not only are Millennials a sizable generation today, but also they will remain a majority for almost two more decades Census Bureau projections say (U.S. Census Bureau, 2021b, 2022). And, in 2040, Millennials will still outnumber the following generation, Generation Z, albeit by a slim margin, with Millennials numbering 89.6 million compared to 89 million Generation Z members (U.S. Census Bureau, 2021b). As such, Millennials will have 19 years from today as the majority cohort to effect change. How will the other generations look in 2040? Generation X will number

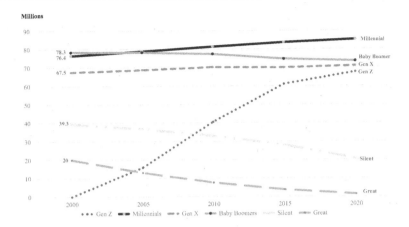

Figure 1.1 Generation Sizes in the United States: 2000 to 2020.

Note. Adapted from *Intercensal Estimates of the Resident Population by Single Year of Age, Sex, Race, and Hispanic origin for the United States: April 1, 2000 to July 1, 2010*, by U.S. Census Bureau, 2018 (https://www.census.gov/data/datasets/time-series/demo/popest/intercensal-2000-2010-state.html). In the public domain; Adapted from *Annual Estimates of the Resident Population by Single Year of Age and Sex for the United States: April 2, 2010 to July 1, 2019*, Main series, by U.S. Census Bureau, 2021a https://www.census.gov/data/tables/time-series/demo/popest/2010s-counties-total.html#par_textimage. In the public domain; Adapted from *National Demographic Analysis Tables: 2020. Total U.S. Resident Population by Age, Sex, and Series: April 1, 2020*. Middle Series, by U.S. Census Bureau, 2022 (https://www.census.gov/data/tables/2020/demo/popest/2020-demographic-analysis-tables.html). In the public domain.

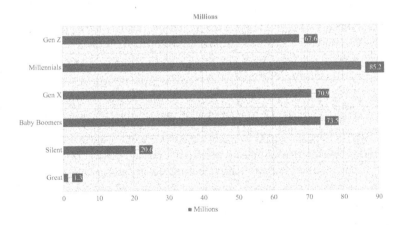

Figure 1.2 Generation Sizes in the United States 2020.

Note. Adapted from *National Demographic Analysis Tables: 2020. Total U.S. Resident Population by Age, Sex, and Series: April 1, 2020*. Middle Series, by U.S. Census Bureau, 2022 (https://www.census.gov/data/tables/2020/demo/popest/2020-demographic-analysis-tables.html). In the public domain.

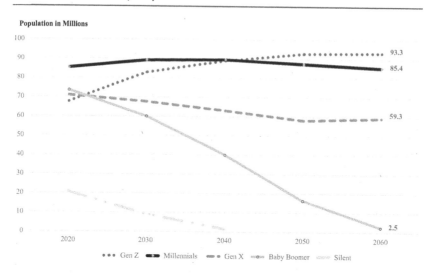

Population in Millions

Figure 1.3 Projected Populations in the United States: 2020 through 2060.

Note. Adapted from 2017 National Population Datasets: Projections for the United States: 2017:2060, by U.S. Census Bureau, 2021b (https://www.census.gov/data/datasets/2017/demo/popproj/2017-popproj.html). In the public domain; Adapted from National Demographic Analysis Tables: 2020. Total U.S. Resident Population by Age, Sex, and Series: April 1, 2020. Middle Series, by U.S. Census Bureau, 2022 (https://www.census.gov/data/tables/2020/demo/popest/2020-demographic-analysis-tables.html). In the public domain.

63.1 million, Baby Boomers 40 million, and Silent Generation will be at 1.5 million (U.S. Census Bureau, 2021b). The turn away from a Millennial majority starts in 2041 when Generation Z is projected to outnumber Millennials and by 2050, Generation Z will number 92.8 million compared to 87.4 million Millennials, 58.1 million Generation Xers, and 16.3 million Baby Boomers (U.S. Census Bureau, 2021b). These population projections are shown in Figure 1.3.

Millennials Enter the Workforce

While there are varying definitions of the Millennial generation, the research presented in this book uses birth dates from 1982 to 2000, dates used by the U.S. Census Bureau when this research project started. As such, Millennials today range in age from 22 to 40, with the majority being in the workforce full-time. The influx of Millennials entering the labor force over the past decade has significantly changed the composition of the workplace. Millennials became the largest generation in the workplace in 2016, and by 2019, there were nearly 65 million Millennials in the workforce compared with about 56 million Gen Xers and 36 million Baby Boomers (U.S. Bureau of Labor Statistics, 2019, 2022). Looking back at 2005 through 2010, the number of Baby Boomer employees declined relative to Generation X employees (U.S. Bureau of Labor Statistics, 2022). By 2010, there were 56.8 million Generation Xers and 55.6 million Baby Boomers (U.S. Bureau of Labor Statistics, 2022). However, as Generation X is a smaller cohort than both Baby Boomers and Millennials, they only held the majority size in the workplace from approximately 2010 to 2015, with Millennials taking the lead in 2016 (U.S. Bureau of Labor Statistics, 2022).

While Baby Boomers had been staying in the workforce longer and delaying retirement, there has been a recent increase in Baby Boomer retirements since the Covid-19 pandemic as reported by Richard Fry (2020) with Pew Research. Sometimes dubbed the "great retirement," similar to the pandemic-related "great resignation" which we'll talk about in Chapter 4, this uptick in retirements will impact the makeup of the labor force, at least in the short term. However, it is important to note that it is too early to say if these retirements are temporary and if these older adults will return to the labor force in other jobs.

By 2021, there were 11.9 million Generation Zs, 66.5 million Millennials, 54.3 million Generation Xers, 27.4 million Baby Boomers, and only 1.2 million Silents in the labor force (U.S. Bureau of Labor Statistics, 2022). The generations in the United States Labor Force from 2000 to 2021 are shown in Figure 1.4.

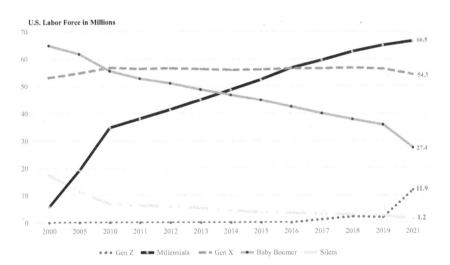

Figure 1.4 Generations in the U.S. Labor Force.

Note. Labor Force includes individuals age 16 or older who are working or looking for work excluding inmates of institutions and active duty in the Armed Forces, Adapted from *Labor Force Statistics from the Current Population: Employment Status of the Civilian Noninstitutional Population Detailed by Age from Annual Average Archived Data 2000 to 2021*, by U.S. Bureau of Labor Statistics, 2022 (https://www.bls.gov/cps/cpsaat03.htm). In the public domain.

To use a term popularized by famed Millennial artist Miley Cyrus, Millennials came into the workplace like a "wrecking ball," armed with their participation trophies, college degrees, and smartphone apps to question the status quo and change the way work is done, but to many older employers, perhaps more familiar with Billy Ray than Miley, this generation still represents something of a mystery. We heard in our interviews that Millennials don't have the same priorities as older workers, who say Millennials want everything handed to them. Many Millennials think they know a better way of doing things or at a minimum want to be able to suggest new ways of doing things. And Millennials may not value company loyalty as much as older workers.

This recently achieved Millennial majority in the workplace results in a new organizational culture where the ideals and decisions of Millennials have substantial impact. For many businesses, this has brought change in the workplace including open office plans, shared workspaces, and rooms for relaxation and downtime during the day. A study from Future Workplace commissioned by Plantronics, now part of global communications company Poly, found that the younger a worker is, the more he or she wants to work in an open office (Poly, 2019). The survey found 56% of Millennials prefer an open floor plan, while only 47% of Gen Xers and 38% of Boomers feel the same.

Matthew, a Baby Boomer executive in the financial industry interviewed for this research project, shared that his company was going through a complete overhaul of their office space to appeal to their Millennial workers. The managers were losing their coveted private offices with windows and being moved to the interior of the office space, freeing up the exterior space with windows for younger workers. He said:

> The outside will have low walls so people can see each other, and, you know, very open and very conducive to getting together and working as a team. It's called 'the neighborhood,' and you can sit there, but you're not supposed to have anything personal left at your station because the next day somebody else may be sitting there when you come in.

In some companies, high-school-style lockers are being installed to accommodate this new style of work where you don't have your own desk. Another recent office design features small rooms for meetings or personal phone calls, providing needed privacy given the lack of individual offices. Even the names of these rooms are non-traditional such as "The Cupboard," "The Junk Drawer" and "The Cookie Jar." But how the office furniture is arranged is just the beginning. In the coming chapters, we'll journey into the world of Millennials to better understand them and what they want in the workplace.

To begin this discussion, it is important to understand the characteristics of Millennials rather than rely on stereotypes. Ask an older worker what adjectives come to mind when they think of Millennials, and you'll probably hear some variation of lazy, privileged, coddled, disloyal, or overly self-focused. But as we reveal in the next chapter, some of these stereotypes are not supported by research. In Chapter 2, we will discuss the historical and social events that occurred when Millennials were growing up as events experienced during one's formative years result in traits and values specific to that group of individuals.

To better understand Millennials, we will examine research which reveals, among other things, that Millennials are more technologically savvy but less skilled at written and oral communication than other generations, have higher expectations in the workplace, are distrustful, prefer working in teams, and think differently about social issues. Understanding these traits will help to explain how Millennials interact and manage conflict in the workplace and how managers can best take advantage of their skills to keep them happy and help the bottom line.

Drexel, a Baby Boomer and business executive for a large organization in the Southeast United States, has watched multiple generations take their place in the world of work. To him, Millennials are less realistic and more transient than preceding generations. "They don't understand the way the work world functions, necessarily," Drexel said. "And that, I think, leads to the transient-ness of it. Instead of working through obstacles, they tend to jettison the work experience and move to something else."

However, Millennials tend to stand up for themselves and are less attached to the old way of doing things, Drexel added:

> They'll prosecute their opinion passionately. Very passionately. They don't take the things that a Boomer would take. Precedent. Established norms. Work flows. Impact on others. They don't see those as being barriers that should contain them into anything that they want to do.

Drexel and Matthew are two of the participants involved in the research leading up to this book. We heard from them and others through one-on-one interviews and focus groups. In subsequent chapters, we'll hear older workers share their observations about getting along with Millennials in the workplace, as well as from Millennials themselves describing their views of conflict in the workplace and what they need to be their best on the job.

The Research

Before we start, we'll briefly touch on the research behind the findings in this book. If you're not fond of statistics and numbers, hang in there as we'll be brief, and this background will help you understand the results we present later on. When we speak about the qualitative research underpinning the findings discussed in this book, we're talking about the interviews and focus groups conducted to hear first-hand accounts from participants. We talked to approximately 50 different people, male and female Millennials and non-Millennials, and continued these discussions until no new information was forthcoming. Throughout the book, you'll hear from Millennials, Generation Xers, and Baby Boomers about what they've seen in the workplace and how they handle conflict in their places of work. This discussion provides insight directly from employees about their personal experiences.

Using this analysis, the interviews and focus groups ultimately revealed the following predominant themes for Millennials: tendency to avoid and withdraw from conflict; preference for a contributing/learning environment that promotes creativity and innovation; the use of online or outside support groups to help with conflict situations; holding high expectations and exhibiting entitled behavior; impatient with a tendency to leave an organization if one's desires are not met; wanting to know why when asked to do something; wanting workplace flexibility including the freedom to establish work hours and schedules; preference for team over individual; desiring and soliciting attention; and feeling judged and defensive. Millennials were also more apt to identify social movements of interest including women's rights, LGBTQ, and the environment. These themes will be further discussed in the later chapters of this book.

Along the way, in addition to meeting more people interviewed for this book, we'll also delve into the statistical analysis of the answers given by 11,000 participants to determine their conflict styles and look at the fascinating results showing how these styles vary by generation. That's where the quantitative portion of our research comes in. Quantitative research means numbers and hard data – things you can count or measure. We'll get into the nitty-gritty starting in Chapter 3, but the nutshell explanation is that we used the results of thousands of questionnaires spanning over a decade that identify the conflict styles of workers from different generations and sort them into five established conflict groups. From there, we were able to dig into the numbers and make comparisons between the generations, separating out important factors like gender, education, and workplace ranking.

This quantitative research was possible due to The Myers Briggs Company supporting a request for conflict styles data for test takers of the Thomas-Kilmann Conflict Mode Instrument with specified birth years over a 13-year span. Data was requested from three distinct time periods, 2006, 2012, and 2018. In order to include the youngest Baby Boomers while still capturing Millennials old enough to be active in the workplace, 2006 was selected as the first database year. Starting with 2006 as the first data collection point, 2012 and 2018 were selected as the other two data collection years to provide equal spacing between data collection, with six years between each included database. For the three time periods of 2006, 2012, and 2018, included in the dataset, Millennial ages are 21/22, 27/28, and 34/35; Generation X ages are 27/28, 33/34, and 40/41; and Baby Boomer ages are 44/45, 50/51, and 57/58.

As there are limitations in both qualitative and quantitative research, we wanted to use both methods in the research leading up to this book to provide the strengths of both methods and allow the strength of one to balance the weakness of the other. The qualitative methods employed in this study may have greater accuracy or validity than quantitative methods as data can be verified with participants. In other words, you are hearing directly from participants and can ask questions to make sure the responses are accurately understood. However, the trustworthiness or reliability of qualitative methods may be less than with quantitative methods. When dealing with numerical data, the results may be more reliable. As such, using both qualitative interviews and focus groups along with the quantitative statistical analysis will improve the rigor of the results.

While many research projects start with quantitative methods, the desire of this study was to begin with interviews and focus groups to obtain individual and group accounts that provide personal anecdotes of intergenerational workplace conflict. The rich data obtained from first-hand accounts of both Millennials and non-Millennials in the workplace sets the stage for the quantitative analysis to further explore the conflict styles of Millennials, Generation Xers, and Baby Boomers.

The Questions

The goal of the research leading up to this book was to answer three main questions starting with "How do Millennials manage conflict in the workplace?" Experts recognize many approaches to conflict. Some people avoid it at all costs, withdrawing and letting others have their way to maintain unity while perhaps building up lingering grudges under the surface. Others view every little dust-up as a chance to compete to show their dominance, succeeding in the short term but alienating coworkers more prone to compromising or collaborating. It's important to note that people are all unique and not everyone utilizes the same conflict style every time a squabble arises. Even the most timid individuals can stand up for themselves when they feel strongly enough, and the most domineering leader can know when it's wiser to back down and live to fight another day. Still, people tend toward certain styles based on a number of factors including their personality and upbringing, which ties into the events that shaped them growing up and their generational cohort. To answer this question of how Millennials manage conflict in the workplace, we relied on the interviews and focus groups we told you about. These findings are presented in Chapter 3.

Our second research question that we'll talk about in this book is "What are the dominant conflict styles of Millennials, Generation Xers, and Baby Boomers?" Older generations we spoke with are prone to say Millennials can't stand conflict and flee to their online safe spaces at the first sign of disagreement. Knowing how Millennials respond to conflicts is one thing, but to truly understand what makes them unique, we need to categorize their conflict style and see how their styles differ from those of other generational cohorts. Our large data spanning a 13-year time period allows us to look at conflict styles by generational cohort, providing insight on the conflict styles in the workplace over the past decade. In Chapter 3, in addition to discussing what we heard in our interviews and focus groups about workplace conflict, we'll present the results from the analysis of data from approximately 11,000 test takers of the Thomas-Kilmann Conflict Mode Instrument.

The Thomas-Kilmann data includes data not only from Millennials, but from Baby Boomers and Generation Xers as well to find out whether Millennials are actually more likely to avoid conflict than their older coworkers. Then, to add another layer to the research, we will also look at differences between same-age Millennials and Generation Xers so we can say with more certainty if the differences we find in conflict styles are due to one's cohort membership rather than simply due to age.

That brings us to our third research question, "How do the conflict styles of Millennials compare with Gen Xers at the same age?" It could be the case that 25-to-30-year-olds are more likely to avoid conflict simply because they are younger and therefore feel less free to ruffle feathers or rock the boat. While our second research question about dominant conflict styles provides insight on the different generational conflict styles in the workplace over the 13-year study period and how those change over time, we will take a deeper look to rule out age as a complicating factor. To accomplish this, we'll go back into the data and make comparisons of Generation Xers when they were 27/28 and 33/34 against same-age Millennials. By isolating age, we can assume that the results we find are due to one's cohort membership. These findings will be discussed in Chapter 3.

As we researched our three main questions, several other findings emerged which we will talk about in this book. While workplace conflict is unavoidable, in an ideal situation the parties will be able to come to a compromise, shake hands, and get back to work congenially. In reality, however, conflict sometimes ends with simmering resentment or when one party says goodbye to the company, an outcome that is often detrimental to the business. And our data and interviews both suggest Millennials are more prone than other generations to bow out when they are not satisfied at work. This has led to stereotypes of the generation as entitled quitters who want benefits that previous generations feel they only received after putting in their time. In Chapter 4, we'll take a look at what our interview subjects and research tell us about what bosses can do to keep their Millennial workforce happy and avoid the stress of a constantly turning-over workforce. These findings are especially helpful in a post-pandemic workplace where employers are vying to attract workers.

In Chapter 4, we'll also talk about several other things we learned in our interviews about workplace interactions, including how Millennials feel they are sometimes judged by older folks and by the media. Other findings from the research include that Millennials desire flexibility and feedback and value workplaces that provide opportunities to learn and grow. In this chapter, we'll dig deep into what Millennials want and desire in their places of work. It's interesting to point out that now that Millennials are the largest cohort in the workplace, they hold some measure of power over employers who may have different thoughts on how the workplace should run and how workers should be compensated.

Another important topic covered in this book is the influence of gender on conflict style which we'll explore in Chapter 5. In this chapter, we'll reveal what we learned in the interviews about how men and women of different generations navigate conflict and salary negotiations. Then, we'll dig into our conflict style data once again to look at how males and females compare. We will look at the conflict styles of male and female Millennials, Generation Xers, and Baby Boomers. First, we'll look at how male conflict styles compare to those of females and whether that varies within and across generations. Then, we will look at same-gender comparisons of conflict styles to look for similarities or differences in male-to-male or female-to-female styles across the generations. For example, are younger females more likely to use a particular conflict style compared to older females? And do males differ in conflict style by generation? The results reveal some interesting findings.

A theme often raised in the interviews is the technological superiority of Millennials, not unexpected for these "digital natives" as they were raised with technology at their fingertips. Millennials grew up connected with their friends and the world through the internet. However, in talking with our participants, we learned some fascinating things about how Millennials use these skills and the significant impact of social media. These findings will be discussed in Chapter 6 where we'll talk about how Millennials harness the power of social media and the impact this has in the workplace, the political realm, and society overall.

Before we say goodbye in Chapter 8, we'll bring in some additional research to look at the politics, diversity, and social views of Millennials and how that relates to the workplace. In Chapter 7, we'll look at the social movements Millennials are engaging in and the impact their generation is having on our society. Millennials want to be part of something bigger than earning a paycheck, to feel like they are making the world a better place every time they punch into work. We'll talk about how one group of Millennials who suffered a terrible tragedy used their anger to lobby for the goals they care about and talk about how leaders can maintain their Millennial morale by making the workplace a space for furthering those issues.

One of the main benefits of this book is to re-introduce the Millennial workforce to older employees, to clear the fog of confusion that sometimes seems to surround this generation. The extensive interviews and research underpinning this book will offer insight into how Millennials resolve conflict. But further, we'll share insights from Millennials themselves with recommendations on how to leverage their considerable skills and make workplaces more Millennial-friendly. Now that you understand what the book and the research are about, let's meet the Millennials.

References

Fry, R. (2020, November 9). *The pace of boomer retirements has accelerated in the past year.* Pew Research Center. https://www.pewresearch.org/fact-tank/2020/11/09/the-pace-of-boomer-retirements-has-accelerated-in-the-past-year/

Fry, R. (2021, November 4). *Amid the pandemic, a rising share of older U.S. adults are now retired.* https://www.pewresearch.org/fact-tank/2021/11/04/amid-the-pandemic-a-rising-share-of-older-u-s-adults-are-now-retired/

Generation Y. (1993, August 30). *Ad Age,* 16.

Horovitz, B. (2012). *After Gen X, Millennials, what should next generation be?* USA Today. https://web.archive.org/web/20200320040227/http://usatoday30.usatoday.com/money/advertising/story/2012-05-03/naming-the-next-generation/54737518/1

Howe, N., & Strauss, W. (2000). *Millennials rising: The next great generation.* Vintage Books.

Kilmann, R.H., & Thomas, K.W. (2009). *Conflict mode instrument.* Mountain View.

Leung, R. (2004). *The echo boomers.* CBS News. https://www.cbsnews.com/news/the-echo-boomers-01-10-2004/

Millennial (adj.). Etymology. (n.d.). https://www.etymonline.com/word/millennial.

Poly. (2019, May 13). *Gen Z says they are most productive when working around noise; Baby boomers say "Shhhh!" They need quiet to get work done. But the biggest open office distraction? Your colleagues.* https://investor.poly.com/news-events/News/news-details/2019/Gen-Z-Says-They-Are-Most-Productive-When-Working-Around-Noise-Baby-Boomers-Say-SHHHH-They-Need-Quiet-to-Get-Work-Done/default

Public Broadcasting Service. (2007). *Generation next.* PBS. https://www.pbs.org/newshour/tag/generationnext

Sharf, S. (2015, August 24). *What is a 'Millennial' anyway? Meet the man who coined the phrase.* Forbes. https://www.forbes.com/sites/samanthasharf/2015/08/24/what-is-a-millennial-anyway-meet-the-man-who-coined-the-phrase/?sh=698d33374a05

Strauss, W., & Howe, N. (1997). *The fourth turning: An American prophecy.* Broadway Books.

U.S. Bureau of Labor Statistics. (2016, August 1). *39 percent of managers in 2015 were women.* https://www.bls.gov/opub/ted/2016/39-percent-of-managers-in-2015-were-women.htm

U.S. Bureau of Labor Statistics. (2019, September 4). *Employment projections: Civilian labor force participation rate by age, sex, race, and ethnicity.* https://www.bls.gov/emp/tables/civilian-labor-force-participation-rate.htm

U.S. Bureau of Labor Statistics. (2022, January 20). *Labor force statistics from the current population: Employment status of the civilian noninstitutional population detailed by age from annual average archived data 2000 to 2021.* https://www.bls.gov/cps/cpsaat03.htm

U.S. Census Bureau. (2015, June 25). *Millennials outnumber baby boomers and are far more diverse, census bureau reports.* https://www.census.gov/newsroom/archives/2015-pr/cb15-113.html

U.S. Census Bureau. (2016). *Annual estimates of the resident population by single year of age and sex for the United States: April 1, 2010 to July 1, 2015.* https://www2.census.gov/programs-surveys/popest/datasets/2010–2015/national/asrh/

U.S. Census Bureau. (2018, September 26). *Intercensal estimates of the resident population by single year of age, sex, race, and Hispanic origin for the United States: April 1, 2000 to July 1, 2010.* https://www.census.gov/data/datasets/time-series/demo/popest/intercensal-2000-2010-state.html

U.S. Census Bureau. (2021a, October 8). *Annual estimates of the resident population by single year of age and sex for the United States: April 2, 2010 to July 1, 2019.* https://www.census.gov/data/tables/time-series/demo/popest/2010s-counties-total.html#par_textimage

U.S. Census Bureau. (2021b). *2017 national population datasets: Projected population by single year of age, sex, race, and Hispanic origin for the United States 2016:2060.* https://www.census.gov/data/datasets/2017/demo/popproj/2017-popproj.html

U.S. Census Bureau. (2022, March 10). *National Demographic Analysis Tables: 2020. Total U.S. Resident Population by Age, Sex, and Series: April 1, 2020.* https://www.census.gov/data/tables/2020/demo/popest/2020-demographic-analysis-tables.html

Chapter 2

Meet the Millennials

Who Are the Millennials?

Thousands of years from now, archeologists combing through the fragments of our civilization will have their work cut out for them describing the Millennial generation. Some sources describe them as coddled narcissists unable to subsist on their own and caring more about social media clout than supporting the economy. Other sources say they were adept at the technology of the time and dedicated to improving the world despite being born into a time of social upheaval. Given their dedication to social causes, it's quite possible that Millennials, along with their Generation Z friends, may be credited with stemming the effects of climate change and addressing social inequities. We can imagine this debate will spark more than a few thrown drinks and shouted threats at the 8264 Interplanetary Archaeology Conference on Ganymede, but let's go ahead and preemptively set the record straight: both sides make some valid points.

Research has found that Millennials are more narcissistic and self-focused than other generations (Foster et al., 2003; Sessa et al., 2007; Twenge at al., 2008). In one study, Jean Twenge from San Diego State University and her colleagues looked at data from college students in the United States who completed the Narcissistic Personality Index between 1979 and 2006, finding higher levels of narcissism in more recent college students (Twenge et al., 2008). Uncoincidentally, Millennials in the research leading to this book were more likely to talk about themselves than Baby Boomers or Generation Xers – analyzing the interview data from Millennials, 73% of the references they made were about themselves, while 27% of the references were about non-Millennials. When asked essentially the same questions, non-Millennials were more apt to talk about Millennials than about themselves. For non-Millennials, the numbers were nearly reversed. Seventy-four percent of their responses were about Millennials with only 26% of the references about themselves. Granted, while this research was introduced as focused on Millennials, this striking difference in responses to the same questions is noteworthy.

DOI: 10.4324/9781003246824-2

While some Millennials we talked to reported that Boomers grew up in idyllic conditions with economic prosperity, Baby Boomers had their own set of challenges, including the Vietnam War, the draft, gas shortages, and the stock market crash in the early 1970s. However, we do hear from Pew Research Center's Richard Fry (2017) that Millennials have higher amounts of student debt and lower income levels compared to Baby Boomers and Generation Xers at the same life stage. In fact, we talked to many Millennials who are overwhelmed by the amount of debt they have accumulated, resulting in some living with friends or parents.

Another often-cited characteristic of Millennials is that they are technologically savvy. They were the first generation of "digital natives," those born into homes with internet connections, and they tend to be more comfortable around technology than other generations. In a study asking Millennials what makes their generation unique, the number one response provided by 24% of respondents was "technology use" (Pew Research, 2010, p. 5). Another survey conducted by PriceWaterhouseCoopers (2012) found 50% of Millennials prefer digital communication over face-to-face. Especially when contrasted with older generations, Millennials are digitally connected and linked by social media, but their tech skills often come at the expense of other skills, namely, face-to-face communication. This influences one of the major differences we found in this study between Millennials and other generations when it comes to conflict, the tendency of Millennials to withdraw and seek support on social media, a topic we'll explore in more detail in Chapter 6.

In this chapter, we will talk about events during their childhoods that shaped Millennials' traits and characteristics. Later on, we'll pay special attention to what this means for how they resolve conflict, what Millennials want and value, and how to embrace this very talented cohort who have the capability to significantly contribute to the workplace in a manner that positively impacts the bottom line.

Understanding Generations in the United States

First, some definitions. Defining a generation is not an exact science, and things can get fuzzy around the edges when a generation is forming. Matthew and Drexel, our friends from the last chapter, are Baby Boomers. Born from 1946 to 1964, Baby Boomers are defined by their upbringing in the prosperous decades following World War II, and they were shaped by the tumultuous social revolutions of the 1960s. They witnessed the assassinations of President John F. Kennedy, Civil Rights leader Martin Luther King, and Robert Kennedy along with civil rights protests and anti-Vietnam war demonstrations.

Today, Baby Boomers range in age from 58 to 76. Pre-pandemic research suggests that these workers were staying in the workforce longer, some not knowing how to "retire," others continuing in jobs they genuinely love, and some continuing to work to achieve their desired retirement income. Robert Clark and Melinda Sandler Morrill, researchers from North Carolina State University, crunched the numbers and found that between 1994 and 2014, the labor force participation rate for men between 62 and 64 grew from 45% to 56%, and for men between 65 and 69, it rose from 27% to 36% (Clark & Morrll, 2016). The rates for women followed a similar pattern, they found, growing from 59% to 66% for women between 55 and 59, and from 45% to 58% for women between 60 and 61, and this trend will only continue as the population ages. As an unintended side effect, younger workers may find it harder to advance with Baby Boomers working longer, since higher ranking jobs may be filled by workers with seniority, possibly leading to more intergenerational conflict.

While historically Baby Boomers have stayed in the workforce longer, it is important to note that there was an uptick in Baby Boomer retirements during the Covid-19 pandemic as discussed in Chapter 1. It remains to be seen if these workers will return to the workforce, whether in similar or different jobs. With decreased concerns about health impacts from the virus, increasing inflation, longer lifespans, and higher age limits to receive full social security benefits, we may see a return of some of these Baby Boomers.

After Baby Boomers came the Generation Xers, sometimes called the MTV Generation, which brought its own perspective to the workforce shaped by a childhood in the so-called Me Decade of the 1970s and the rapid technological expansion of the 1980s. Gen Xers were born between 1965 and 1981. They experienced Watergate, the birth of the Environmental Protection Agency, the Arab Oil embargo leading to gas shortages, the end of the Vietnam war, and the Camp David peace accords with Menachem Begin from Israel and Anwar Sadat from Egypt. Also, Microsoft was founded in 1975 and a few years later Steve Jobs, Steve Wozniak, and Ronald Wayne founded Apple. Ranging in age from 41 to 57 in 2022, Generation X is a smaller generation than the Millennials or the Baby Boomers.

Following Generation X are the Millennials. The U.S. Census Bureau (2015) defines Millennials as born between 1982 and 2000, which is the definition used in this book. However, there remains a lack of consensus on the beginning and end dates for this generation. Some researchers define the end date for Millennials as 2002, while others, including Pew Research, push the end date as early as 1996. Under the definition we'll be using, the youngest members of this group turned 18 in 2018, with most of them either entering college or the workforce. We'll address the events they experienced in their youth in the next section of this chapter.

The newcomers on the scene are the members of Generation Z, sometimes called Zoomers, a play on Boomers that became darkly ironic when the COVID-19 pandemic forced much of their school and work life onto digital platforms like Zoom. This generation began in 2001 with an approximate end date of 2016, so older Zoomers are entering college and the workforce, while younger Zoomers are still quite young. Early research on this generation shows they are similar to Millennials in their dedication to addressing climate change and social equality (Parker et al., 2019). In their youth, they experienced the wars in Iraq and Afghanistan and numerous school and religious site shootings.

Predating the Boomers are the Silent Generation, a comparatively small generation due to low birth rates during the Great Depression. Born from 1928 to 1945, the youngest members of this generation are 77 years old, so few are still actively working. A major event experienced by older Silents was the great depression, the effects of which spanned the 1930s. Also, World War II was declared in 1941. Lastly, the Greatest Generation was born from 1901 to 1927. Many from this generation were raised during the Great Depression and were of fighting age in World War II. As the youngest members of this cohort turn 95 years old in 2022, they are not assumed to be currently active in the workplace. The generations in the United States are shown in Table 2.1, with an estimated end date for Generation Z of 2016.

Table 2.1 The United States Generations Defined

Generation	Birth Dates	Age in 2022
Generation Z	2001–2016	6–21
Millennial	1982–2000	22–40
Generation X	1965–1981	41–57
Baby Boomers	1946–1964	58–76
Silent	1928–1945	77–94
Greatest	1901–1927	95+

Note. For Generation Z to Generation X: From Millennials Outnumber Baby Boomers and Are Far More Diverse, Census Bureau Reports, by U.S Census Bureau, 2015 (https://www. census.gov/newsroom/press-releases/2015/cb15-113.html). In the public domain. For Generation X to Greatest Generation: From Resident Population in the United States in 2019, by generation, by E. Duffin, 2020, Statista (https://www. statista.com/statistics/797321/us-population-by-generation/).

Events That Shaped Millennials

Every generation is shaped by the events they experienced, and Millennials saw their share of turmoil and chaos unfold on their TV and computer screens. Research shows that key events that occurred during formative years, from the onset of puberty to the end of one's physical growth, are potentially the most impactful for determining one's attitudes and disposition. Our definition places formative years for the majority of Millennials as approximately 1990 to 2017.

Millennials list the attacks on the World Trade Center and the Pentagon as one of the most formative events of their youths (Deane et al., 2016). They watched from classrooms and living rooms as the planes smashed into the towers. Like all Americans, they were afraid, sad, and angry. Young men who had reached their 18th birthday had already registered for the draft, an act which suddenly gained new significance – though the draft was not reinstated, many Millennials would serve in the ensuing wars in Iraq and Afghanistan or watch friends and family go off to war. Many of those who stayed stateside felt the world of their childhood disappear overnight. Shelley, a Millennial who works in the art business on the east coast of the United States, said:

> I was two weeks out of leaving home, I was in my second week of college when 9/11 happened. And I was in Virginia. So, like, I mean, everyone in my dorm, we knew somebody. Then we had, in Virginia, there were shooters on the highway that whole fall.

Shelley was referring to the DC sniper attacks of 2002, which took ten lives along the highway in Virginia, Washington D.C., and Maryland and panicked motorists at a time of heightened fear of terrorism. She said:

> Our formative coming-of-age was in this time of the apocalypse. And then the Iraq War, then the Afghan War, and then the recession and people telling us we'd never get jobs and how dare we think we'd have a good life.

The oldest Millennials witnessed the fall of the Berlin Wall from TV screens in their grade school classrooms, but the end of the Soviet Union would not bring about a period of affluence as the fall of the Third Reich did for Boomers. By the time Millennials were turning 18, a bachelor's degree was becoming more important for middle-class jobs, and Millennials are the most educated generation – 39% of them have at least a bachelor's degree, compared with 29% for Gen Xers, 25% for Boomers, and 15% for the Silent Generation, as reported by Kristen Bialik and Richard Fry with Pew Research Center (Bialik & Fry, 2019). The Pew researchers further note that an additional 28% of Millennials have some college compared with 28% of Gen Xers, 21% of Baby Boomers, and 13% of Silents.

With 67% of Millennials having attended college, it's interesting to point out that studies have supported a link between attending college and an increase in critical thinking (McMillan, 1987; Pascarella, 1989; Pascarella et al., 1996). This critical thinking involves the ability to reason, think critically, analyze arguments, and make decisions based on that analysis. As such, this critical thinking, widely thought to be a positive outcome in education, may contribute to Millennials naturally asking "why" as found in this study. This may explain Janelle's wonderment at the Millennials she oversees at work. The Generation X attorney in the Southeast United States shares:

> But when it comes time to – You're going to do this, you're going to do this and you're going to do this – I think we're more likely to hear the 'Why? Why do we have to do it this way?

But while Millennials were working toward their degrees, college was becoming more expensive than for previous generations. In 2007 and 2008, a student at a public university could expect to pay $6,190 per year (Insler, 2018). Twenty years earlier, that student would have paid $1,490 per year for the same diploma, according to data reported by Insler (2018) on the online lending marketplace Student Loan Hero owned by LendingTree. As a result, Millennials graduated saddled with student loan debt – just as the Great Recession decimated the job and housing markets, putting important life milestones like getting married, starting a family, and buying a home in question for many college-educated Millennials.

Millennials grew up in the midst of the Enron scandal, the bankruptcy of Lehman Brothers, and the enactment of the Emergency Economic Stabilization Act of 2008 in response to the subprime mortgage crisis, emboldening some of them to take a stand against what they see as corporate greed. They made up the core of the 2011 Occupy Wall Street movement, running in age from 11 to 29 at the time. Sociologist Ruth Milkman and her colleagues from City University of New York note that the protest was not spontaneous but planned by political activists who took their cues from other worldwide protests during that time, including the Arab Spring (Milkman et al., 2013). Milkman and her team surveyed 729 people who attended the May 1, 2012 rally with half of those surveyed actively involved in the movement – meaning they participated in at least 6 or more Occupy Wall Street initiatives. They found that 40% of the actively involved respondents were under 30 and many were unemployed or underemployed. Further, looking at respondents under age 30, 37% reported that they had been laid off from or lost a job and more than half had $1,000 or more in student debt.

Another survey of the Zuccotti Park protesters in Lower Manhattan by Douglas Schoen (2011), a Democratic Party pollster, found that 49% were under the age of 30. One more study, by Baruch College professor Hector R. Codero-Guzman and business analyst Harrison Schultz, was cited by Amanda Greenfield (2011) in *The Atlantic*. Focusing on the OccupyWallSt.org website, the pair conducted a survey of 1,619 people who visited the site, finding that 64% in the Occupy Wall movement were under the age of 34. They also found 15% of the protestors were unemployed and 18% worked part-time work or were underemployed.

Some Millennials have the perception that older people, especially Baby Boomers, who grew up in a time of relative economic prosperity for many, just don't understand the financial world they are dealing with. But some older folks we talked to say they get it, like in this exchange from one of our focus groups. Jack, a Generation Xer and Vice President working for a large service industry in the Southeast United States, said:

> They came up in the worst economy that we've seen for years, the guys that work for me, one's a little bit older and one's a little bit younger, so it's interesting. I think there's different Millennial mindsets, cause there's a lost generation there.

"When the real estate market crashed," said lawyer Janelle.

"Yeah, 2008, the economy," Jack said.

"You couldn't get a job," said Saddie, a Baby Boomer education professional in the Southeast United States.

"You couldn't get a job," Jack agreed. "You came out of college with a good degree--"

"-- And huge student loan debt," Janelle chimed in.

"Student loans and you just can't get a decent job, so I think there's a whole different mindset," Jack said.

"It kind of broke their spirit," said Mary, a Generation X archivist in the Southeast United States.

Don, a Baby Boomer engineer working in the Southeast United States, added:

> Well, the other comparison to that is people who went through the Depression. You know, my parents are really different from their parents. So, it definitely impacts how you operate. You know, how much you're willing to hang out there. You're sailing, are you willing to hike it out or are you going to take the sails down and go plodding along?

Frank, a Baby Boomer attorney in the Southeast United States, shared similar sentiments in an interview. He said:

> Millennials, you know, it's interesting. They seem to get a bad rap, but in retrospect, I think they are all working and trying to do well, but their job prospects aren't as good, and also a lot of them have a lot of student debt. It seems like education was a lot cheaper when I went, when Baby Boomers went through it, and they're also in bad

housing markets that seem to be delaying their family choices, having children, unable to buy a house, and the houses they do get are very expensive and not quite what they wanted. So, the Millennials seem sort of disappointed in the hand that they've been dealt. They think they should be better off than they are at this point in their lives.

He added:

I hear a lot of stuff on the news and that the Millennials don't like to work. That they're lazy. They don't have a sense of going anywhere. And I think mainly that they haven't had much opportunity, and that I think as the time goes on and people do retire — from what I'm reading the Baby Boomers are retiring slower than previous generations — but when more jobs become available and they're able to work I think that they will do very well with what they're doing.

Many Millennial interview subjects agreed with these points, and some said they view the hurdles they have jumped as fodder for changing the world. Hala, a Millennial who works for a fortune 500 company in the Southeast United States, told us:

I think our generation will be the next generation to lead a major revolution. The reason I say that is right now there is so much corruption in our society. The top 1% literally has so much power that I don't think that it's just civil rights issues any longer, it's classist. Because they're doing everything. I'm passionate about that, but also, the war on drugs stuff because I don't see a reason to continually make marijuana illegal. Not that I'm a user or anything, but I know the benefits for some people, and it's a waste of money to put people in jail for this type of thing.

Looking at events that occurred during their youth provides perspective on the developmental environment experienced by Millennials. Following is a list of major events that occurred during their formative years. While not meant to be inclusive, these happenings are provided to offer perspective. While some of the earlier events affected older Millennials more than younger Millennials, the earliest listed event occurred in 1991. At that time, the youngest Millennial was nine years old and capable of recognizing events in the surrounding environment. While all these events impacted the Millennials, a certain number of these events were more widely publicized and may have had a more direct influence. Table 2.2 provides a list of major events that occurred during their formative years.

Table 2.2 Significant Events Experienced by Millennials in Their Formative Years

Year	Event	Year	Event	Year	Event
1991	World Wide Web debuts	1999	Columbine shooting	2010	Don't Ask Don't Tell repealed
1991	Gulf War	2001	Enron scandal	2011	Japan earthquake and tsunami
1991	End of the Cold War	2001	9/11 attacks	2012	Sandy Hook shooting
1992	Rodney King riots	2001	Afghan War begins	2012	Trayvon Martin killed
1992	Hurricane Andrew	2001–2009	George W. Bush president	2013	Black Lives Matter formed
1993–2001	Bill Clinton president	2002	Department of Homeland Security formed	2013	Navy Yard shooting
1993	Don't Ask Don't Tell	2003	Iraq War begins	2014	Border crisis declared
1995	Oklahoma City bombing	2003	Columbia disaster	2015	Gay marriage authorized
1995	O.J. Simpson trial	2004	Indian Ocean tsunami	2015	Shooting at Emanuel African Methodist Episcopal Church
1995	Million Man March	2004	Massachusetts legalizes same-sex marriage	2015	"Build the Wall" introduced by Trump
1995–1996	21-Day federal government shutdown	2005	Hurricane Katrina	2016	Pulse Nightclub shooting
1996	DOMA signed by Clinton	2007	Great Recession starts	2017	Hurricanes Maria and Irma
1997	Ellen DeGeneres comes out	2007	Virginia Tech massacre	2017–2021	Donald Trump president
1998	War in Kosovo	2009–2017	Barack Obama president	2017	Sutherland Springs church shooting
1998	Clinton impeached	2009	Fort Hood shooting	2017	Las Vegas shooting
1998	Matthew Shepard murdered	2010	Chile earthquake	2018	Marjory Stoneman Douglas High School shooting
		2010	Deepwater Horizon spill		

Helicopter Parents

Millennials grew up experiencing a radically different style of parenting than those in prior generations. Researchers Neil Howe and William Strauss in their *Helicopter Parents in the Workplace* describe the parents of Millennials as having a close and intertwined relationship with their children, more so than previous generations (Howe & Strauss, 2007). "Throughout their childhood and adolescence, today's youth have been more likely to trust their parents, depend on their support and guidance, and tell them about their lives than prior generations at the same-age" (Howe & Strauss, 2007, p. 2).

Child nurturing as described by Strauss and Howe (2007) was relaxed for Baby Boomers, under-protective for the Gen X latchkey kids, and tightened for Millennials who experienced a more protective childhood. This protective environment provided Millennials frequent support and interaction, consistent with their desire for a nurturing work environment. The term "helicopter parenting" became popular in the late 1980s and early 1990s, often uttered by exasperated teachers describing how their students' parents always seemed to be hovering over their shoulders. You probably have heard the description – the parent who is constantly shuffling their child from soccer to ballet practice to the piano recital while doing the science fair project and drafting the college application – all for the child's own good, of course. The parent who has the teacher on speed dial to speak his or her mind whenever the child gets a bad grade.

One study by Patricia Somers with the University of Texas at Austin and Jim Settle with Shawnee State University estimated 40%–60% of parents on college campuses throughout the United States could be classified as helicopter parents (Somers & Settle, 2010). Somers and Settle classified these parents into different types, including the consumer advocate, who believes her financial contribution to her child's education makes her an equal partner and is eager to negotiate with the admissions office for a better deal on tuition and fees; the toxic parent, a meddler who sometimes goes so far as to plant electronic bugs or cameras in their child's dorm room; and the safety patrol parent who is always nervous about their child's safety and ready to swoop in to bring supplies or perform a rescue mission at the first sign of trouble. The two other types of helicopter parents identified by Somers and Settle are the vicarious college student, attending all the college activities and "living" the college experience, and the equity and fairness advocate, who focuses on requesting services for their child.

Somers and Settle (2010) found helicoptering diminished as students got closer to graduation, but the rotors often started spinning again once a student nears graduation and begins preparing for the next phase of life, with parents involved in graduate school applications or job interviews. In fact, employers report parents conducting their adult children's job searches, filling out applications and calling employers to complain if their child doesn't land the gig.

Phil Gardner, Director of the Collegiate Employment Research Institute at Michigan State University, surveyed 725 employers about parental involvement in the workplace and found 40% of parents gather company information for their children, 31% submit a resume on behalf of their child, and 26% are involved in promoting their child for a position (Gardner, 2007). Several large companies have taken notice, and they've adapted their hiring process to accommodate Millennial students and their helicopter parents.

The ways in which companies have adapted to target Millennial employees are discussed by Joy Peluchette with Lindenwood University and her colleagues (Peluchette et al., 2013). For example, General Electric has advertised directly to parents with the slogan "Let us take your son or daughter off your payroll and put them on ours" (Peluchette et al., 2013, p. 606). Howe and Strauss (2007) also talk about parent-focused initiatives by other companies including Enterprise-Rent-A-Car and Ferguson Enterprises sending letters to parents of potential employees who have been offered a job explaining the position and highlighting the benefits of working for the company. Further, Ernst and Young has provided packets for parents along with their recruiting materials, including a memory stick with company information, and Office Depot has provided web pages specifically designed for parents of potential hires. Lastly, companies like Merrill Lynch have invited parents into the workplace, allowing helicopter parents to finally meet the bosses they've been emailing face-to-face.

While caution is recommended asking questions about family during an employment interview, with any questions pre-screened by your Human Resource department, Calvin, a Baby Boomer, and senior manager in the communications industry in the Southeast United States, said he has adopted this approach as well. He said:

> If I was going to recruit a Millennial today for a specific job, I'd say 'have you had a chance to talk to your parents about the position and what have they told you?' That has to be part of the interview process and, I might even invite them if we got close to the final round — 'Bring your parents down, we'd like them to see the place and meet them and let them look at our organization and all that.' That HAS [emphasis added] to be the new way to recruit. Otherwise, the likelihood of them staying much longer, unless they get entangled in a long-term relationship, get married or something like that, is unlikely.

Calvin highlights the different environment in which Millennials were raised: Hand-in-hand with helicopter parenting, many Millennials grew up with a heightened concern for their safety. They grew up in the age of "stranger danger," watching colorful puppets lecture them about the terrible things that could happen if they spoke with an adult they did not know, contributing to Millennials' low level of trust in others as found by Kali Trzesniewski and M. Brent Donnellan, with the University of Western Ontario and Michigan State University, respectively, as well as Pew Research Center (Trzesniewski & Donnellan, 2010; Pew Research, 2014). This heightened concern kicked into overdrive after September 11, 2001, when international terrorists were added to the list of people to be worried about.

Millennials are also known as the participation trophy generation, the idea being that when they played sports, each participant got to take home a trophy, so they never learned the importance of winning. Some child psychologists say participation trophies are harmless trinkets that remind kids of the hard work they put in and the fun they had and encourage them to keep playing in the future. Some say the attitude of uplifting everyone contributes to Millennials' predilection for working in a team, which we'll explore further in Chapter 4. Others blame the trophies for what they call Millennials' unreasonable demands in the workplace and their desire for rapid career advancement, which we'll also dig into more deeply in Chapter 4.

Those who call Millennials "entitled" may not be entirely off base, however – remember the research mentioned above finding Millennials are more narcissistic than older generations? Both the Millennials and non-Millennials we spoke with in our interviews describe Millennials as entitled. And Millennials were more apt to talk about themselves than other generations which we'll explore in Chapter 4. This is consistent with Millennials receiving frequent attention from their helicopter parents and numerous trophies during their youth, which may drive their habit of seeking recognition at the workplace.

What We Know about Generational Differences

Millennials have been a hot topic of conversation in politics and media. And while there has been research on this generation, it often does not take into account differences based on age rather than generation – that is to say, it does not try to detangle what differences between generations can be attributed to one's age versus the unique circumstances experienced during one's formative years. But intergenerational conflict is nothing new. Take this quote, often misattributed to Socrates:

> The children now love luxury; they have bad manners, contempt for authority; they show disrespect for elders and love chatter in place of exercise. Children are now tyrants, not the servants of their

households. They no longer rise when elders enter the room. They contradict their parents, chatter before company, gobble up dainties at the table, cross their legs, and tyrannize their teachers.

Author Garson O'Toole (2018) attributes the quote not to Socrates but to a Cambridge student named Kenneth John Freeman, who included a summary of complaints registered against young people in his 1907 Cambridge dissertation. But the conflict went both ways, even in ancient times. Here's what Aristotle (ca. 350 B.C.E./2004) had to say about the old men of his day:

> They are small-minded because they have been humbled by life: their desires are set upon nothing more exalted or unusual than what will help them to keep alive. They are not generous, because money is one of the things they must have, and at the same time, their experience has taught them how hard it is to get and how easy to lose. They are cowardly, and are always anticipating danger; unlike that of the young, who are warm-blooded, their temperament is chilly; old age has paved the way for cowardice; fear is, in fact, a form of chill. (Book II, Chapter 13, p. 1)

The ancients recognized the difference between young and old, but if they also pondered the effects historical shifts had on age cohorts, that discussion is lost to time. While the dialogue of generational discord between young and old may have continued over time, that broad discourse does not focus on attributes that arise due to the specific time period. There may be commonality with youth or age, but there are also differences. For example, Millennials may have been raised with technology at their fingertips, seeing the terrorist attacks of 9/11 on TV, and feeling the effects of the great recession. In contrast, members of the Silent Generation grew up with World War II and recovering from the Great Depressions. While both Millennials and the Silent Generation experienced the fear and insecurity of war along with economic uncertainty, the early 1930s and 1940s provided a different cultural experience than the 1980s and 1990s.

Interest in generational changes grew among western thinkers in the 19th and 20th centuries as war and revolt spread across Europe and North America. Karl Mannheim is most often cited as the father of generational research. He introduced the concept in his 1928 essay "Das Problem der Generationen," which was translated into English in 1952 as "The Problem of Generations." For Mannheim (1952), generational cohorts are defined by significant historical events witnessed by the people of that generation during their youth. In other words, people who are born in a specific time frame experience the same childhood events that shape them. As such, individuals are influenced by the culture in which they are raised, resulting in traits and values specific to that group of individuals. Then, those individuals influence society based on their unique traits and characteristics.

Other researchers have built on Mannheim's theory, maintaining the focus on the effects of major historical disruptions in shaping generations. Researchers William Strauss and Neil Howe in their 1997 work *The Fourth Turning: An American Prophecy* suggest that there are four generational types that reoccur over time, aligning with historical events. "Looking back over American history, we find a correspondence between recurring patterns in the generational constellations and recurring types of historical events" (Strauss and Howe, 1991, p.33).

Strauss and Howe (1997) suggest a cycle of four recurring generational types that remain consistently ordered over time. These include: (1) Idealists, (2) Reactives, (3) Civics, and (4) Adaptives. Each generation throughout history is typified as one of these types, with each lasting approximately 20 years in length, consistent with generational cohort definitions. As such, there is what Strauss and Howe refer to as a "turning" every 80 years, returning the cycle to begin again. Significant historical events are suggested to precipitate these turnings. In the past, these have included (1) the Boston Tea Party and American Revolution, (2) the Civil War and formation of the confederacy, and (3) the stock market crash of 1929 and Roosevelt's New Deal (Strauss & Howe, 1997).

Strauss and Howe predicted in 1997 that Millennials would lead the fourth turning and the 2008 financial crisis and great recession are at the forefront of this transition. Within Strauss and Howe's classifications, Millennials are classified as "Civics," known to bring about political realignment, impacting elections and voting behaviors (Strauss & Howe, 1997). While bringing about great change, this period is also known to be marked by strife and often violence. This is an interesting prediction in that it was made in 1997, and we are currently experiencing youth-dominated protests in 2022.

If we look at current protests on racial inequality, 41% of the people participating are in the 18 to 29 age group according to Amanda Barroso and Rachel Minkin with Pew Research Center (Barroso & Minkin, 2020). Comparatively, the pair report that 19% of all adults in the United States are in this 18 to 29 age group. The same researchers report that age 50 and older individuals represent 26% of the overall adult population in the United States with only 15% of this age group engaged in the recent racial protests. Of course, younger individuals may be more available to protest, while older individuals may be constrained by jobs and child-rearing.

The cyclical theory suggested by Strauss and Howe can be compared to another framework called world-systems theory developed by Immanuel Wallerstein. In his 2007 book *World Systems, Analysis, an Introduction,*

Wallerstein suggests that historical systems operate within their own structures until they eventually encounter problems they cannot resolve, which he terms "systemic crisis" (Wallerstein, 2007). At that point, a transition occurs to an alternate course. Per Wallerstein, this happens only when crises occur, not to be confused with difficulties within a system that can be resolved. When Wallerstein wrote this in 2007, he postulated that we were in such a crisis and speculated that it could last 25 to 50 years. This timing is consistent with Strauss and Howe's theory of a "Fourth Turning" beginning in 2008, with similarly expected instability and conflict.

Mannheim says that we can gain insight by studying generations and the impact of shared historical events, but scholars disagree on how much weight we can put on generational research. One perspective questions whether generational differences exist based on the results of studies. Kali Trzesniewski and M. Brent Donnellan with the University of Western Ontario and Michigan State University, respectively, conducted a study of 477,380 high school seniors in the United States spanning 1976 through 2006 (Trzesniewski & Donnellan, 2010). Looking at numerous values and behaviors, while they found some evidence that younger individuals today may be less trusting and have higher educational goals than older generations, they conclude that there is insignificant evidence of widespread cohort-based differences.

Another study that found limited evidence of generational differences was conducted by Lucy Cennamo with Louis Vuitton Moet Hennessy and Dianne Gardner with Massey University (Cennamo & Gardner, 2008). Using an online questionnaire completed by 504 Auckland employees, Cennamo and Gardner did find generational differences in work values, albeit smaller than expected. In another paper, researchers Emma Parry and Peter Urwin, with Cranfield University and University of Westminster, respectively, state that research on generational differences in the workplace has contradictory findings (Parry & Urwin, 2011). However, while noting other considerations when conducting generational research, they suggest that it is necessary to engage in research that separates generational effects from time period and age effects.

The second perspective is that differences do exist between generations. In a study looking at generational differences in leader values and leadership behaviors, Valerie Sessa from Montclair State University, along with her colleagues, used data from two large databases totaling more than 20,000 participants who completed a leadership behavior survey (Sessa et al., 2007). They found that managers from different generational cohorts do differ in work values and behaviors, both those that are self-reported and those that are reported by others. Likewise, Jean Twenge from San Diego State University and her colleagues found higher levels of narcissism in more recent college students using data from college students in the United States who completed the Narcissistic Personality Index between 1979 and 2006 (Twenge et al., 2008).

So, what gives? Why do some researchers find generational differences are significant while others do not? What we find by looking at studies is that several scholars agree that contradictory generational study results may be due to methodological approach. Namely, research needs to separate generational effects from time period and age effects. In other words, if a 30-year-old and a 60-year-old have different attitudes about workplace expectations, how confident can we be that the reason is that one is a Millennial, and the other is a Baby Boomer? Maybe the Baby Boomer felt differently when he was 30, or maybe the Millennial will change her mind when she reaches 60?

David Costanza with The George Washington University and Lisa Finkelstein with Northern Illinois University state the main challenge in the study of generational differences is separating out age, specific time period, and cohort or generational aspects (Costanza & Finkelstein, 2015). Relatedly, W. Keith Campbell from the University of Georgia and his colleagues conclude that generational differences do exist and can be measured if the correct methodologies and data are used (W. K. Campbell et al., 2015). Campbell, along with his colleagues, acknowledges that not only does culture shape generations, but generational cohorts in turn influence and shape culture.

To better understand what we can learn from generational research, Sean Lyons with the University of Guelph and Lisa Kuron with Wilfrid Laurier University conducted a comprehensive review of academic studies (Lyons & Kuron, 2013). They found that time-lag and cross-sectional approaches, while finding some similarities across generations, also found some key differences in values, preferences, and behaviors. Relatedly, in the study mentioned above by Jean Twenge and her colleagues that found higher levels of narcissism in more recent college students, a cross-temporal approach was utilized (Twenge et al., 2008).

Another study by Stacy Campbell at Kennesaw State University and her colleagues utilized a time-lag design (S. Campbell et al., 2017). Their research, using Monitor the Future data for high school seniors from 1976 to 2014, finds generational differences in workplace attitudes and values, although these are best described as gradual trends rather than abrupt changes between generations. In designing their study, Campbell and her colleagues noted the importance of including same-age individuals born at different times to control for age effects. They conclude that generational differences exist but further clarify that the end of one generational cohort and the beginning of another is not marked by a definitive point in time. Rather, these beginning and end points are "fuzzy."

Studies designed to look at data over time and compare same-age individuals at different time periods are more likely to obtain accurate results.

Addressing these recommendations, this study combines several methods to ensure robust and meaningful results. First, we'll look at what participants say in interviews and focus groups. Then, we'll look at both cross-sectional and longitudinal data, using the results of the TKI Conflict Mode Inventory over a 13-year time span for approximately 11,000 Millennials, Generation Xers, and Baby Boomers. Next, we'll compare same-age Millennials and Generation Xers to tease age from cohort effect. Lastly, we'll look across all the results to see where findings are corroborated across methods.

In the next chapter, we'll start with what our interview and focus group participants say about how Millennials deal with conflict in the workplace and then we'll look at our analysis of the Thomas-Kilmann Conflict Mode Instrument data to see what it tells us about the conflict styles of Millennials versus Generation Xers and Baby Boomers.

References

Alsop, R. (2008a). *The trophy kids grow up: How the Millennial generation is shaking up the workplace.* Jossey-Bass.

Alsop, R. (2008b, October 21). *The trophy kids go to work.* The Wall Street Journal, Eastern Edition. https://www.wsj.com/articles/SB122455219391652725

Aristotle. (2004). *Aristotle's Rhetoric.* Book II, Chapter 13. (L. Honeycutt, Trans.). https://kairos.technorhetoric.net/stasis/2017/honeycutt/aristotle/rhet2-13.html (Original work published ca. 350 B.C.E.)

Barroso, A., & Minkin, R. (2020, June 24). *Recent protest attendees are more racially and ethnically diverse, younger than Americans overall.* Pew Research Center. http://www.pewresearch.org/fact-tank/2020/06/24/recent-protest-attendees-are-more-racially-and-ethnically-diverse-younger-than-americans-overall/

Bialik, K., & Fry, R. (2019). *Millennial life: How young adulthood today compares with prior generations.* Pew Research Center. https://www.pewsocialtrends.org/essay/millennial-life-how-young-adulthood-today-compares-with-prior-generations/

Campbell, S.M., Twenge, J.M., & Campbell, W.K. (2017). Fuzzy but useful constructs: Making sense of the differences between generations. *Work, Aging and Retirement, 3*(2), 130–139. https://doi.org/10.1093/workar/wax001

Campbell, W.K., Campbell, S.M., Siedor, L.E., & Twenge, J.M. (2015). Generational differences are real and useful. *Industrial and Organizational Psychology, 8*(3), 1–8.

Cennamo, L., & Gardner, D. (2008). Generational differences in work values, outcomes, and person-organization values fit. *Journal of Managerial Psychology, 23*(8), 891–906. https://doi.org/10.1108/02683940810904385

Clark, R.L., & Morril, M.S. (2016). Working longer, retiring later: Are employers ready for the new employment trend? *Employment Research, 24*(2), 4–6. https://doi.org/10.17848/

Costanza, D.P., & Finkelstein, L.M. (2015). Generationally based differences in the workplace: Is there a there there? *Industrial and Organizational Psychology: Perspectives on Science and Practice, 8*(3), 308–323.

Cutler, N.E. (2015). Millennials and finance: The "Amazon generation." *Journal of Financial Service Professionals, 66*(6), 33–39.

Deane, C., Duggan, M., & Morin, R. (2016). *Americans name the 10 most significant historic events of their lifetimes; 9/11, Obama election and the tech revolution among those with greatest impact on the country.* Pew Research Center. https://www.pewresearch.org/politics/2016/12/15/americans-name-the-10-most-significant-historic-events-of-their-lifetimes/

DeVaney, S.A. (2015). Understanding the millennial generation. *Journal of Financial Service Professionals, 69*(6), 11–14.

Duffin, E. (2020, June). *Resident population in the United States in 2019, by generation.* Statista. https://www.statista.com/statistics/797321/us-population-by-generation/

Duffin, E. (2020, July 20). *Gender distribution of the resident population of the United States from 1980 to 2019: U.S population by sex 1980–2019.* Statista. https://www.statista.com/statistics/241495/us-population-by-sex/

Foster, J., Campbell, K., & Twenge, J. (2003). Individual differences in narcissism: Inflated self-views across the lifespan and around the world. *Journal of Research in Personality, 37*, 469–486. doi:10.1016/S0092-6566(03)00026-6

Fry, R. (2017, September 6). *5 facts about Millennial households.* Pew Research Center. http://www.pewresearch.org/fact-tank/2017/09/06/5-facts-about-millennial-households/

Gardner, P. (2007). *Parent involvement in the college recruiting process.* Collegiate Employment Research Institute. http://ceri.msu.edu/publications/pdf/ceri2-07.pdf

Greenfield, R. (2011, October 19). *The Occupy Wall Street protesters aren't just a bunch of kids. While the movement has been identified as a millennial driven movement, the demographics are much more diverse than that.* The Atlantic. https://www.theatlantic.com/national/archive/2011/10/occupy-wall-street-protesters-arent-just-bunch-kids/336581/

Graf, N. (2017, May 16). *Today's young workers are more likely than ever to have a bachelor's degree.* Pew Research Center. https://www.pewresearch.org/fact-tank/2017/05/16/todays-young-workers-are-more-likely-than-ever-to-have-a-bachelors-degree/

Howe, N., & Strauss, W. (2000). *Millennials rising: The next great generation.* Vintage Books.

Howe, N., & Strauss, W. (2007). *Helicopter parents in the workplace.* NGEN. https://www.lifecourse.com/assets/files/article_pdfs/Helicopter_Parents_Workplace_112007.pdf

Insler, S. (2018). *Do Millennials have it better or worse than generations past?* Student Loan Hero. https://studentloanhero.com/featured/millennials-have-better-worse-than-generations-past

Lyons, S., & Kuron, L. (2013). Generational differences in the workplace: A review of the evidence and directions for future research. *Journal of Organizational Behavior, 35*(1), 139–157.

Mannheim, K. (1952). The problem of generations. In P. Kecskemeti (Ed.) *Karl Mannheim: Essays* (pp. 276–322). Routledge.

Matthews, V. (2008). *Debunking the myths about Generation Y.* Personnel Today. https://www.personneltoday.com/hr/debunking-the-myths-about-generation-y/

McMillan, J. (1987). Enhancing college students' critical thinking: A review of studies. *Research in Higher Education, 26*(1), 3–29.

Milkman, R., Luce, S., & Lewis, P. (2013). *Changing the subject: A bottom-up account of Occupy Wall Street in New York City.* Russell Sage Foundation. https://www.russellsage.org/research/reports/occupy-wall-street-movement

Ng, E.S.W., Schweitzer, L., & Lyons, S.T. (2010). New generation, great expectations: A field study of the Millennial generation. *Journal of Business and Psychology, 25*(2), 281–292.

O'Toole, G. (2018, October 4). *Misbehaving children in ancient times.* Quote Investigator. https://quoteinvestigator.com/2010/05/01/misbehave/

Parker, K., Graf, N., & Igielnik, R. (2019, January 17). *Generation Z looks a lot like Millennials on key social and political issues.* Pew Research. https://www.pewresearch.org/social-trends/2019/01/17/generation-z-looks-a-lot-like-millennials-on-key-social-and-political-issues/

Parry, E., & Urwin, P. Generational differences in work values: A review of theory and evidence. *International Journal of Management, 13*, 79–96.

Pascarella, E. (1989). The development of critical thinking: Does college make a difference? *Journal of College Student Development, 30*(1), 19–26.

Pascarella, E., Bohr, L., Nora, A., & Terenzini, P. (1996). Is differential exposure to college linked to the development of critical thinking? *Research in Higher Education, 37*(2), 159–174.

Peluchette, J.V., Kovanic, N., & Partridge, D. (2013). Helicopter parents hovering in the workplace: What should HR managers do? *Business Horizons, 56*(5), 601–609.

Pew Research Center. (2010, February 24). *Millennials: Confident. Connected. Open to change.* www.pewsocialtrends.org/files/2010/10/millennials-confident-connected-open-to-change.pdf

Pew Research Center. (2014, March). *Millennials in adulthood: Detached from institutions, networked with friends.* http://www.pewsocialtrends.org/2014/03/07/millennials-in-adulthood/

PricewaterhouseCoopers. (2012). *Millennials at work: Reshaping the workplace in financial services.* https://www.pwc.com/gx/en/financial-services/publications/assets/pwc-millenials-at-work.pdf

Rentz, J.O., Reynolds, F.D., & Stout, R.G. (1983). Analyzing changing consumption patterns and cohort analysis. *Journal of Marketing Research, 20*(1), 12–20.

Rogler, L.H. (2002). Historical generations and psychology: The case of the great depression and WWII. *The American Psychologist, 57*(12), 1013–1023.

Rutkoff, A. (2011, October 19). *Who occupies? A pollster surveys the protestors.* The Wall Street Journal. https://www.wsj.com/articles/BL-METROB-14122

Ryder, N.B. (1965). The cohort as a concept in the study of social change. *American Sociological Review, 30*(6), 843–861.

Schoen, D. (2011, October 18). *Polling the Occupy Wall Street crowd. In interviews, protesters show that they are leftists out of step with most American voters. Yet Democrats are embracing them anyway.* The Wall Street Journal. https://www.wsj.com/articles/SB10001424052970204479504576637082965745362

Sessa, V.I., Kabacoff, R.I., Deal, J., & Brown, H. (2007). Generational differences in leader values and leadership behaviors. *The Psychologist-Manager Journal, 10*(1), 47–74.

Somers, P., & Settle, J. (2010). The helicopter parent: Research toward a typology (Part I). *College and University, 86*, 18–27.

Strauss, W., & Howe, N. (1991). *Generations: The history of America's future, 1584 to 2069.* Quill.

Strauss, W., & Howe, N. (1997). *The fourth turning: An American prophecy.* Broadway Books.

The Associated Press – NORC Center for Public Affairs. (2016, May). *Working longer: The disappearing divide between work life and retirement.* https://apnorc. org/wp-content/uploads/2020/02/AP-NORC-2016_Working-Longer-Poll_Report1.pdf

Trzesniewski, K.H., & Donnellan, M.B. (2010). Rethinking "Generation Me": A study of cohort effects from 1976–2006. *Perspectives on Psychological Science, 5*(1), 58–75.

Twenge, J.M., Konrath, S., Foster, J.D., Campbell, W.K., & Bushman, B.J. (2008). Egos inflating over time: A crosstemporal meta-analysis of the Narcissistic Personality Inventory. *Journal of Personality, 76*(4), 875–901.

U.S. Census Bureau. (2015, June 25). *Millennials outnumber baby Boomers and are far more diverse, census bureau reports.* https://www.census.gov/newsroom/press-releases/2015/cb15-113.html

U.S. Census Bureau. (2020, June 22). *Annual estimates of the resident population by single year of age and sex for the United States: April 2, 2010 to July 1, 2019.* https:// www.census.gov/data/tables/time-series/demo/popest/2010s-counties-total. html#par_textimage

Wallerstein, I. (2007). *World-systems analysis. An Introduction.* Duke University Press.

Winograd, M., & Hais, M.D. (2014). *How Millennials could upend wall street and corporate America.* Brookings Institute. https://www.brookings.edu/research/-how-millennials-could-upend-wall-street-and-corporate-america/

Chapter 3

How Millennials Deal with Conflict

Millennials in the Workplace: What We Hear from Employees

"Fuzzy" though they may be, understanding generational differences in how employees approach conflict can be vital for creating a work environment with minimal discord, and a wise manager will take them into account to help achieve the best-performing workplace. And when it comes to Millennials, there's a fundamental mismatch between the traits they tend toward, and the traditionally defined skills required for successful conflict resolution that focus on face-to-face communication. We'll talk about how Millennials are bringing a new facet to resolving conflict with their technology-driven approaches.

Successful conflict resolution requires significant communication and interpersonal skills based on a foundation of honesty and trust to achieve a win/win outcome in negotiating or avoid a suboptimal outcome where a party gives up some of the gains that could be achieved. But Millennials are less trustful than any generation before them – a Pew Research Center report from 2014 found only 19% of Millennials say that most people can be trusted, less than half the rate of Baby Boomers at 40% (Pew Research, 2014). Furthermore, the process of resolving a dispute is impacted by expectations and one's willingness to compromise, but research indicates Millennials are opinionated (Alsop, 2008a; DeVaney, 2015; Hartman & McCambridge, 2011) and have higher expectations than other generations (Alsop, 2008b; Cutler, 2015; Myers & Sadaghiani, 2010), calling into question how these traits impact their approach to conflict resolution, specifically their expectations and willingness to compromise.

Another consideration is that Millennials have technological proficiencies that surpass their oral, written, or interpersonal competencies (Anderson & Rainie, 2012; Hartmann & McCambridge, 2011). So, do they approach conflict differently, and perhaps in a more technological and less face-to-face way, than other generations? The question addressed in

DOI: 10.4324/9781003246824-3

the interviews and focus groups is "How do Millennials manage conflict in the workplace?" So, what did we hear from these employees? A theme expressed in the interviews and focus groups leading up to this book, by both Millennials and non-Millennials, is that Millennials are more likely to withdraw from and avoid conflict. Drexel, the Baby Boomer executive for a large organization, said:

> Most Millennials, when there's conflict - they don't like confrontation. They understand that conflict has occurred. They know there's disagreement. They tend to withdraw and say 'I'll just go figure this out'... Whereas non-Millennials are more comfortable, not always in the confrontation, but trying to work it out with the individual, not go away.

Millennials recognize this trend as well. In the interviews and focus groups that led to this book, just over three quarters of Millennials – 77% – self-reported avoiding conflict, while 46% of non-Millennials also stated that Millennials avoid conflict. This was in response to open-ended questions asking interviewees to describe conflicts at work, including their thoughts, how they reacted and dealt with it, and how it was solved. There was no mention of a particular conflict style in the questions asked.

Jada, a Millennial supervisor for a large manufacturing company in the Southeast, shared in one of our focus groups:

> When there's a conflict, I do not speak up. Let's say there was a work problem, then let's say a group of us is trying to work together and you're not working. Then, instead of saying 'Hey, you've got to work', I just do it myself and hold it back.

Brianna, a Millennial who works for a government agency in the Mid-Atlantic United States, spoke not only about how the individuals she manages avoid conflict, but how she does, as well:

> At my work, I currently supervise 8 interns. Their ages are 18 to 26. We have frequent meetings. Also, in these meetings, among myself and the 8 interns, we have directors of various agency locations. Now, I've noticed that when a conflict comes up and we're addressing these concerns that the interns, they tend to not approach the conflict. They tend to hold back sometimes their views. Sometimes in passing after the meeting is over, they'll give me a suggestion, but they're too afraid to speak up. I've noticed I, myself, I'm not as confident as some of the directors.

Ellie, a Millennial advertising manager who works with Millennials and Gen Xers, said she has noticed a difference between the generations, as well. She told us in an interview:

> I find Gen Xers much more direct in addressing conflict, whereas I think my Millennial colleagues are much more passive about not wanting to address an issue or not wanting to make more out of an issue where there is one and it has to be addressed. I think they are a little bit more passive about making it an issue and would rather sweep it under the rug and not have an issue at work.

Another manager sheds further light on his Millennial employees by describing how they do not engage in conflict. Jay, a Millennial himself, works for a large retail organization in the Southeast United States. He said:

> I feel like non-Millennials are more likely to hear both sides before they jump to a conclusion, whereas a Millennial might, you disagree with them and they don't want to hear that, and so they don't even give you the time of day because they don't agree with you.

Nate, a Millennial entrepreneur in the Southeast United States agrees, describing Millennials tendency to avoid conflict:

> You know, I find that the younger people that are in that age range are pretty non-confrontational, so it can be hard to pull information out of them. So, you have to sort of approach that confrontation a lot differently than you would with maybe somebody that's older.

Negotiation and Conflict Resolution

So how do people approach conflict? Looking at the basic tenets of negotiation theory can shed some light. When looking at how people negotiate, researchers tend to agree there are two main types of negotiation: distributive, also referred to as positional, and principled, also referred to as integrative. Distributive negotiation looks at a fixed sum that must be divided. It's often thought of as a pie to be divided among two or more people. Some people may get more than others, but there's only one pie to be split up. Principled negotiation, however, is more time-consuming and looks to expand the outcomes.

In describing distributive negotiations, Gregory Brazeal of the University of South Dakota states "each side adopts an extreme position, knowing that it will not be accepted, and then employs a combination of guile, bluffing, and brinksmanship in order to cede as little as possible before reaching a deal" (Brazeal, 2009, p. 1). Distributive negotiation is considered a type of win-lose negotiation with competing and dominating styles pursuing their interests and ignoring the interests of the other party.

Principled negotiations are more complex. For example, rather than splitting one pie, think about baking a second pie. Or if pie is not your thing, imagine two friends arguing over an orange who discover that one only wants the inside for juice, while the other only wants the peel for baking. With principled negotiation, both parties win, hence, it is referred to as win-win negotiation.

When examining conflict in the workplace, it's useful to understand how experts understand conflict and the approaches people take to mitigate it. Researchers and human resource specialists use a tool called the Thomas-Kilmann Conflict Mode Instrument (TKI) to better understand how people deal with conflict (Thomas & Kilmann, 1977). Developed by Kenneth Thomas and Ralph Kilmann in 1977, it's a questionnaire with 30 pairs of statements, and test takers must choose which of the two choices best describes them for each of the 30 statements.

In designing the test, Thomas and Kilmann wanted to eliminate the possibility of test takers choosing a response perceived as socially desirable – one that has positive connotations in society. For example, employees may feel their employer would prefer collaborative behavior over competing or avoiding behavior. To reduce this result, the TKI was designed so that each subject must choose between two statements that are equally desirable. Both choices are framed in a positive way so the test taker will not be swayed to select an answer that makes them look better and instead can select the answer that best fits their style.

In their approach to understanding conflict styles, Thomas and Kilmann (1977) utilize the two elements of assertiveness and cooperation, identifying five conflict styles. These styles are competing (high assertiveness and low cooperation); accommodating styles (high cooperation and low assertiveness); compromising (mid-level assertive and mid-level cooperation); avoiding (low assertiveness and low cooperative); and collaborating (high assertiveness and high cooperation). The five conflict responses identified by Thomas-Kilmann are described below:

Competing – Those with a competing style have high assertiveness and low cooperativeness. The priority of individuals with this style is to pursue their needs without concern for the needs of others. As described by Thomas and Kilmann, while this type of conflict response can be useful in an emergency or situation when a leader needs to direct the action of others, it can result in others being afraid to speak up. As such, dire consequences may result if subordinates follow the poor decisions of leaders without being able to provide their advice. The competing style of assertiveness and low cooperation leads to win/lose outcomes as with distributive negotiations.

Accommodating – Those proficient in this conflict style are unassertive and cooperative. They will abandon their own needs in the interest of co-operating with others. At times this strategy can be helpful when concessions can help preserve unity or pave the way to long-term success. Over time, however, those with accommodating behaviors may be walked over and ignored, and the good ideas they have may not be recognized. This can be categorized as a neglect-lose/win style.

Compromising – People who favor compromise score in the middle of the road for both assertiveness and cooperation. The focus is on finding a solution with a willingness to be somewhat cooperative but without the effort required to identify and explore creative solutions as with a collaborative style. So, compromising individuals look for a middle ground. Thomas and Kilmann say compromising can be an effective style when there is a time constraint, but compromise can also lead to abandoning important principles. This can be viewed as mid-level win/mid-level lose type of style.

Avoiding – This style has low assertiveness and low cooperation. Avoiders will remove themselves from conflict and forego a win result. As with all styles, sometimes this style can be effective. For example, when there is a power imbalance and you know you cannot win, or when an issue is irrelevant, and it is better to lose the battle but later win the war. However, too much avoidance will impact your effectiveness in negotiations. This style results in avoid-lose/win outcomes.

Collaborative – Collaborators have high assertiveness and high cooperation. This style will pursue a win/win solution and individuals with this style will work to accommodate their needs while working to similarly satisfy the other party's needs. However, this style is more time-consuming than other styles and may not fit all conflict situations. This win/win outcome is captured in principled forms of negotiation.

There is no "correct" conflict resolution style. While we are able to use different conflict styles, some people are more effective at using a particular style than others. A timid individual may have difficulty employing a competitive style, especially in a conflict with a competitive individual. And different styles are more effective in different situations. As noted above, if you are negotiating with a power imbalance, avoiding may preserve a relationship better than an assertive style. However, while we are able to use different styles, we often tend to gravitate toward one or two predominant styles as a result of our personalities, culture, upbringing, and gender. In fact, approximately 85% of the individuals included in this study who completed the TKI had one predominant conflict style, while the remaining had conflict style ties. Before we begin our review of the Thomas-Kilmann data used in this research study, let's look at what M. Afzalur Rahim has to say about conflict styles.

Adding to research on interpersonal conflict, in 1983, M. Afzalur Rahim, from Western Kentucky University but publishing this research from Youngstown State University where he also taught, created another instrument called the Rahim Organizational Conflict Inventory-II, or ROCI-II (Rahim, 1983). The inventory is focused on two dimensions, concern for self and concern for others, similar to how the Thomas-Kilmann Conflict Instrument focuses on assertiveness and cooperation. This results in the five conflict styles described as:

> *Integrating* - These people show high concern for others as well as high concern for themselves and want to work collaboratively to reach a solution that will be mutually satisfying. Rahim's integrating style is representative of principled negotiations with win/win outcomes.
>
> *Obliging* - This style shows high concern for others and low concern for self, and individuals with this style will sacrifice their personal concerns in favor of the other party.
>
> *Dominating* - Those with this style show low concern for others and high concern for themselves, hoping to come out on top of any conflict regardless of the cost. This is similar to a distributive negotiation with a win/lose outcome.
>
> *Avoiding* - People with this style show low concern for others and low concern for themselves. Like in the Thomas-Kilmann Conflict Instrument, they respond to conflict by withdrawing.
>
> *Compromising* - People with this style have mid-level concern for self and mid-level concern for others. They often will come up with solutions such as let's just spilt the difference.

Now, with this background on conflict resolution and instruments to identify conflict styles, let's look at the Thomas-Kilmann data used in this study.

Thomas-Kilmann Conflict Mode Instrument Data

We shared what some of our interview and focus group participants have to say about how the Millennials manage conflict in the workplace and their tendency to avoid conflict. These first-hand accounts from Millennial and non-Millennial employees give us a view of conflict styles in the workplace. While over 77% of Millennials and 46% of non-Millennials in the qualitative study reported that Millennials avoid conflict, we know that subordinates may avoid confrontational situations, understanding that the power imbalance may result in people being less apt to speak up. And people may use different styles depending on the specific situation and environment. So, to further investigate conflict styles, we will add another layer and explore data from the TKI to look at the conflict styles for approximately 11,000 test takers spanning Millennials, Generation Xers, and Baby Boomers. The data will tell us the dominant conflict styles of the different generations, including whether Millennials have an avoiding style per this instrument. Special thanks to The Myers Briggs Company for providing the data for this research study.

In the initial analysis, we start with aggregated data over the 13-year time period for Millennials, Generation Xers, and Baby Boomers. Next, we examine generational conflict styles for each database year of 2006, 2012, and 2018 so we can account for changes over time and look at the stability of conflict styles. Lastly, we will look at same-age Millennials and Generation Xers to isolate age from cohort effect as same-age differences are not due to age. Given the large number of Millennials in today's workplace, this comprehensive data is important to help understand how generational cohorts manage workplace conflict.

To answer the question on the dominant conflict styles for Millennials, Generation Xers, and Baby Boomers, we conducted a binary logistic regression for each of the three cohorts for the five conflict styles – a binary logistic regression is a fancy term for a statistical tool that codes the approximate 11,000 participants in the data by the two variables of conflict style (dependent variable) and generational cohort (independent variable). Then, the analysis tells us whether each cohort predicts a conflict style at a statistically significant level, meaning that something more than chance is explaining the relationship between the two variables. In other words, we can say which of the test takers are more or less likely to have a certain conflict style. So, when you read in the upcoming chapters that a particular cohort is more or less likely to have a certain conflict style, this means the results were statistically significant. At times, we may also mention non-significant results, simply meaning that we cannot conclude that the relationship is meaningful. Looking at the dominant conflict styles, three generations and five conflict styles mean 15 regressions, and we'll touch on each of them.

In our analysis, we also looked at one's education level and work level at the time the questionnaire was completed. Organizational level was included based on research showing that higher level employees may have more integrating or collaborative conflict management styles (Brewer et al., 2002). Also, research shows that Millennials are more highly educated than previous generations (Barroso et al., 2020; Bialik & Fry, 2019). Given the possible significance of these variables, they are held constant in the quantitative results to ensure they are not influencing the results.

Another statistical test you will hear about in this book are z-tests to compare sample populations and look for significance. For example, when we look at conflict style changes over time, the weighted percent of each of the five conflict styles is calculated across the three-time frames of 2006, 2012, and 2018 for Millennials, Generation Xers, and Baby Boomers.

Then, we employ two-proportion z-tests to compare the percent of conflict styles of the different generational cohorts and look for significance. Essentially, we are testing to see if the styles are statistically different between the generations by each individual time period. These same z-tests will be used when we look at gender differences and in the same-age analysis.

Looking at the individuals in the sample we analyzed, 48% of Millennials held bachelor's degrees compared with 42% of Gen Xers and 36% of Baby Boomers. Another 25% of Millennials had master's degrees, with 28% of Gen Xers and 25% of Baby Boomers at the same level, and 2% of the Millennial participants had doctoral degrees, while 3% of Gen Xers and 4% of Boomers did. These education levels are shown in Table 3.1. The larger number of advanced degrees among Generation Xers and Baby Boomers is potentially impacted by the younger ages of the Millennials in this study, including those that are age 21 and 22. At that age, Millennials would not yet have had time to complete a doctoral degree, a master's level degree, or a professional degree. However, even with the younger number of Millennials in this study, the number of Millennials with master's and professional degrees is very similar to Generation Xers and Baby Boomers, consistent with research showing that Millennials are a highly educated cohort with a higher percentage of college education compared to other generational cohorts.

Looking at work level, consistent with their younger age, 10% of Millennials in the sample were working in entry-level jobs, compared with only 3% of Gen Xers and 2% of Baby Boomers. Further, as expected, members of the Millennial generation were less represented among the middle management, senior management, and executive levels than the more experienced Gen Xers and Boomers. Only 4% of Millennials in the sample were senior management or higher, compared with 7% for Gen Xers and 20% for Baby Boomers as shown in Table 3.2.

Dominant Conflict Styles of Millennials, Generation Xers, and Baby Boomers

To answer the question: "What are the dominant conflict styles for Millennials, Generation Xers, and Baby Boomers," we used the binary logistic regression we talked about earlier. Starting off with Millennials, there are three conflict styles with significant findings – accommodating, competing, and collaborating. And remember, significant results will be either positive, meaning a cohort is more likely to use a conflict style compared to other generations, or negative, meaning a cohort is less likely to use a conflict style compared to the other cohorts.

For an accommodating conflict style, Millennials are *more* likely to use this conflict style than non-Millennials. Remember, individuals with this

Table 3.1 Percentage of Millennials, Generation Xers, and Baby Boomers by Level of Education

	High School	Trade/ Tech	Some College	Community College	Bachelor's Degree	Master's Degree	Prof Degree	Doc Degree
Millennials (%)	4	1	10	5	48	25	5	2
Gen Xers (%)	4	2	10	6	42	28	5	3
Baby Boomers (%)	6	3	14	8	36	25	6	4

Note. Education levels of individuals in the Thomas-Kilmann Conflict Mode Instrument data. N = 10,687.

Table 3.2 Percentage of Millennials, Generation Xers, and Baby Boomers by Current Work Level/Rank

	Entry	Non-Management	1st Line Management	Mid-Management	Senior Management	Executive
Millennials (%)	10	39	16	31	3	1
Generation Xers (%)	3	31	19	39	6	1
Baby Boomers (%)	2	22	17	40	16	4

Note. Work level/rank of individuals in the Thomas-Kilmann Conflict Mode Instrument data. N = 10,687.

style are more cooperative and less assertive per the TKI. Yet, if we look at the competing conflict style, more assertive and less cooperative, the results of our analysis show that Millennials are *more* likely to employ a competing conflict style compared to other generations. So, Millennials are found more likely to employ the opposite styles of competitive and accommodating styles, one highly assertive and uncooperative, and the other unassertive and uncooperative. However, it is important to remember that this is consistent with differences within cohorts and the key finding is the likelihood of Millennials using these two styles is more likely compared to non-Millennials. Our third finding for Millennials is that they are *less* likely to use the assertive and cooperative style of collaborating compared to Generation Xers and Baby Boomers.

Looking at our analysis, the results are not significant for Millennials having an avoiding style which is unassertive and uncooperative. Why was this finding not significant given what we heard in our interviews and focus groups about the tendency of Millennials to avoid conflict? One thing to keep in mind is that the regression results may be impacted by the inclusion of age 21/22-year-old Millennials in this Thomas-Kilmann data analysis who may be emboldened by youth, while the average age of Millennials included in our interviews and focus groups is 30.4 with a mean age of 31. In fact, looking at data from the 2006 time frame for age 21- and 22-year-old Millennials, the percent with an avoiding style is 17% for females and 9% for males. By 2012, the percent of Millennial females with an avoiding style increases to 23% and 20% for males, and by 2018 the percent for females is 22%, while the percentage of Millennial males with this style rises to 23%.

Another consideration is that many of our non-Millennial interviewees were from executive and professional fields and employees under their supervision many have included those with more tenure versus younger age Millennials. Still, we know that the avoiding style increases over time as Millennials age, and further on in this chapter we will look at the statistical significance at these later time periods to see how that compares with this aggregated 13-year finding. And, we find evidence of Millennials having an avoiding conflict style when we break it down by gender in Chapter 5 and when we compare same-age Generation Xers versus Millennials further on in this chapter. So, stand by for a deeper dive.

Turning to Generation X, four conflict styles were found to be significant – competing, compromising, collaborating, and avoiding. For the competing style, characterized as assertive and uncooperative, the results indicate that Generation X members are *more* apt to employ a competing conflict style than non-Generation Xers. Note, as both Millennials (compared to Generation Xers and Baby Boomers combined) and Generation Xers (compared to Millennials and Baby Boomers combined) are more likely to compete, we'll take a further look at this finding when we compare same-age Millennials and Gen Xers further on in this chapter.

Generation X is also *more* likely than Millennials and Baby Boomers to have a compromising style, or mid-level assertive and mid-level co-operative. Looking at the conflict styles Generation Xers are less likely to use, we find that they are *less* likely to employ a collaborative, or assertive and cooperative, conflict style compared to non-Generation Xers. We also found that Gen X is *less* likely to have an avoiding conflict style, characterized as uncooperative and unassertive, compared to Millennials and Boomers.

Last but not least, we'll take a look at our Baby Boomers. Our analysis found significant result for all five conflict styles but perhaps not in the way you may be thinking. Despite their reputation for being competitive, the results for Baby Boomers show they are *less* likely to use a competitive, or assertive and uncooperative conflict style, compared to the other generations. And, interestingly, Baby Boomers are *more* likely to avoid conflict than Millennials and Gen Xers. Baby Boomers are also found to be *less* likely than Millennials and Gen Xers to utilize an accommodating conflict style which is cooperative and unassertive. Lastly, Baby Boomers are *less* likely to compromise, characterized by mid-level assertiveness and mid-level cooperation. Of all three generations, only Baby Boomers are found *more* likely to collaborate, with assertive and cooperative elements.

When we look at the results for education level and work rank/level, we find consistent results across all generations. Millennials, Generation Xers, and Baby Boomers with higher levels of education are *more* likely to compromise and *less* likely to collaborate and avoid than less educated members of their cohorts. Looking at work level, across all generations, higher level employees are *less* likely to accommodate and avoid than lower level employees. However, higher level employees are *more* likely to have competing, collaborative, and compromising styles than lower rank employees. This consistent finding for all three cohorts may indicate the importance of using competing, collaborating, and compromising styles when climbing the corporate ladder. As both competing and collaborating are assertive, and compromising is mid-level assertive, this assertiveness may be an asset in advancing one's career. Further, it may be that less assertive styles are detrimental to career advancement as higher level employees in this study are less likely to have avoiding and accommodating styles, both of which include an unassertive component.

An unexpected result of these regressions is that Millennials are *more* likely than non-Millennials to employ a competitive conflict style. In addition, Generation Xers are also *more* likely to utilize a competitive conflict style. Interestingly, Baby Boomers in this analysis are found to be *less* likely to use a competitive conflict style compared to Millennials and

Generation Xers, despite previous research that describes them as confrontational and competitive.

Summarizing our results by conflict style comparing one generational cohort to the individuals outside that generation, Millennials are *more* likely to accommodate, while Baby Boomers are *less* likely to do so. Looking at an avoiding style, Baby Boomers are *more* likely to employ this style, while Generation Xers are *less* likely to avoid. For the competing style, Millennials and Generation Xers are *more* likely to compete, while Baby Boomers are *less* likely to do so. For collaboration, Millennials and Generation Xers have the same result of being *less* likely to collaborate, while Baby Boomer are *more* likely to be collaborative. Lastly, Generation X is *more* likely to compromise, while Baby Boomers are *less* likely to compromise. It's interesting to note that the only consistent results for conflict styles are that both Millennials and Generation Xers have the same results for competing (more likely to use) and collaborating (less likely to use) conflict styles. Meanwhile, the other significant findings for conflict styles finds one generation more likely to use a particular style, while another generation is less likely to use that style. These results are shown in Table 3.3.

Table 3.3 Dominant Conflict Styles: Significant Findings

Conflict Style	Significant Findings: Cohorts More Or Less Likely to Use Conflict Style versus Non-Cohorts
Accommodating	Millennials more likely Baby Boomers less likely
Avoiding	Gen Xers less likely Baby Boomers more likely
Competing	Millennials more likely Gen Xers are more likely Baby Boomers less likely
Collaborating	Millennials less likely Gen Xers less likely Baby Boomers more likely
Compromising	Gen Xers more likely Baby Boomers less likely

To further illustrate the conflict styles of Millennials, Generation Xers, and Baby Boomers, Figure 3.1 provides a comparison of conflict styles for each generation as a weighted average. Each conflict style is displayed as percent of the total conflict styles for each generation, utilizing weighted averages. As an example, for Millennials and an avoiding conflict style, this comparison shows the percent of avoiding style as a percent of the total conflict styles for Millennials, including avoiding, accommodating, competing, collaborating, and compromising. It shows percent of styles within

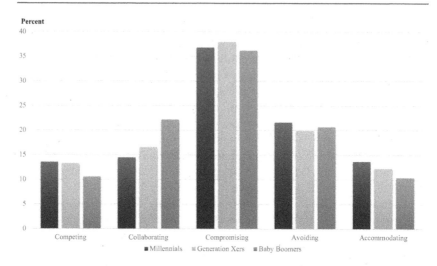

Figure 3.1 Conflict Styles of Millennials, Generation Xers, and Baby Boomers by Weighted Averages.

Note. Weighted averages of conflict styles from the Thomas-Kilmann Conflict Mode Instrument data.

generations and does not compare across generations. However, the results show predominant styles within a generation. The consistency in conflict styles across generations is observed, with compromising the predominant conflict style across all three cohorts. In addition, while the avoiding style was not significant for Millennials in the statistical analysis, Figure 3.1 shows the higher weighted average of this conflict style for this cohort.

Changes over Time

One thing that's true about people of any generation is that they will age. While not included as a primary focus in this study, various research has examined personality and conflict style changes over time. Research suggests that there is a link between one's age and how one interacts in the workplace, says Julian Birkinshaw of the London Business School in research he conducted with his colleagues (Birkinshaw et al., 2019). The researchers note that while age diversity in the workplace has positive benefits, this diversity can also bring challenges. As Birkinshaw (2019) writes, "Different generations have their own expectations and demands, and working relationships can become strained. It's not always easy to report to someone who is significantly older or younger than you are" (p. 75).

To investigate, Birkinshaw and his colleagues conducted a survey of more than 10,000 managers ranging in age from 21 to 70 (Birkinshaw et al., 2019). What they found was that age was an influential factor impacting management style. In particular, they found that older workers are more focused on working collaboratively and building coalitions, consistent with our findings of Baby Boomers being more likely to employ a collaborative conflict style, while Millennials and Gen Xers are less likely to use this style. More mature employees were also found to be more empathic than younger workers. Regarding recognizing how one's actions impact others, per Birkinshaw and his colleagues 71% of older employees felt this recognition was important versus 45% of younger employees.

In a related 2008 meta-analysis examining age relative to job performance, the University of Hong Kong's Thomas Ng and the University of Georgia's Daniel Feldman found higher levels of organizational citizenship among older workers, signifying a greater cooperation and conformity to corporate norms (Ng & Feldman, 2008). Similarly, a team of researchers led by Brent Roberts at the University of Illinois at Urbana-Champaign conducted a meta-analysis of 92 different studies, examining data on changes in personality traits over time (Roberts et al., 2006). One of the goals of the study was to address the difference in opinions as to whether personality is fixed or subject to change with age. Roberts and colleagues found that changes in traits varied across lifetime frames, with some traits changing in early adulthood, but with the most change occurring in the age 20-to-40-year time frame. Specifically, they found that agreeableness and conscientiousness were shown to increase as people age.

Given that personality traits and characteristics may vary with age, and likewise impact approaches to conflict, examining if and how conflict styles change over time will provide insight on the stability or variability of these styles. Utilizing available data in this 13-year time span study, the weighted percent of each of the five conflict styles was calculated across the three time frames of 2006, 2012, and 2018 for Millennials, Generation Xers, and Baby Boomers. Then, we will use the two-proportion z-tests we've told you about to look for a difference between the two proportions comparing (1) Millennials and Generation Xers, (2) Millennials and Baby Boomers, and (3) Generation Xers and Baby Boomers for each of the three time periods. In this analysis, we will be reporting conflict styles that a particular cohort is more likely to employ from a statistical standpoint.

While the ages of participants from each of the three cohorts differ, the changes within the specific cohorts are examined. Given these age differences, each analysis provides insights on specific age spans. For Millennials, ranging in age from 21-to-34, the time frame reflects changes in earlier developmental time frames. Meanwhile, for Generation Xers, the age 27-to-40 time frame is examined. Note that both Millennials and Generation Xers include ages that fit within the age 20-to-40 time period with the most personality trait changes, per Roberts. For Baby Boomers, the included ages of 44 to 57 will reflect more mature stages of development.

When we look at the competing conflict style over the 13-year span, we find that this style decreases with age for all three generations in this

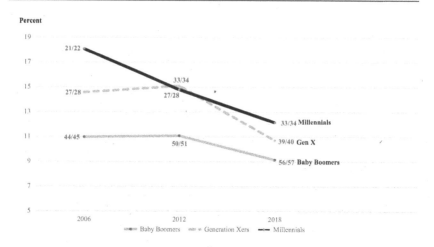

Figure 3.2 Competing Conflict Style over Time by Generation with Ages.
Note. Average competing conflict styles from the Thomas-Kilmann Conflict Mode Instrument 2006, 2012, and 2018 data as a percent of all conflict styles.

study, with a 33% decrease for Millennials, a 27% decrease for Generation Xers, and a 17% decrease for Baby Boomers. These findings are shown in Figure 3.2. The greater change in this conflict style for employees in the 20-to-40-year time frame is consistent with the previously noted findings by Roberts and his colleagues. One interesting observation is that the percent of competing style for Millennials at age 33 and 34 is lower than the percent of competing style for Generation Xers at the same age. This will be examined further on in this chapter when we look at same-age Millennials versus Generation Xers.

So, what did we learn about how the competing conflict styles change over time for our cohorts? What we find is that Millennials in the workplace are *more* likely to compete than Baby Boomers for all three time periods. And, looking at Generation Xers compared to Baby Boomers, Generation Xers are *more* likely to employ a competitive style in 2006 and 2012. This significant difference in competing behavior between Millennials and Generation Xers versus Baby Boomers may contribute to workplace conflict. Lastly, there is no significant difference in any time period in the results for Millennials versus Generation Xers and a competing style.

Consistent with the competing style, there is a decrease in the percent of people across generations with a collaborative style over the 13-year time frame. There is a 16% decrease for Baby Boomers, an 11% decrease for Generation Xers, and a 6% decrease for Millennials. This is an interesting finding as Julian Birkinshaw and his colleagues found that collaboration increases with age. However, this study looks at Baby Boomers from 44- to 57-years-old, Generation Xers from 27-to-40, and Millennials from

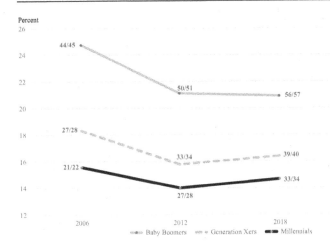

Figure 3.3 Collaborating Conflict Style over Time by Generation with Ages.
Note. Average collaborative conflict styles from the Thomas-Kilmann Conflict Mode Instrument 2006, 2012, and 2018 data as a percent of all conflict styles.

21-to-34, while Birkinshaw et al. included individuals from age 21 to 70. The collaborative conflict style percent over time for Millennials, Generation Xers, and Baby Boomers is shown in Figure 3.3.

Consistent with what we found with the competing conflict style, results for the collaborative style for both Millennials and Generation Xers are not significant for any of the individual time frames. However, Baby Boomers are *more* likely to collaborate than both Millennials and Generation Xers over each of the three time frames, consistent with our previous findings that Baby Boomers are *more* likely to collaborate. This is also consistent with Birkinshaw's findings that older workers are more focused on working collaboratively. And, as collaborative conflict style has a cooperative component, our finding also supports the research by Ng and Feldman (2008) showing older workers are more cooperative. Another observation – as with the competing style, we see differences in the percent of collaborative style for same-age Millennials and Generation Xers which we'll explore in the next section.

The compromising conflict has less variation over time, increasing 2% for Baby Boomers, increasing 13% for Generation Xers, and staying essentially stable for Millennials. Once again, we see a difference for same-age Millennials and Generation Xers at age 27 and 28, with Generation Xers having a lower percent of compromising style compared to same-age Millennials, to be explored. These conflict style percentages are shown in Figure 3.4. We did find that Generation Xers in the 2018 data are *more* likely to employ a compromising style versus both Millennials and Baby Boomers, consistent with the previous findings that Generation Xers are *more* likely to compromise.

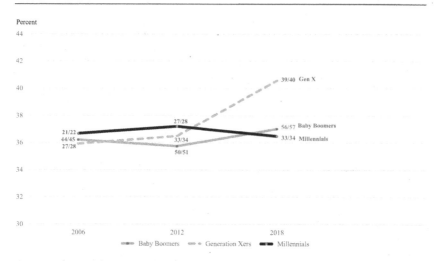

Figure 3.4 Compromising Conflict Style over Time by Generation with Ages.
Note. Average compromising conflict styles from the Thomas-Kilmann Conflict Mode Instrument 2006, 2012, and 2018 data as a percent of all conflict styles.

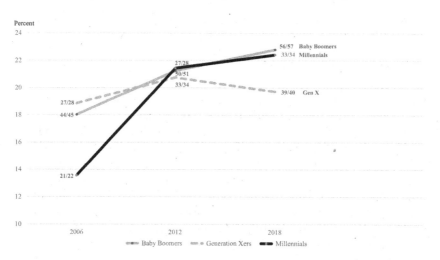

Figure 3.5 Avoiding Conflict Style over Time by Generation with Ages.
Note. Average avoiding conflict styles from the Thomas-Kilmann Conflict Mode Instrument 2006, 2012, and 2018 data as a percent of all conflict styles.

In contrast to the more stable compromising style, the avoiding conflict style shows the most change over time, with a 26% increase for Baby Boomers, a 5% increase for Generation Xers, and a 65% increase for Millennials. These results are shown in Figure 3.5. While our earlier analysis was not significant for Millennials having an avoiding conflict style over the 13-year aggregated data, here we see that Millennials have a higher percent of avoiding style compared to Generation Xers at ages 27/ 28 and 33/34. We'll look further at this in the next section.

What does our analysis show? In 2006, Generation Xers are *more* likely than Millennials to employ the avoiding style. However, by 2018, at age 33/34, Millennials are *more* likely than Generation Xers to use an avoiding style. Also, in 2018, Baby Boomers are *more* likely to employ an avoiding conflict style compared to Generation Xers consistent with previous results that Baby Boomers are more likely to avoid compared to non–Baby Boomers.

Lastly, the accommodating conflict style stayed essentially unchanged for Baby Boomers, increased 2% for Generation Xers, and decreased 11% for Millennials as displayed in Figure 3.6. Once again, we see differences in same-age Millennials and Generation Xers at age 27/28 and age 33/ 34 which we'll address shortly. What did our statistical tests show? Both Millennials and Generation Xers are *more* likely to accommodate than Baby Boomers in 2006 and 2018. Comparing this with the results for the aggregated data, Millennials are *more* likely to accommodate over the 13-year period, but Generation Xers were not likely to accommodate when looking at all three periods.

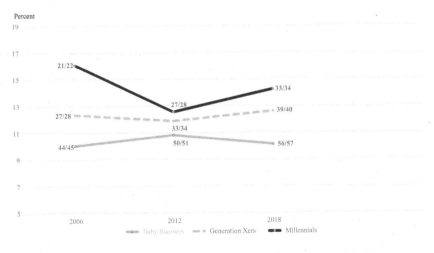

Figure 3.6 Accommodating Style over Time by Generation with Ages.
Note. Average accommodating conflict styles from the Thomas-Kilmann Conflict Mode Instrument 2006, 2012, and 2018 data as a percent of all conflict styles.

So, what did we learn about how conflict styles change for the three cohorts over time? For the avoiding conflict style, all three cohorts have an increase in this style with 65% for Millennials, 5% for Generation Xers, and 26% for Baby Boomers. Consistent with research findings, we see more change in the younger Millennial generation. For the competing style, Millennials again see the greatest change over time with a 33%

decrease versus a 27% and 17% decrease for Gen Xers and Baby Boomers, respectively. Millennials also see an 11% decrease in accommodating, while this style is fairly stable for Gen X and Baby Boomers. And, over the 13-year time frame, the collaborative style decreased 6% for Millennials, while Gen X and Baby Boomers have an 11% and 16% decrease, respectively, in this style over the 13-year time frame. The only cohort seeing a substantial change in compromising style is Gen X, with a 13% increase.

Same-Age Analysis: Millennials versus Generation Xers

When we looked at conflict styles over time by examining each of the three time periods, we noticed some differences in the percentages of these styles between same-age Millennials and Generation Xers. Now, we'll look at these same-age differences to see if they are statistically significant, meaning that something more than chance is explaining the relationship between the two variables. In this analysis, we will look at conflict style data for Millennials and Gen Xers at two different combined age groups: 27/28 and 33/34. This includes a comparison of accommodating avoiding, collaborating, compromising, and competing conflict styles.

By looking at same-age data, we can tease age from the equation and truly see if Millennials in their 20s and 30s were different from Generation Xers in their 20s and 30s. Millennials and Generation Xers were included in this analysis as they comprise the largest percent of the current workforce with a combined 120.8 million workers in 2021, including 66.5 million Millennials and 54.3 million Generation Xers (U.S. Bureau of Labor Statistics, 2022). Comparatively, there were only 27.4 million Baby Boomers in the workforce in 2021 (U.S. Bureau of Labor Statistics, 2022). Further, our available data did not have same-aged data for Baby Boomers that overlapped the other cohorts.

We often hear about conflict between Millennials and Baby Boomers, but in our interviews, we also heard about conflict between Millennials and Generation Xers. Jesse, a Millennial entrepreneur in the Southeastern United States, describes a conflict with a Generation X boss:

> The worst person I ever worked for was a Gen-Xer. And the second worst person I ever worked for was a Gen-Xer... I'm trying, there was one conflict that comes to mind. You know it ends up with me, you know, resigning and starting my own business.

So, let's look at the analysis of same-age Generation Xers and Millennials to see how their conflict styles differ. We start by looking at an accommodating style. Individuals with this style are cooperative and unassertive. Based on what we heard in our interviews and focus groups, we hypothesized that Millennials are more likely to have this style than Generation Xers since accommodating includes a low assertiveness component. When we looked at ages 27/28, the percent of Millennials with an accommodating style is 12.63% versus 12.28% for Generation X, very similar and not statistically significant. However, by ages 33/34, the percentage of Millennials with this style is almost 3% higher compared to Generation Xers. Our statistical tests tell us that by ages 33/34, Millennials are *more* likely than Generation Xers to accommodate.

In our interviews, Chloe, a Millennial in the art business in the Mid-Atlantic region of the United States, talks about how Millennials are less assertive in salary negotiations, impacted by entering the workplace in the midst of the 2007 to 2009 recession. As a result, they were less assertive and more cooperative in their approach:

> I got my master's degree in 2007, so I pretty much integrated into the Recession in the workplace... it was almost unheard of to negotiate. You know, 'How dare you negotiate?' And I did negotiate, and it was terrifying. But most of my co-workers, who were Millennials, didn't because they were just so grateful to have a job and there was the fear that if we did negotiate, we'd get fired for someone who wasn't going to negotiate. They would just sit there and take the... you know... the salary you couldn't live on.

And Chloe describes how she felt during these negotiations. She shared, "I hated it, I was just shaking."

The avoiding style is the second most predominant conflict style behind the compromising style, representing approximately 21% of the five overall conflict styles. Looking at Millennials and Generation Xers when they were both 27 and 28 years old, the avoiding style is almost 3% higher for Millennials than Generation Xers, and Millennials at this age are *more* likely to avoid compared to same-age Generation Xers. By ages 33 and 34, the percent of Millennials with an avoiding style fell approximately 2% relative to Generation Xers. While not statistically significant at this later age comparison, the percent of Millennials with an avoiding style remained higher than the percent of Gen Xers with an avoiding style.

In our interviews, we heard how Millennials avoid conflict compared to Gen Xers. Dominique, a Millennial working for a consulting firm in the Midwest region of the United States, shares the following when asked how Millennials in the workplace deal with conflict:

> So, it seems to me that just from the few that I've seen, it seems to boil up. And then it explodes or implodes rather than addressing it earlier. I think Millennials will tend to wait until it's at a breaking point.

Andrew, a Baby Boomer and Vice President for a large communications company in the Southeast United States, talks about a Millennial going around his back to get approval to come in late:

> Well, I just gave the example of the Millennial who didn't like what I told them, so they went to their manager, and sort of went around my back, and only heard what they wanted to hear and came back to me and said 'We've figured it out, and I can come in late. I'm gonna readjust my schedule.

Andrew went on to say that, in actuality, the situation had not been resolved and the Millennial misconstrued the conversation when she said the schedule change had been worked out. He added to his comments by saying that he thinks Millennials avoid conflict.

Another example comes from Samuel, a Generation Xer in the financial industry in the southeast United States, who describes Millennials as preferring less direct methods of communication: "the method of communication and issue resolution is more via written communication, electronic communication than it is verbal or face to face."

A noticeable difference between the generations can be seen in the collaborative style at age 27/28, with the percent of Generation Xers with a collaborative style 5% higher than the percent for same-age Millennials. So, Generation Xers at this age are *more* likely to collaborate than Millennials. But by ages 33 and 34, this gap narrows, with Generation Xers approximately 1% higher in collaborative style than Millennials at the same age, though this result is not statistically significant.

Some of our participants did say that Generation Xers are more apt to lend a hand. Dominique, the Millennial in the consulting business, reveals: "It's rare that I've found another Millennial who was, who took the time to help me learn something or helped me reach the next point. All of that has always come from a Gen-Xer..."

Drexel, our Baby Boomer executive, adds:

> I think Millennials are much more interested in singular activity and not in a bad way because one person can certainly get the job done. But they prefer to be much more isolated and want to be their own boss. They want to pursue things in their own time and skill levels and be given that opportunity. Whereas I think... Gen Xers are more inclusive to bring in people to assist them with their projects in teamwork and where millennials seem to me to be much more isolated.

While we hear that Millennials prefer working in teams, we'll pursue the particulars around that desire in Chapter 4.

Compromising is the predominant conflict style, representing about 37% of respondents in the data, and there is minimal difference in the percent of Millennials and Generation Xers with this style. At ages 27/28, the percent of Millennials with this style is approximately 1% higher than for Generation Xers at the same age, but by ages 33/34, the percent of Millennials and Generation Xers with a compromising style is essentially the same for both generational cohorts. The statistical analysis shows no significant difference at either age comparison.

Turning to a competing style, the percentage of Millennials with a competing style is slightly higher at ages 27/28, but by ages 33/34, the percentage of Generation Xers with a competing style is 3% higher than the percent of Millennials with this style. In that six-year time frame, the percent of Millennials with a competing style decreased almost 3%, while Gen Xers only had a 0.5% increase in this conflict style. Looking at the statistics, the age 27/28 comparison is not significant, but by ages 33/34, Generation Xers are significantly *more* likely to employ a competing style compared to Millennials due to the decrease in Millennials with a competing style over the time period.

A summary of our findings on the conflict styles of Millennials versus Generation Xers at age 27/28 and 33/34 is summarized in Figure 3.7.

Now that we've had a chance to hear what Millennials and non-Millennials say about conflict in the workplace and looked at the results of the TKI analysis, we'll turn to other issues that were revealed in our

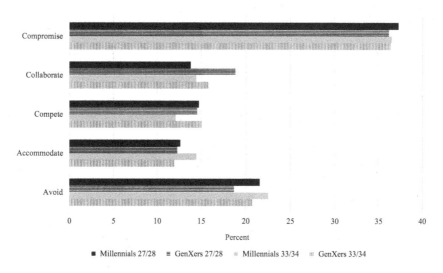

Figure 3.7 Same-Age Comparison of Conflict Styles: Millennials versus Generation Xers.

Note. Same-Age Comparison of Conflict Styles Millennials and Generation Xers from the Thomas-Kilmann Conflict Mode Instrument.

interviews in Chapter 4. We'll address the often-heard complaint that Millennials are more likely to quit their jobs if not satisfied and share what Millennials want and value in the workplace.

References

Alfredson, A., & Cungu', A. (2008). *Negotiation theory and practice: A review of the literature.* Food and Agricultural Organization of the United Nations, FAO. www.fao.org/docs/up/easypol/550/4-5_Negotiation_background_paper_179EN.pdf

Alsop, R. (2008a). *The trophy kids grow up: How the Millennial generation is shaking up the workplace.* Jossey-Bass.

Alsop, R. (2008b, October 21). The trophy kids go to work. *The Wall Street Journal, Eastern Edition.* https://www.wsj.com/articles/SB122455219391652725

Anderson, J.Q., & Rainie, L. (2012). *Millennials will benefit and suffer due to their hyperconnected lives.* Pew Research Center. http://www.pewinternet.org/2012/02/29/millennials-will-benefit-and-suffer-due-to-their-hyperconnected-lives/

Barroso, A., Parker, K., & Bennett, J. (2020, May 27). *As Millennials near 40, They're approaching family life differently than previous generations.* Pew Research Center. https://www.pewsocialtrends.org/2020/05/27/as-millennials-near-40-theyre-approaching-family-life-differently-than-previous-generations/

Bialik, K., & Fry, R. (2019). *Millennial life: How young adulthood today compares with prior generations.* Pew Research Center. https://www.pewsocialtrends.org/essay/millennial-life-how-young-adulthood-today-compares-with-prior-generations/

Birkinshaw, J., Manktelow, J., D'Amato, V., Tosca, & E. Macchi, F. (2019). Older and wiser? How management style varies with age. *MIT Sloan Management Review, 60*(4), 75–81.

Brazeal, G. (2009, April 23). Against gridlock: The viability of interest-based legislative negotiation. *Harvard Law and Policy Review Online, 3,* 1–14. https://papers.ssrn.com/sol3/papers.cfm?abstract_id=1730725

Brewer, N., Mitchell, P., & Weber, N. (2002). Gender role, organizational status, and conflict management styles. *The International Journal of Conflict Management, 13*(1), 78–94.

Campbell, W.K., Campbell, S.M., Siedor, L.E., & Twenge, J.M. (2015). Generational differences are real and useful. *Industrial and Organizational Psychology, 8*(3), 1–8.

Campbell, S.M., Twenge, J.M., & Campbell, W.K. (2017). Fuzzy but useful constructs: Making sense of the differences between generations. *Work, Aging and Retirement, 3*(2), 130–139.

Cutler, N. E. (2015). Millennials and finance: The "amazon generation". *Journal of Financial Service Professionals, 66*(6), 33–39.

DeVaney, S.A. (2015). Understanding the millennial generation. *Journal of Financial Service Professionals, 69*(6), 11–14.

Druckman, D., Olekalns, M., & Smith, P.L. (2009). Interpretive filters: Social cognition and the impact of turning points in negotiations. *Negotiations Journal, 25,* 13–40.

Druckman, D., & Olekalns, M. (2011). Turning points in negotiation. *Negotiation and Conflict Management Research, 4*(1), 1–7.

Fisher, R., & Ury, W. (1982). Getting to yes. *Management Review, 71*(2), 16–21.

Fisher, R., & Shapiro, D. (2005). *Beyond reason: Using emotions as you negotiate.* Penguin Books.

Fisher, R., Ury, W., & Patton, B. (2011). *Getting to yes: Negotiating agreement without giving in.* Penguin Books.

Hartman, J.L., & McCambridge, J. (2011). Optimizing Millennials' communication styles. *Business Communication Quarterly, 74*(1), 22–44. https://doi.org/10.1177/1080569910395564

Kilmann, R., & Thomas, K. (1977). Developing a forced-choice measure of conflict handling behavior: The "mode" instrument. *Educational and Psychological Measurement, 37*(2), 309–325.

Kilmann, R.H., & Thomas, K.W. (2009). *Conflict mode instrument.* Mountain View. *Business Communication Quarterly, 74*(1), 22–44.

Myers, K., & Sadaghiani, K. (2010, March 5). Millennials in the workplace: A communication perspective on millennials' organizational relationships and performance. *Journal of Business and Psychology, 25*, 225–238. https://doi.org/10.1007/s10869-010-917207

Ng, T.W.H., & Feldman, D. (2008) The relationship of age to ten dimensions of job performance. *Journal of Applied Psychology, 93*(2), 392–423. https://doi.org/10.1037/0021-9010.93.2.392

Patton, B. (2005). Negotiation. In M.L. Moffitt & R.C. Bordone (Eds.) *The handbook of dispute resolution* (pp. 279–303). Jossey-Bass.

Pew Research Center. (2014, March). *Millennials in adulthood: Detached from institutions, networked with friends.* http://www.pewsocialtrends.org/2014/03/07/millennials-in-adulthood/

Rahim, M.A. (1983). A measure of styles of handling interpersonal conflict. *Academy of Management Journal, 26*(2), 368–376.

Raiffa, H. (1982). *The art and science negotiating: How to resolve conflicts and get the best out of bargaining.* The Belknap Press of Harvard University Press.

Roberts, B., Walton, K., & Viechtbauer, W. (2006). Patterns of mean-level change in personality traits across the life course: A meta-analysis of longitudinal studies. *Psychological Bulletin, 132*(1), 1–25.

Thompson, L., Peterson, E., & Brodt, S.E. (1996). Team negotiation: An examination of integrative and distributive bargaining. *Journal of Personality and Social Psychology, 70*(1), 66–78.

U.S. Bureau of Labor Statistics. (2022, January 20). *Labor force statistics from the current population: Employment status of the civilian noninstitutional population detailed by age from annual average archived data 2000 to 2021.* https://www.bls.gov/cps/cpsaat03.htm

Zariski, A. (2010, April). A theory matrix for mediators. *Negotiation Journal,* 203–235.

Chapter 4

Millennials Are Born to Scram

How to Keep Them Satisfied

Get What I Want or Leave

Ellie, the Millennial advertising manager, was gunning for a raise at the time of our interview. She said:

> I took my negotiation to my manager, who is in the very low Gen X range. I outlined what I was currently making and what I felt I should be making based on the new skills I had acquired and new projects I had recently taken on, as well as prior projects I had taken on as a workload to hopefully get a higher salary.

Unfortunately, the manager didn't bite. She continued:

> They shared that at that time, unless you are up for a level promotion, they did not do salaries outside of a 3%, for kind of like year over year increases, so I did not get one at that time. And it has since caused me to start looking for a new position because I feel that I am underpaid for the work I am doing.

When Millennials are not happy with their work, they are more likely to make their dissatisfaction known in the form of handing over their two weeks' notice, much to the chagrin of many of the employers in the interviews leading up to this book. Calvin, the Baby Boomer senior manager, said he has noticed this. He shared:

> Millennials have probably the least amount of loyalty of any employees that I've worked with. Meaning if they don't get what they want – this frustration level of, if I can't convince this person to see it my way, to give them what they want, they're gone. And they use that. Some say it overtly, but most do it covertly – you just get the sense that 'well if I don't get what I want, I'm out of here' and sure enough within months, that's what happens, So, their lack of loyalty to the company

DOI: 10.4324/9781003246824-4

or the product or sometimes even the organization is transparent. Their loyalty tends to be to their friends and family and network they've created online. That's where they tend to have their greatest amount of value of what relationships are. Relationships at work are all based on people like them hanging out doing things together. Everyone else that doesn't do that -- if you have kids and you're not a single Millennial - they're like – 'Ehhh I don't have time for you.' So, they're very self-absorbed.

Calvin illustrated this with a story of a young supervisor who wanted to be promoted to manager.

She was very capable and doing a great job, but she had not the experience - she had been on the job a little over a year and the job required two years of experience or more before they could be eligible. She felt that she was already eligible, that she was entitled to the position because she felt she was better than everyone else she was working with and was anxious to get the promotion immediately. I had to explain to her -- there are a set of guidelines and rules set up to make sure that people have enough experience and are ready to go. And I didn't think she was ready for that yet.

The young supervisor did not take that well. Calvin further shared:

She was very frustrated and very upset with me and was convinced that the rules just needed to be changed for her. So, I felt that was a sort of a misunderstanding of why these guidelines exist and she was not patient enough to understand why more time on the job would have benefited her a great deal. So, it was frustrating for me to have to explain to her over and over again - I think you're capable, I think you're very good, but to become a manager it takes a certain amount of time on the job. She wasn't willing to accept that. And, by the way, she later left. Ultimately, three months later, she left and took another job. I'm pretty sure it was out of that frustration.

Calvin described a similar story about a non-Millennial who also came to him for a promotion that he did not receive, but he had a different response. "He wasn't happy," Calvin said. "Frustrated. But he buckled down and started to do more work and took my recommendation to include more people critiquing his work and expanding his repertoire." Calvin went on to explain how the employee expanded his skill set by taking on additional responsibilities and getting involved in projects where he could learn new things. And Calvin reported that the employee he told us about has moved up the ladder and is very successful at the same company that challenged him.

These two stories illustrate a popular opinion among our interview subjects – 85% of non-Millennials reported that Millennials are impatient and will leave if not satisfied. In addition, 62% of Millennials reported the same finding. Nate, the Millennial entrepreneur, said his Millennial employees expect raises and advancement within a short period of time and will leave if they do not get what they want. He said:

> You know, it's like, OK, I've done all of these things for so long, so, you know, that's got to happen now or I'm out. And making yourself so valuable that it's…. I mean I don't want to say it's backing anyone into a corner, but kind of. Yeah. So, they're kind of shooting really high without actually putting time in just because they can go and get another job… So, you know, it's sort of like, if I don't get this raise by six months on the dot, then I'm just going to go.

Hala, the Millennial working for a fortune 500 company in the Southeast United States, shares:

> I think Millennials are not tolerant of the things that our parents were willing to take just to stay in the job. So, for me, it doesn't take a lot if my expectations are not being met. I'm completely ok with leaving. I can go to work somewhere else, or I can go to work for myself.

George, a Baby Boomer business executive in the Southeast United States, had a similar experience of Millennials leaving if they did not get what they wanted. He described a previous management role supervising Millennials:

> Almost all the employees I had were Millennials - if they didn't get what they wanted, if it became unsatisfactory, they would just leave. There's no loyalty to the company. There's only loyalty to themselves and their friends and their collective group. They just turn to you and say, 'I'm just not gonna do this anymore,' And you go, 'what do you mean? You have a contract.' 'Well, yeah, sue me.' And sure enough, they felt like all those skills were very transportable. I can just go move to Utah. 'Why would you move to Utah?' 'Because there's a buddy of mine that works there.' Right. So, to handle conflict - 'I just don't want to deal with this, I'll go somewhere else.…' And I think that is indicative of that Millennial group, whereas Baby Boomers are very dedicated to the work ethic of 'you need to hang in there, figure it

out, stick with it.' You got benefits that you might be involved in, and you want to maintain loyalty to the company. Those are very different philosophical views.

He added:

Non-Millennials are much easier to deal with in negotiations. non-Millennials, they tend to refer to historical facts, things that they've experienced and then bring to the table. Hard to refute that, right? And they also have, if you're a non-Millennial Baby Boomer manager, they have more in common, so there's less need for conflict. I find that they're more about 'let's talk about how we can get this done, how we can compromise,' because they understand the makings of the business better. Where the Millennial comes in, they've been there a year and a half, and they think they should get everything that person works 20 years for. 'I've been here a year and a half and I'm better.'

In our interviews, non-Millennials repeatedly said they valued the concept of loyalty to one's company and were perplexed that Millennials do not appear to feel the same way. Janelle, the Generation X attorney, described it as Millennials "looking at employers as plugging in and unplugging." She said:

What's in it for me right now? Because if I'm working for you and, you know, I'm reaping what I sow, I might stay. But if I'm at PQR Company and the reaping is not sowing, you know, I'm out of here... So, they are looking at employers as plugging in and unplugging.

But Mary, the Generation X archivist, said she gets it. "I think they're smart in that they have seen that companies are not loyal to their parents, so why should they be loyal to a company?" she said.

Backing up what we heard in our interviews about Millennials having higher turnover, a Gallup poll found that 21% of Millennials reported changing jobs and that number is triple the number reported by non-Millennials (Gallup, 2016). Also, supporting the longer tenure of older workers, an Associated Press-NORC Center for Public Affairs Research study of workers aged 50 and older found that 41% have been with the same employer for 20 years and 18% have been with the same organization for 30 years (The Associated Press – NORC Center for Public Affairs Research, 2016). Further, the U.S. Bureau of Labor Statistics (2020) reported that 54% of workers aged 60 to 64 had been employed for ten years versus 10% of those aged 30 to 34.

There may be several reasons for the higher turnover rate among Millennials. First, younger employees are less apt to be married with children, perhaps giving them a greater sense of freedom to risk leaving a job. Another consideration is that younger employees can more easily shift jobs than senior employees who are well-established in their roles. However, as Millennials age, given the economy, business environment, and change in retirement benefits, they may not have the same job tenure as previous generations. Defined benefit pension benefits that calculate a monthly pension payment based on income and tenure have mostly gone by the wayside. Also gone are the golden handcuffs those benefits created, with employees staying so they don't lose their retirement money. Instead, younger employees can contribute money to more portable 401(k) plans, with companies often matching what the employee contributes.

Per a survey conducted by XpertHR (2021) of 222 organizations that offer 401k plans with a matching contribution, 28% have no wait period to be fully vested, meaning the employer matching contributions are immediately 100% owned by the employee. Further, XpertHR reports that 13% of the companies vest their employees' 401(k) contributions after one year, 7% after two years, and 14% after three years. So, 62% of companies provide 100% vesting within three years or less. As a result, this lessens the need to stay longer with a company so as not to lose these funds. Also, the amount of money saved in the first couple of years of employment may be minimal, and it may not be worth staying in a lower paying job if you are offered a higher paying job elsewhere.

The COVID-19 pandemic has brought change to the workplace, including the "great resignation" which we'll talk more about further on in this chapter. While COVID-related resignations have spanned the generations, we still see younger cohorts leaving jobs more frequently than older generations. A recent survey by CareerBuilder (2021) found the average time spent in a job was two years nine months for Millennials versus five years two months for Generation X, and eight years three months for Baby Boomers. One reason we heard in our interviews and focus groups for the shorter tenure of Millennials is that their expectations are not met by their employers.

High Expectations

A consistent finding in our interviews and focus group is that Millennials have high expectations and are often described as "entitled," even by Millennials themselves. This was a very strong theme with many consistent remarks across all generations, reported by over 92% of Millennials and 100% of non-Millennials. Typically, when high expectations were mentioned, it was tied to a sense of entitlement, including receiving pay and promotions more quickly than dictated by previous corporate practice. And being dissatisfied if that did not occur. The findings in this research suggest that these expectations result in conflict in the workplace.

"Millennials think they shouldn't be on weekends anymore, they think they should be moving on" shared Kelly, a Baby Boomer executive for a large company in the southeast United States. She added:

> You know, I've done that already. So more of a sense of entitlement. That they deserve things more - they think they do. So, the folks that are older tend to feel like they have to work harder to earn what the Millennials feel like they deserve... And they want it because they think they've put in a certain amount of time and now they should get it.

Maya, a Generation X retail manager in the northeast United States, recalled a Millennial she worked with previously:

> Younger, but very much a hustler, from Brooklyn. The problem that he represented which was very consistent in Millennials is a kind of an 'I deserve this.' ... 'Entitled,' that's the word. Consistently with the demographic that is even, I would just say two to five years younger than me, there is an entitlement that has been across the board. Where I can say that you need to get from Point A to Point B before you get the raise. Usually, it is them approaching me for a raise or me giving them a review and them not thinking that's enough of a raise, then not having any kind of explanation or any kind of physical, actionable results that show that they deserve that raise.

In our interviews and focus groups we also heard that Millennials are self-focused, affecting their sense of entitlement. Almost 50% of non-Millennials said that Millennials are self-focused and 25% of Millennials report the same finding about their own cohort. This is consistent with other research showing Millennials have higher levels of narcissism than previous generations (Foster et al., 2003; Lyons & Kuron, 2013; Sessa et al., 2007; Twenge at al., 2008).

Abe, a Millennial manager for a large retail chain in the Southeast United States, reiterated this sense of entitlement in his own generation. He said:

> Millennials are entitled. They are gonna be a little full of themselves, think the world should be given to them.... and, therefore, assume that within a few months they can be a leader or a manager regardless

of how much they've actually learned, just because. And they feel that way just because of who they are.

Carrie, a Generation X retail store manager in the Southeast United States, talks about her experience with a part-time Millennial employee who called her about his work schedule:

> I had somebody call me the other day. And part-time for us is anything from 4 hours to 32 hours. I just have to give them between 4 and 32. And this guy got 22 hours. And he called me on the phone and the first thing he said was 'I'm calling you about my hours. You need to give me my 32 hours. I get 32 hours. And I said, 'No you don't. You're part time.' So, I get a lot of I'm entitled to the max of everything.

Viewed from Carrie's perspective, in allocating available hours among all part-time workers, she may not be able to give the employee 32 hours and 22 is considerably higher than the minimum 4 hours. From the worker's perspective, he may need more hours to make ends meet. It would therefore not be surprising if he were to leave the job for another opportunity that allows him to consistently know the hours he will be working and to make enough money to get by.

A title frequently associated with Millennials is "entitled." During my training sessions I ask the audience, including Millennials and non-Millennials, for words they would use to describe Millennials. And I hear "entitled" 100% of the time. Given stereotypes that influence how we view each other, we looked further at the behaviors described by our interview and focus groups participants when they use the word "entitled." We found that the behaviors were often associated with having high expectations, wanting to quickly move up the ladder. Yet, more often than not, Millennials were described as wanting, with minimal effort, what other Generations feel they had to work for.

Knowing that younger employees have high expectations and are more likely to leave their jobs compared to older employees, what did we learn from the individuals we spoke to about how to keep Millennials satisfied? As we'll discuss in this chapter, there are other things that Millennials want and value in a work environment that will prove more important than pay. This is backed up by Gallup (2016) polling that finds that Millennials who are engaged and emotionally connected with the work they are doing are more likely to stay, while those who are detached or not connected are likely looking to switch jobs. However, Gallup (2016) finds that only 29% of Millennials are engaged at work, while 55% are not engaged and 16% are actively disengaged. In the following pages, we will share what Millennials told us about what they want from their places of work and how to keep them from exiting stage right.

Value-Added Work

In this research, Millennials were asked "what do you want from work and what do you value in a work environment?" Sixty-two percent reported the desire to be contributing and adding value to a larger cause beyond themselves. Millennials are a socially conscious group of individuals and will relate well to organizations that are socially conscious, as well. Companies directly working in fields that positively impact social efforts of interest to Millennials, or supporting such programs through donations or other efforts, will appeal. In our interviews, we also heard from Millennials that they appreciate companies that provide time off for volunteer work. This will be discussed in more detail in Chapter 7.

In response to the above question on what is valued in a work environment, Rebecca, a Millennial working in Human Resources for a large manufacturer in the Southeast United States, replied "Value-added work, right? Things where I feel I'm contributing to something bigger than myself is really important to me. And knowing I'm helping other people to be successful."

Similarly, Shelley, the Millennial working in the art business who watched 9/11 unfold from her dorm room, says "The one thing I really strive to do in my work is to truly help people… That's what really lights me up. I could care less about the market."

Julia, a Millennial working in Human Resources in the Southeast United States, shares "From my work I most want to feel fulfilled. I want to feel that what I'm doing is important and that it matters and that is making a difference to people."

A 2017 Deloitte survey of Millennials found that 86% of Millennials believe that a company's success should encompass more than simply financial gain (Deloitte, 2017). The study further found that Millennials stay longer with companies that support social issues. Deloitte's 2020 survey of Millennials and Generation Zs likewise found that loyalty increases when companies address employee needs such as diversity and sustainability (Deloitte, 2020). In another Deloitte survey from 2021, the commitment of Millennials to address issues of concern is demonstrated by Millennials avoiding companies that clash with their values and causes (Deloitte, 2021). Deloitte found that 44% of Millennials made choices about the work they will do and the companies they will work for based on their personal ethics (Deloitte, 2021). In Chapter 7, we'll talk about the specific causes that are important to Millennials.

A Learning Environment

In addition to doing value-added work, 54% of the Millennials in our interviews and focus groups expressed a desire to be in an environment that provides training and promotes learning. Similarly, Gallup (2016) reports that 59% of Millennials want to be in an environment that promotes growth and learning, and that training opportunities are an important consideration for Millennials when looking at potential employers. This should not be surprising since Millennials are a highly educated cohort, and this educational foundation may have instilled a curiosity and appreciation for learning that carries over into the workplace. And, similar to the correlation between commitment to social causes and longer tenure, Gallup consultant Cassandra Fritzsche notes that 68% of Millennials who were provided an opportunity to learn and grow in their places of employment plan to be with that employer next year (Fritzsche, 2019).

Issac, a Millennial manager for a small firm in the Southeast United States, tells us about the type of work environment he values.

> I would say I really value the opportunity for education, and for training. I really value open communication, between team members, from supervisor to worker. That way there are clear expectations and clear boundaries set. And I want to work for someone who is invested in me as a person, and cares about me as a person so they are understanding of my work/life balance, that they value my happiness, because my happiness in the workplace a lot of time directly correlates with the productivity and efficiency of my work.

Want to Know Why

A common theme from the interviews and focus groups that were a part of this research is Millennials' curiosity, their propensity to always want to know the "why" when they are asked to do something. Almost 50% of Millennials and 40% of non-Millennials noted this trait. As such, Millennials were often described as more difficult to manage. Interviewees noted that when you give non-Millennials a task, they go complete it without asking questions. Millennials, however, want to ask questions and debate. They want to understand why they are doing it and why they are doing it the way they are asked to do it, said Jay, the Millennial manager for a large retail chain. He shared:

> You tell them something to do at work and they question you about it. 'Why do I have to do this?' And they're not exactly like 'OK, you're my boss, I should listen to what you say.' They want to question stuff.

"You need to walk them through EVERYTHING [emphasis added]," lamented Carrie, the Generation X retail manager. "You really got to break it down.... You got to tell them the why behind it."

Janelle, the Generation X attorney, mentioned this same theme of Millennials questioning and wanting to know why. She said:

> When it comes time to - You're going to do this, you're going to do this and you're going to do this - I think we're more likely to hear the 'Why? Why do we have to do it this way?

Nate, the Millennial entrepreneur who manages several employees, shared his experience with his employees:

> So, the non-Millennials typically don't have any questions when they're told something. Whereas I would say Millennials are a little bit more prying, curious about why. With a non-Millennial it's a little bit easier. But with the Millennial - wanting to know why and having questions...

Kiyanna, the Millennial social worker, said she's seen questioning behavior both from herself and from younger Millennial employees. She said:

> There have been times when I've been trained by Gen Xers and Baby Boomers, and when it's my turn to be the trainer, I have a hard time explaining why we do things the way we do sometimes. In the sense that I would say this is the way we've always done it, and when that's been questioned or challenged I kind of get stuck in the middle. 'Oh, I don't know why we do it that way.' You know, having a newer perspective, it's interesting to see. I feel that I am on the older side of the Millennials. We get our baby social workers who are 22 or 23, and I'm like, 'Oh my gosh, this is, like, totally different from my experience starting out as a social worker.' So, it's the challenge when it comes to being a trainer in that sense, but also its challenging in the fact that when I have a new idea or a way that I think things can be done more efficiently, sometimes that idea is rejected or scoffed at because it's not the way things have always been done.

Peter, a Millennial working for an accounting firm in the Southeast United States, flipped the script saying that the problem is not with Millennials but with older generations. In an interview he told us:

> I think a lot of the generations before Millennials, they don't know how to give feedback, right? So, they have a task from their management – this is what we're supposed to be doing, right? And then they just string that down the pipeline, this is what you are supposed to do while Millennials want to know why we're doing this task - what's the benefit and what's the outcome? And so that's not ever explained.

We have people leave the organization because of that. They want to feel like they're working on a project and not working on a task.

When examining the questioning behavior of Millennials, it is helpful to revisit the educational levels of Millennials we discussed in Chapter 2. Namely, 39% of Millennials have a bachelor's degree or higher compared with 29% for Generation Xers, approximately 25% for Baby Boomers, and 15% for Silents, and studies have supported the link between attending college and an increase in critical thinking (McMillan, 1987; Pascarella, 1989; Pascarella et al., 1996). In 2016, the University of Minnesota's Christopher Huber and Nathan Kuncel performed a meta-analysis investigating whether college teaches critical thinking (Huber & Kuncel, 2016). While they found that targeted efforts to teach critical thinking did not necessarily improve this type of thinking long term, they did conclude that a college education does foster critical thinking, whether that was a specific goal of the curriculum or not. So, there is an increase in critical thinking from normal college coursework.

This critical thinking involves the ability to reason, think critically, analyze arguments, and make decisions based on that analysis. As such, this critical thinking, widely thought to be a positive outcome in education, may contribute to Millennials naturally asking "why" as found in this study. To Peter, the Millennial working for an accounting firm, this questioning behavior is preferable to being stuck in the past as he shares:

> I think the thing that stood most out to me is problem solving and how that is done differently among the different generations of where, I feel like, I've worked with, especially Baby Boomers, it's a lot of the 'same stuff that we've always done.' Whereas, when I've worked with Millennials that are my age and Millennials that are younger than me, coming up with new ideas and new ways to do things is an exciting and challenging way to get people engaged, and Millennials are kinda turned off by the 'this is the way we do it because this is the way we have always done it.'

Tell Me How I'm Doing

Almost 40% of non-Millennials we spoke with mentioned that Millennials desire frequent feedback and attention in the workplace, and 54% of Millennials mentioned a desire for recurrent attention and feedback. Maya, the Generation X retail manager, shared her thoughts on Millennials' desire for feedback: "There has to be support through all of it. They have a need for constant or more validation. And some kind of reciprocal effect to what they're doing immediately."

Similarly, Andrew, the Baby Boomer Vice President, remarked "What do Millennials value in their work environment and what do they want from work? They want recognition. And they value supervision."

Millennials express the same opinion about Millennial employees under their supervision. Angie, a Millennial retail supervisor in the Atlanta, Georgia area, commented:

> So, I'm constantly having to tell myself that you have to reinforce them, constantly having to give feedback. But sometimes I'm not even understanding why I'm giving feedback cause it's just like you know, doing a good job. Why do I have to pat you on the back every time for doing the same task?

Historically, employee feedback in many companies came in the form of an annual review. But how do most employees feel about the annual review? In my many years in corporate life, I've heard few positive remarks about these performance evaluations and significant moaning and groaning when it comes time for these reviews. And we know that feedback provided close to the activity one is evaluating is much more effective. Therefore, Millennials requesting more timely feedback can be efficient and helpful if this feedback is managed so as not to be overly burdensome or time-consuming. Many managers schedule bi-weekly meetings with their employees to touch base and get updates on current activities. To meet the needs of your Millennial employees, rather than simply reviewing a list of current tasks or assignments, take this opportunity to tell your employees how they are doing and solicit their feedback and suggestions.

Another tool that has been adopted by some companies is to use a performance app to provide or request feedback. We'll talk more about that in Chapter 8 but it's worth mentioning that this type of feedback makes sense as Millennials are connected to digital platforms and accustomed to getting information at the touch of a key. They have grown up in this environment with access to what's happening now. No waiting for letters in the mail, or someone to call on the family landline. Instead, they immediately connect.

Do Millennials Really Like Working in Teams?

We hear that Millennials like frequent feedback, but do they like to work in teams? With the importance they place on diversity and inclusion, we would expect Millennials to prefer working as a team rather than as individuals, and the research bears that out, in a sense. Regarding preference for team or individual work, 70% of Millennials mentioned a preference for teamwork, but 46% also mentioned a preference for individual work in certain situations. For non-Millennials, 70% also reported a preference for teams, while only 39% reported a preference for individual work. Since our interview questions were not either/or, some employees we spoke with said that they prefer to work on a team but prefer individual work for certain tasks. As such, our percentages will not add to 100%.

Peter, the Millennial working for an accounting firm, said:

> I'd rather work with other colleagues in a team environment. It kind of distributes the workload and makes it more collaborative. And you possibly get better solutions than if you were to do it all yourself. You have other people to catch your mistakes. And you're able to catch theirs. So, I'd rather work collaboratively than alone.

Jada, the Millennial supervisor for a large manufacturing company, summarizes the sentiments expressed by several Millennials:

> It's good for me to work in a team or assigned as a team *if* [emphasis added] there are exact rules that I have to do. Meaning I am happy that we're in a team together. It's just that I do not want to step in for your work if you didn't do it. That's what I don't like. So, if there's a criteria of individual work and performance check, then I would be happy to be in a team.

In the analysis of team versus individual preference, a prevailing sentiment that emerged was that Millennials prefer teamwork for the social aspect, while non-Millennials mentioned the probability of a better outcome or end product when individuals work together. In fact, Matteo, a Millennial employed by a not-for-profit headquartered in Washington, D.C., said "I like group work for the social aspect of it."

This social facet is consistent with a study published by Lucy Cennamo and Diane Gardner in the Journal of Managerial Psychology (Cennamo & Gardner, 2008). Their research discovered that younger workers may prefer a psychological contract with the organization that emphasizes "freedom, status, and social involvement." (Cennamo & Gardner, 2008, p. 904). Conversely, non-Millennials in our interviews and focus groups describe teams as having a team leader and designated roles, while Millennials describe teams having an equality aspect. As such, Millennials mention the possibility of a stalemate in teams as there is an assumption that there is no assigned leader to make decisions given conflicting opinions.

One suggestion to keep your Millennial employees happy is to form working groups for certain activities where employees can share what they are working on and allow the group to provide suggestions and feedback. The age-old saying is that two heads are better than one and rather than having a pre-determined task or outcome, it is suggested that these groups simply provide a forum for feedback. These working groups will provide a social aspect along with the feedback that Millennials desire while not having a group task.

Cut Me Some Slack

What else do Millennials want? Almost 50% of Millennials in the research leading up to this book mentioned that they are defensive and feel judged as a generation. Chloe, the Millennial who works in the art business, commented:

> I feel that there's a lot of external judgment about the generation that I don't feel that previously Gen Xers experienced. I find in the workplace it's almost like the word Millennial is discriminatory. If you replace that with race or gender or age, the way it is often used in the workplace would actually be a bit more negative. But because they're Millennials, it's OK to disparage.

Ellie, the Millennial advertising manager, said she hears stereotypes about Millennials, but these do not match up with what she encounters in the workplace.

> I know that people just kind of view Millennials as the burn-out generation or they're lazy or entitled. I just know that from my experience in the workplace for the last seven years, that at least in the creative field that I work in, that the opposite is true. That Millennials kind of bring the spark and the energy to the companies where I'm at. Whereas the Gen Xers are more set in their ways and have a particular mindset... I feel that Millennials bring more to the table in terms of creative ideas.

Similarly, Shelley, the Millennial in the art business, states:

> So, I've never seen such a bashed generation. And I don't think we've really done anything to deserve that... It is just my absolute pet peeve when I see the trashing of Millennials in our culture now. And I mean it's not that we're perfect. I do not claim perfection, but I just don't think it's a constructive dynamic. I think all of the generations really have a lot to give to each other. And if we stop having this generational tribal warfare, we could all benefit from it.

In a study by Michael J. Urick of Saint Vincent College and his colleagues on understanding and managing intergenerational conflict, they discuss how perceptions of generational differences, including portrayals of different cohorts in popular media, can predispose these groups to conflict (Urick et al., 2017). These preconceived notions are carried into the workplace, setting the stage for interactions. This harkens back to our introduction of the age-old phenomenon discussed in Chapter 2 of how older generations view younger folks and vice versa. The difference today is the impact and global reach of our technology, with information at one's fingertips.

We find portrayals in the media for all generations that emphasize stereotypes. In May 2013, the cover of Time Magazine featured a photo of a young woman taking a selfie with her iPhone with the title "The ME ME ME Generation: Millennials are lazy entitled narcissists who still live with their parents. Why they'll save us all." In the article, Gen X author Joel Stein describes Millennials as cellphone obsessed, entitled, and self-focused but then concludes that Millennials are impressive and have the ability to bring about great social change (Stein, 2013). In a video attached to his article, Stein portrayed himself living like a Millennial for a day by wearing a T-shirt featuring The Who, a band that broke up in 1983, and checking his phone a lot. Even though the video was done tongue in cheek, Stein's widely circulated piece influences how Millennials are viewed.

Are Millennials Killing Industries?

One comment from a Millennial I spoke with during the research leading up to this book was that Millennials are even blamed for killing industries. During the 2010s, it was common to point your browser to your favorite news aggregator and find a think piece about how Millennials were impacting the business world. In 2014, Wall Street Journal reporter Julie Jargon, referring to data compiled by restaurant consultant Technomic Inc., cited young consumers for a slump in sales at McDonald's (Jargon, 2014). "Customers in their 20s and 30s—long a mainstay of McDonald's business—are defecting to competitors, in particular so-called fast-casual restaurants like Chipotle Mexican Grill Inc. and gourmet-burger chain Five Guys Holdings LLC" (Jargon, 2014, para. 2).

In 2016, Wall Street Journal reported that Millennials were purchasing fewer groceries than other generations, citing government records, survey data, and shopper analytics (Haddon, 2016). The Journal's Heather Haddon's story is titled "Grocers Feel Chill From Millennials – Younger shoppers spread purchases across many new options." She noted that 154 Wal-Mart stores had closed, with the company planning for slower growth in brick and mortar stores and a greater emphasis on e-commerce. It's quite interesting to note, given consumer purchasing changes brought on by the COVID-19 pandemic, that Haddon went on to talk about efforts to win over the Millennial demographic, including testing apps to place grocery orders in advance. Such efforts included partnering with services such as Instacart and Shipt. So, we can thank our young consumers for being the catalyst that brought about the services that so many people relied on during the COVID-19 pandemic.

The Atlantic published a response piece to the Wall Street Journal article. Author Derek Thompson talked about the cultural shift away from grocery stores to eating out more often (Thompson, 2016). Analyzing data from the Bureau of Labor Statistics, Thompson found that people from multiple age groups were actually spending more at restaurants and less at grocery stores, citing the increase in restaurant spending across all age groups from approximately the mid-1990s to the mid-2000s. So, there was a broader societal shift occurring that was impacting grocery sales and the trend was not confined to Millennials.

By 2019, restaurant industry types were lamenting that Millennials were not eating at casual restaurants enough. Jonathan Maze for restaurantbusinessonline.com, citing the decreased number of restaurant visits by this cohort, said "I hate to say this, but Millennials are killing restaurants. In particular, they are killing casual dining" (Maze, 2019, paras. 1-2). His article was titled "Why is Restaurant Traffic Falling? Blame Millennials." In 2019, Tim Nelson with Yahoo News reported on Millennials killing breakfast cereal, with General Mills supposedly abandoning advertising targeted at Millennials in favor of trying to promote their cereals to older and younger cohorts. (Nelson, 2019).

Three years earlier, the Washington Post found that Millennials were similarly impacting the napkin industry, opting instead to use paper towels in their place settings as reported by Jura Koncius (Koncius, 2019). That same year, Claire Atkinson with the New York Post worried about Millennials killing movie theaters (Atkinson, 2016) and the Wall Street Journal's Sharon Terlep reported that Proctor and Gamble cited Millennials behind the decline in sales of fabric softener (Terlep, 2016). And in 2018, Millennials dealt a blow to cookouts everywhere, supposedly targeting American cheese, according to Bloomberg's Lydia Mulvany and Leslie Patton (Mulvany & Patton, 2018) and mayonnaise, according to Sandy Hingston with Philadelphia Magazine (Hingston, 2018).

Malory Schlossberg with Business Insider worried over Millennials not playing enough golf (Schlossberg, 2016), and Mike Pomranz with Food & Wine reported that Millennials were not drinking enough wine (Pomranz, 2019). The same year, Twitter users piled on the Economist after the newspaper asked in an unintentionally viral tweet why Millennials are not buying diamonds (The Economist, 2018).

"I work at a grocery store," replied @cowlonfull (Fullerton, 2016).

"Why isn't a debt-addled generation in an era of obscene wealth inequality buying cheap gems acquired in shitty conditions?!" asked @HorrorFilms101 (Van Fleet, 2016).

"We're all investing in rubies," joked @zdroberts. "Oh, & trying to pay back 25K in student loans while unemployed" (Roberts, 2016).

"The shambling remains of the Boomers' economy plus 1000x higher student loan rates generally leave us barely able to eat," said @ZhaelKavanagh (Collins, 2016).

"That and people realize it's just a rock," added @SirHaakon (Haakon, 2016).

One measure of a post's population on Twitter is its ratio of likes and retweets to comments. Generally, when a post receives many more comments than likes or retweets, it's a sign that people are criticizing the post in the comments. The Economist's diamond tweet received about 2,000 retweets and more than 21,000 comments as of 2021. Another example of a discussion that prompted a flurry of twitter comments and a sarcastic stereotype was focused on avocado toast.

In 2017, Australian real estate millionaire Tim Gurner, a Millennial himself, was profiled on 60 Minutes Australia (2017) noting Millennials' wasteful spending habits. When asked about the possibility that young folks may never own a home Gurner said:

> Absolutely when you're spending $40 a day on smashed avocado and coffees and not working. Yeah, of course. Absolutely. When I had my first business when I was 19, I was in the gym at 6 a.m. in the morning and I finished at 10:30 at night and I did it seven days a week. And I did it 'til I could afford my first home and there was no discussion around going out for breakfast, or could I go out for dinner or whatever it was. I just worked. (60 Minutes Australia, 2017, 0:14)

Gurner talked about the necessity to work hard and save money to realize the dream of home ownership but described Millennials as traveling and dining out. Several news outlets picked up the story including David Johnson with Time who penned an article titled "How much Avocado Toast Would You Have to Give Up to Buy A Home" (Johnson, 2017)? Another article by Sam Levin with the Guardian was titled "Millionaire tells millennials: If you want a house, stop buying avocado toast (Levin, 2015). The Millennial response was swift. Writer Kaleb Horton wrote a sarcastic takedown for MTV News in which he calculated that if he cut avocados from his budget, he would be able to afford a house in 642 years (Horton, 2017). A couple of the other responses posted on Twitter follow:

"if millennials stopped eating avocado toast and started collecting all the uneaten toast, they cld use the toast as material to build homes," opined Twitter user @miragonz (Gonzalez, 2017).

"Recs for other cholesterol-lowering food that pair nicely w/ unstable job market, unattainable housing & never-ending student loan debt?" asked @ehernandez (Hernandez, 2017).

Do Millennials feel they are blamed for killing industries and unjustly stereotyped? Many of the Millennials we spoke with in our interviews and focus groups think so. However, if you look, you can find stories about Baby Boomers killing industries, including the housing market and live Christmas tree businesses. There are also memes depicting older generations in a less than ideal light. The key is the discourse which sets perceptions and Millennials are very aware of how they are portrayed in the media. We'll talk more about this in Chapter 6.

Millennials Want Flexibility

One of the most common manifestations of Millennials' questioning behavior often comes in the form of a request for flexibility. To the Millennial mind, if the goal is productivity, why should I be in the office from 9 to 6 every day if I can get the work done in half the time at home and spare myself the commute and interminable meetings? Kelly, the Baby Boomer executive for a large company, shares:

> They want to have free time. They want to have time to do things. I think my generation was more willing to work 12-hour days with the idea that we will get ahead and make some money and then down the road we can enjoy ourselves. I think that generation may have a better idea about social and time value in that working 40 hours a week is fine, but not going crazy, that having more time to have a social life, family life or have activities is something that Millennials have, which I think is actually better than some of the work ethic that the Baby Boomers had.

In 2018, a group of researchers led by Baiyun Gong with Nova Southeastern University found that Millennials are more likely than other generational cohorts to engage in role innovation, defining this role innovation as "an individual's practice of redefining an organizational role in order to satisfy personal needs" (Gong et al., 2018, p. 83). Perhaps, influenced by helicopter parenting or stemming from higher levels of narcissism, Millennials appear to desire environments that can adapt to their needs. The Millennials we spoke with agreed and said they like having input on their roles and how work is accomplished. Gong and company further note that role innovation is key to keeping an organization adaptable (Gong, 2018). As such, innovation brought about by Millennials may accrue positive benefits to organizations, allowing them to evolve over time and remain viable and competitive.

Millennials also desire flexible schedules. Seventy-seven percent of Millennials in our interviews and focus groups indicated they want flexible schedules and the ability to work from home at least part of the time. In addition, 54% of the non-Millennials we spoke with mentioned that the Millennials they work with want flexible work arrangements. For bosses trying to keep Millennials happy, flexibility is the name of the game. Rebecca, the Millennial Human Resource manager working for a large manufacturer, said:

> I guess for me it's not necessarily moving up but being able to work in other departments or locations. That flexibility. And when I need, I can take a day off, I can take PTO because I work overtime on weekends. And I don't get paid for overtime cause I'm salaried. So, the flexibility not to come in Monday and work about 40 hours but work Tuesday through Friday. Just that flexibility to work wherever I want but I get the work done.

Holly, a Millennial working in the public sector in the Southeast United States, expresses this same sentiment saying, "Most of my work friends have been able to negotiate some sort of arrangement like that because we just don't feel like we need to be 9 to 5 at an office anymore."

While many Millennials said they do not want a set work schedule that requires them to be in an office every day, some traditional organizations were slower to adapt these flexible solutions, creating dissatisfaction and conflict for their Millennial employees. As discussed by Crystal Kadakia, in her book *The millennial myth: Transforming misunderstanding into workplace breakthroughs*, Millennials bring a modern approach to the workplace and are not motivated by the same things that motivated older generations (Kadakia, 2017). She writes "In the highly cognitive, complex skills world that we are moving into, I'd like to posit that 9 to 5 is not likely to be the most productive work structure" (Kadakia, 2017, pp. 21–22). The good news for Millennials is that the pandemic has changed how many companies look at flexible work schedules, as we'll discuss in the next section of this chapter. However, the amount of flexibility will depend on the specific workplace.

Abe, the Millennial manager for a large retail store, talks about struggling to accommodate a Millennial's schedule:

> He (the employee) had said 'It's too hard for me to get to work in the morning.' So, we had come to the agreement that he could work in the evenings because it would be easier for him to get to work. And then he still kept coming late to work. And so, we bumped it back further, and still late to work. And it got to the point where he was late a remarkable number of times. I don't know how you can be late that many number of times.

While Abe tried to accommodate the Millennial's request for different hours, he was clearly frustrated that no matter what he did, the employee was still late. He did say that the employee was a very good worker when he was at work, but the retail environment managed by Abe required employees to be there during specific time frames. And Mary, the Generation X archivist, described a Millennial coworker who has had similar problems. She tells how he slept in through three alarms and showed up two and a half hours late to work:

> This is the second time in the short time that I've worked there that this person has overslept. The first time he was supposed to have gone to a big workshop on our collection which is like Christmas for us. And he overslept and he missed it and he didn't get the flash drive that had all the templates and brochures and everything on it. So that was kind of a big deal, and then he came in late to work right in the middle of the day because he just slept through these alarms.

While Millennials desire flexibility, over 50% of our interviewees reported that non-Millennials are rigid and resist change. This results in conflict as Millennials want flexibility and the opportunity to bring new ideas, yet they report to or work alongside non-Millennials who they describe as rigid and resistant to change. Jamie, a Millennial government sector employee in the Southeast United States, describes an interaction with her non-Millennial boss. She shares:

> We had one day a week that we could work from home, and that was like our kind of agreement, and it was across the whole agency. But I had a new supervisor, and this was a very foreign idea to her. And I actually really liked the supervisor, but around the work from home component, we'd be on conference calls, and she would say 'Well, Jamie is probably at home with a cocktail - she's working from home today.' And it really did irk me. I was like, 'I am so productive – I'm getting so much more work done than you are!' So that was a conflict that got under my skin. But even with time - I just needed to show her that I was producing on deliverables.

Kiyanna, the Millennial social worker, described the nightmare of dealing with one Baby Boomer manager who had an attitude she felt was unrealistic and harmful. She said:

> Her mentality was that as your supervisor, you work until the job is done, and if your home life suffers because of that or if you have emotional trauma because of the job you were doing, then suck it up and do the job anyway. It was expected that you stayed at work until the job was done, which in the field of social work, the job is never done. So, her influence created a really unhealthy culture for the team that I was working on, and, she and I had a lot of conflict when I would

try to draw the line of saying, 'No, I am leaving at 5 o'clock tonight, I cannot work late, I can't come in early tomorrow.' She would really be just passive aggressive towards you and treat you differently and even be unprofessional with you by cussing you out and yelling at you.

In our interviews, we heard that Millennials want more than a steady paycheck. They want flexibility to experience life more holistically. They want to travel and have time to pursue other interests outside the workplace. It's important to note that this does not mean that Millennials do not want to work. Millennials are very hardworking – they just want to work according to their own time frames.

Andrew, the Baby Boomer Vice President, describes Millennials as the "this is how I want to do it generation." However, he describes non-Millennials as the "that's not how we do it generation." On a similar note, approximately 25% of both Millennials and non-Millennials mentioned that Millennials feel that rules do not apply to them. That held true in the research leading up to this book as well – 55% of the Millennial interview participants were late for our scheduled interview, and they were late by an average of 35 minutes. For non-Millennials, only one was late for our interview by approximately eight minutes. Andrew shared his views on the Millennials he works with:

> With me being a Baby Boomer, if you showed up for work late, you were frightened, you were scared. If you came in and your manager was there, you would immediately go and apologize, 'Oh my God, I'm late, I'm sorry. It's never gonna happen again.' And you stuck to your word. But my thing is, a Millennial will just walk right by you and sit at their desk late. I think that Millennials for a lot of reasons have gotten passes, you know, by their teachers, by their parents, by others that 'oh well, you know, such is life, you're late.' You need to try to be here by 5 o'clock, but if you can't, OMG, life will still go on.

Flexible hours can be a major factor for Millennials looking to balance work and the rest of their life, but there are plenty of other areas where they and older managers do not see eye to eye, including attire and workplace behavior. In our interviews, 54% of non-Millennials describe Millennials as unprofessional or laid back. These non-Millennials express surprise at Millennials' more relaxed attitudes at work. Catherine, a Baby Boomer who works in education in the Southeast United States, said she has noticed this phenomenon. She shared:

> We would have meetings and the younger group would come into a meeting, it's just their approach, the way they would dress sometimes was maybe not quite as professional. They sit there and they bring

their drinks and their food and they're acting like it is okay to have their stuff at the table.

Jack, the Generation Xer Vice President, remembered one case in which a promising job candidate didn't impress because of his appearance.

I had a guy who was interested in a job that might come down the road. Young guy and pretty well respected. So, he wants to meet with me when I'm in the office. So, I schedule a time… So, he comes, and comes in unshaven wearing a rumpled shirt, really, and was a nice young man and, we're talking, and he's telling me about his ambitions, and I say great, great.

But Jack continued:

He didn't present it. He didn't put the time in to impress me. The first impression was not there. I think that was really interesting, kind of like, I couldn't imagine anyone ever doing that. I mean why would you ever come to a meeting not prepared if you want the job? He could have put on a nice shirt and a pair of slacks.

Pandemic Spurs Change

Just as Millennials were advocating for flexibility in the workplace and remote work schedules, the COVID-19 pandemic turned the world upside down. Overnight, many organizations were forced into virtual work and Millennials led the way with their technological expertise. Now, the success of remote work has set the stage for continuing this type of arrangement as employees across generations are requesting virtual work for at least part of their schedules. It will be interesting to see how much virtual work continues after the pandemic which will be organization dependent as some companies are better able to adapt to this arrangement than others. However, the gate has opened, and companies have become more comfortable with virtual work.

One company that has embraced the change to remote work is Quora. CEO Adam D'Angelo announced in 2020 that Quora was switching to "remote first," meaning virtual will be the principal mode of work. The pandemic-led transition to remote work was discussed by D'Angelo in an interview on KQED (Jamali, 2020). In that discussion, he shared that they would not have made the transition to remote work without the education gained from the COVID-19 pandemic. During the pandemic, many organizations experienced a learning curve as they transitioned to a virtual environment, taking the lessons learned during COVID to create a virtual work system that operates effectively and efficiently. This proof of concept is allowing some organizations to continue remote work post-pandemic.

While Quora expects some employees to come back to the office, most of their employees have expressed a desire to continue to work remotely (D'Angelo, 2020). One of the benefits is that as companies downsize their office space, they will recognize savings in terms of rent and overhead. However, the decrease in demand for office space will have an economic impact on commercial office buildings. Another advantage of remote work is the ability to hire the best people for the job from numerous locations around the world. In May 2020, Salvador Rodriguez with CNBC reported that Facebook CEO Mark Zuckerberg, known to be the world's richest Millennial, predicted half of the company's workers could be working remotely within five to ten years, providing a much greater talent pool for the social media behemoth (Rodriguez, 2020). Then in 2021, Zuckerberg announced that employees of all levels can request to work from home, not just senior-level folks (Porterfield, 2021). He further discussed hybrid schedules for employees that need to be in office at least part of the time.

In a similar vein, Amazon is allowing some employees to work remotely as reported in the Seattle Times by Katherine Anne Long and Heidi Groover (Long & Groover, 2021). And Google is supporting a hybrid work model going forward as reported by Gerrit De Vynck with The Washington Post (De Vynck, 2022). Another company reimaging their workplace is Twitter. On March 3, 2022, Twitter CEO Parag Agrawal announced how Twitter will manage their work environment going forward saying "Wherever you feel most productive and creative is where you will work and that includes working from home full-time forever. Office every day? That works too. Some days in office, some days from home? Of course" (Agawal, 2022, para. 3). Agrawal noted that they would continue to face challenges with remote meetings and other facets of virtual work but reiterated Twitter's commitment to allowing employees to choose where they work from. While a change in control could impact the type and amount of virtual work offered by these companies, the COVID-19 pandemic has opened up a world with flexible and remote work schedules that are especially appealing to Millennials and align with their preference for digital versus face-to-face communication.

Still, not everyone has the luxury of working for companies that can easily accommodate remote work and employers less flexible or requiring onsite employees have been flummoxed by their Millennial employee's desire for flexibility. As an example, Janelle, our Generation X attorney, talked about the requirement for some jobs, like receptionists, to be onsite from 9 to 5 to answer the phones. She had struggled with a Millennial receptionist for whom punctuality was not a strong suit. Janelle describes her experience:

> Her first day there, she showed up around ten. I mean this is a secretarial, receptionist job. I mean there was, you know, you have to be at

the phones. We're not forwarding this to your cell phone. And every time I would sit down and talk with her, she was looking at her phone.

While some organizations need to personally greet guests or clients coming to their offices, other companies are abandoning traditional reception desks and instead allowing visitors to directly phone the person they are visiting from the reception area. Or, if a more personalized welcome is desired, interacting with a remote receptionist. Perhaps, changes brought about by the pandemic will result in companies reimagining the traditional reception area.

Another industry undergoing change is Wall Street. Historically known as an industry with onsite employees working long hours, this industry pivoted during the COVID-19 pandemic to a virtual work environment. Lananh Nguyen with the New York Time recently reported on numerous firms implementing flexible work arrangements (Nguyen, 2022). She quotes Tom Naratil with UBS as endorsing greater work-life balance for employees. Further, Nguyen notes that Citigroup, Wells Fargo, BNY Mellon, and JP Morgan Chase, among others, intend to provide flexible work incorporating virtual work.

Are Millennials Driving the Great Resignation?

In April of 2021, the number of Americans who quit their jobs reached an all-time high of about 4 million, according to the Bureau of Labor Statistics (2021). By November, that number had increased to 4.5 million (U.S. Bureau of Labor Statistics, 2022). While there has been a recent increase in the number of employees across all age groups who are quitting their jobs, Ian Cook's analysis of 9 million records across 4,000 firms found that employees between the ages of 30 and 45, capturing a large portion of our Millennial cohort, have the greatest resignation rates with an average increase of over 20% from 2019 to 2020 (Cook, 2021).

In addition to the higher resignation rate among 30- to 45-year-olds, Cook (2021) reported a higher resignation rate among mid-level employees, which may comprise a greater number of Millennials given their ages. The researchers also found higher resignation rates by industry, with higher rates in tech and health care, both impacted by an increase in demand for services which translates to a corresponding increase in employee workloads and stress.

Economists list a number of factors behind the recent increase in resignations – some were afraid of catching COVID-19 at work, others were spurred by the pandemic to seek new careers with better work-life balance, and still others, especially those responsible for child-rearing, said they could not work because pandemic shutdowns kept their children out of school or daycare. Some economists argue that expanded unemployment insurance benefits from the federal government, designed to help those who were laid off due to the pandemic, incentivized people to collect unemployment money rather than return to work. However, these benefits were a lifeline to many.

There may be other factors specific to Millennials. A 2021 study by Adobe (2021) of 5,500 participants found that people are increasingly feeling the need to always be on and available from a work perspective especially now that work and home life have blended with virtual pandemic-induced work. In fact, a majority of respondents told Adobe they are working longer hours now than before the pandemic. Younger workers feel the pressure to be "always on" more than other generations. Generation Zs and Millennials were more likely to tell the pollsters they feel more pressured to be accessible outside of normal work hours. For Gen Z, 57% said they feel that way, followed by 54% for Millennials, 47% for Gen Xers, and 39% for Boomers and older (Adobe, 2021).

The Adobe (2021) survey finds Millennials were also the generation most likely to say they felt pressured to work during normal office hours, even if that's not when they feel the most productive – 63% of Millennials said so, followed by 62% of Generation Zs, 52% of Gen Xers, and 42% of Baby Boomers. However, respondents say they would like more flexibility to work when it's convenient for them. With this pressure to be "on" and wanting more flexible hours, Adobe found that Millennials and Gen Zs are the most likely to plan to pursue a new job in the next year. A majority of Generation Zs said so, at 56%, followed by 49% of Millennials. Only 31% of Generation Xers and 18% of Baby Boomers and older said they have plans to seek a new job in the near future. Consistent with what we heard about pandemic-related changes, leaders surveyed by Adobe said they are making changes to retain employees with the biggest change being adapting flexible working hours rather than simply allowing employees to work remotely.

Large majorities of Millennials surveyed by Accenture also said they would switch jobs for better work-life balance (78%), more control of their work schedules (73%), or the option to work remotely (66%) (Smith et al., 2021). These numbers were the highest of any generational cohort. In addition, looking at responses from more than 9,000 workers worldwide, Accenture finds that 83% of employees prefer a hybrid work model. As noted by Accenture, different employees will want different work arrangements that meet their needs. The key for employers is having the flexibility to allow each employee to work in a manner that maximizes their performance while meeting their work-life balance needs.

There are other factors driving Millennials to seek work opportunities that better meet their needs. Millennials are more likely to be in lower ranked positions than older generations and may therefore be less inclined to stick with a job. Their heavier-than-average student debt load and desire for more work-life balance may also spur them to seek better working conditions elsewhere, and with plenty of firms now looking to hire, they may believe themselves to be in a better position to bargain for better pay and benefits than they were pre-pandemic.

Hillary Hoffower in Business Insider quotes a Millennial interviewee named Sana as saying she felt empowered resigning during the pandemic (Hoffower, 2022). Hoffower describes how many Millennials joined recession-impacted companies, accepting jobs below their qualifications just to get employed. Now, the current market is allowing some Millennials to secure positions that offer better salaries and increased flexibility.

While older workers may be desiring more flexibility and work-life balance based on their experience with remote work during the pandemic, younger workers are more apt to leave their jobs. Bottomline, the workplace of the future, is different from the pre-pandemic workplace. The lesson we have learned from virtual work combined with the desire by many workers to have flexible work locations and schedules is spurring companies to adapt new work models. And, as Accenture found that 31% of employees are disgruntled, 15% apathetic, 12% ambivalent, and only 42% are thriving (Smith et al., 2021), reconceptualizing workplace practices to better meet the needs of employees will hopefully result in better employee engagement and satisfaction.

References

Adkins, A. (2019, December 16). *Millennials: The job-hopping generation.* Gallup.com. https://www.gallup.com/workplace/231587/millennials-job-hopping-generation.aspx

Adobe. (2021). *The future of time: A global study fielded by Adobe Document Cloud.* https://www.adobe.com/documentcloud/business/reports/the-future-of-time.html

Agrawal, P. [@parga]. (2022, March 3). *Here's the announcement to the company about our approach and commitment to truly flexible work.* [Tweet]. Twitter. https://twitter.com/paraga/status/1499422876134371329?ref_src=twsrc%5Etfw

Atkinson, C. (2016, April 16). *Millennials are killing The Movie Business.* New York Post. https://nypost.com/2016/04/15/millennials-are-killing-the-movie-business/

CareerBuilder. (2021, October 5). *Millennials or Gen Z; who's doing the most job hopping.* https://www.careerbuilder.com/advice/how-long-should-you-stay-in-a-job

Cennamo, L., & Gardner, D. (2008). Generational differences in work values, outcomes, and person-organisation values fit. *Journal of Managerial Psychology, 23*(8), 891–906.

Collins, P. [@ZhaelKavanagh]. (2016, July 4). *The shambling remains of the Boomers' economy plus 1000x higher student loan rates generally leave us barely able to eat.* [Tweet]. Twitter. https://twitter.com/ZhaelKavanagh/status/749873883482714113

Cook, I. (2021, September 15). *Who is driving the great resignation?* Harvard Business Review. https://hbr.org/2021/09/who-is-driving-the-great-resignation

D'Angelo, A. (2020, October 30). *Remote first at Quora.* Quora. https://quorablog.quora.com/Remote-First-at-Quora

Deloitte. (2017). *The Deloitte Millennial Survey 2017. Apprehensive Millennials: Seeking stability and opportunities in an uncertain world*. https://www2.deloitte.com/us/en/pages/about-deloitte/articles/millennial-survey.html

Deloitte. (2020) *The Deloitte Global Millennial Survey 2020. Resilient generations hold the key to creating a "better normal"*. https://www2.deloitte.com/gr/en/pages/-about-deloitte/articles/MillennialSurvey2020.html

Deloitte. (2021). *The Deloitte Global 2021 Millennial and Gen Z Survey. A call for accountability and action*. https://www2.deloitte.com/global/en/pages/about-deloitte/articles/millennialsurvey.html

De Vynck, G. (2022, March 2). *Google says its workers will have to be back in the office April 4*. The Washington Post. https://www.washingtonpost.com/technology/2022/03/02/google-back-to-work/

Fritzsche, C. (2019, June 26). *Engaging and retaining your millennial employees*. Gallup.com. https://www.gallup.com/cliftonstrengths/en266396/engaging-retaining-millennial-employees.aspx

Fry, R. (2017, April 19). *Millennials aren't job-hopping any faster than Gen X did*. Pew Research Center. https://www.pewresearch.org/fact-tank/2017/04/19/millennials-arent-job-hopping-any-faster-than-generation-x-did/

Fullerton, K. [@cowlonfull]. (2016, July 1). *I work at a grocery store*. [Tweet]. Twitter. https://twitter.com/cowlonfull/status/748670936069476353

Gallup. (2016). *How Millennials want to work and live*. https://www.gallup.com/workplace/238073/millennials-work-live.aspx

Gong, B., Ramkissoon, A., Greenwood, R.A., & Hoyte, D.S. (2018). The generation for change: Millennials, their career orientation, and role innovation. *Journal of Managerial Issues, 30*(1), 82–96. https://search.proquest.com/docview/2186484901?accountid=11824

Gonzalez, M. [@miragonz]. (2017, May 15). *If millennials stopped eating avocado toast and started collecting all the uneaten toast, they cld use the toast as material to build homes*. [Tweet]. Twitter. https://mobile.twitter.com/miragonz/status/864217792412737536

Graf, N. (2017, May 16). *Today's young workers are more likely than ever to have a bachelor's degree*. Pew Research Center. https://www.pewresearch.org/fact-tank/2017/05/16/todays-young-workers-are-more-likely-than-ever-to-have-a-bachelors-degree/

Haakon. [@SirHaakon]. (2019, May 4). *That and people realize it's just a rock*. [Tweet]. Twitter. https://twitter.com/SirHaakon/status/1124778493122715649

Haddon, H. (2016, October 27). *Grocers feel chill from millennials*. The Wall Street Journal. https://www.wsj.com/articles/grocers-feel-chill-from-millennials-1477579072

Hernandez, E. [@ehernandez]. (2017, May 15). *Recs for other cholesterol-lowering food that pair nicely w/ unstable job market, unattainable housing & never-ending student loan debt?* [Tweet]. Twitter. https://mobile.twitter.com/ehernandez/status/864213033442095104

Hingston, S. (2018, August 12). *How Millennials killed Mayonnaise*. Philadelphia Magazine. https://www.phillymag.com/news/2018/08/11/mayonnaise-industry-millennials/

Hoffower, H. (2022, February 6). *A 36-year-old millennial explains 4 reasons she has no regrets about joining the great resignation: "I made a choice for me."* Business Insider. https://www.businessinsider.com/why-millennial-joined-great-resignation-career-switch-better-pay-promtion-2022-2

Horton, K. (2017, May 16). *Just how much do I have to reduce my avocado budget to buy a house?* MTV News. http://www.mtv.com/news/3013436/no-war-but-the-class-war-bougie-breakfast-edition/

Huber, C.R., & Kuncel, N.R. (2016). Does college teach critical thinking? A meta-analysis. *Review of Educational Research, 86*(2), 431–468. https://doi.org/10.3102/0034654315605917

Jamali, L. (2020, July 10). *Quora CEO Adam D'Angelo on his company's shift to 'remote-first.'* KQED. https://www.kqed.org/news/11828168/quora-ceo-adam-dangelo-on-his-companys-shift-to-remote-first

Jargon, J. (2014, August 25). *McDonald's faces 'Millennial' challenge.* The Wall Street Journal. https://www.wsj.com/articles/mcdonalds-faces-millennial-challenge-1408928743

Kadakia, C. (2017). *The millennial myth: Transforming misunderstanding into workplace breakthroughs.* Berrett-Koehler Publishers.

Kantrowitz, A. (2020, May 14). *Twitter will allow employees to work at home forever.* BuzzFeed News. https://www.buzzfeednews.com/article/alexkantrowitz/-twitter-will-allow-employees-to-work-at-home-forever

Koncius, J. (2016, March 28). *Do you use paper towels as napkins at the dinner table? You are not alone.* The Washington Post. https://www.washingtonpost.com/lifestyle/home/do-you-use-paper-towels-as-napkins-at-the-dinner-table-you-are-not-alone/2016/03/25/d0d076b0-eb8c-11e5-b0fd-073d5930a7b7_story.html

Long, K.A., & Groover, H. (2021, October 12). *Amazon will allow many employees to work remotely, indefinitely. Affected businesses react.* The Seattle Times. https://www.seattletimes.com/business/amazon/amazon-will-allow-many-employees-to-work-remotely-indefinitely/

Levin, S. (2017, May 15). *Millionaire tells millennials: If you want a house, stop buying avocado toast.* The Guardian. https://www.theguardian.com/lifeandstyle/2017/may/15/australian-millionaire-millennials-avocado-toast-house

Mays, J.C. (2018, March 31). *Laura Ingraham takes a week off as advertisers drop her show.* The New York Times. Retrieved April 27, 2022, from https://www.nytimes.com/2018/03/31/business/media/laura-ingraham-david-hogg.html

Maze, J. (2019, April 26). *Why is restaurant traffic falling? Blame millennials.* Restaurant Business. https://www.restaurantbusinessonline.com/financing/why-restaurant-traffic-falling-blame-millennials

McMillan, J. (1987). Enhancing college students' critical thinking: A review of studies. *Research in Higher Education, 26*(1), 3–29.

Mulvany, L., & Patton, L. (2018, October 10). *Millennials kill again. The latest victim? American cheese.* Bloomberg.com. https://www.bloomberg.com/news/articles/2018-10-10/american-cheese-is-no-longer-america-s-big-cheese

Nelson, T. (2019, July 22). *Millennials are killing Cereal. Can Boomers and Gen Z save it?* Yahoo! News. https://news.yahoo.com/millennials-killing-chttps://news.yahoo.com/millennials-killing-cereal-boomers-gen-190613585.htmlereal-boomers-gen-190613585.html

Nguyen, L. (2022, April 5). *Wall Street's rigid culture bends to demands for flexibility.* New York Times. https://www.nytimes.com/2022/04/04/business/wall-street-remote-work.html

Oh, H., Cho, H., & Yim, S. (2021). Influence of perceived helicopter parenting, critical thinking disposition, cognitive ability, and learning motivation on learning behavior among nursing students. *International Journal of Environmental Research and Public Health.* https://pubmed.ncbi.nlm.nih.gov/33540930/

Pascarella, E. (1989). The development of critical thinking: Does college make a difference? *Journal of College Student Development, 30*(1), 19–26.

Pascarella, E., Bohr, L., Nora, A., & Terenzini, P. (1996). Is differential exposure to college linked to the development of critical thinking? *Research in Higher Education, 37*(2), 159–174.

Pew Research Center. (2010, February 24). *Millennials: Confident. Connected. Open to change.* www.pewsocialtrends.org/files/2010/10/millennials-confident-connected-open-to-change.pdf

Pomranz, M. (2019). *Adults under 35 are behind a 'marked decline' in wine consumption.* Food and Wine. https://www.foodandwine.com/news/millennials-wine-study-2019

Porterfield, C. (2021, June 9). *Facebook will allow nearly all employees to work remotely post-pandemic.* Forbes. https://www.forbes.com/sites/carlieporterfield/2021/06/09/facebook-will-allow-nearly-all-employees-to-work-remotely-post-pandemic/?sh=1a7b22dd26a7

Roberts, Z. [@zdroberts]. (2016, July 3). *NAHHH we're all investing in rubies. Oh, & trying to pay back 25K in student loans while unemployed.* [Tweet]. Twitter. https://twitter.com/zdroberts/status/749785479017558020

Rodriguez, S. (2020, May 21). *Zuckerberg says employees moving out of Silicon Valley may face pay cuts.* CNBC. https://www.cnbc.com/2020/05/21/zuckerberg-50percent-of-facebook-employees-could-be-working-remotely.html

Rodriguez, S. (2021, June 9). *Facebook extends its work at home policy to most employees.* CNBC. https://www.cnbc.com/2021/06/09/facebook-will-let-all-employees-who-can-work-remotely-to-request-full-time-remote-work.html

Schlossberg, M. (2016, July 1). *Millennials are killing the golf industry.* Business Insider. https://www.businessinsider.com/millennials-are-hurting-the-golf-industry-2016-7

Sessa, V.I., Kabacoff, R.I., Deal, J., & Brown, H. (2007). Generational differences in leader values and leadership behaviors. *The Psychologist-Manager Journal, 10*(1), 47–74.

60 Minutes Australia. [@60Mins]. (2017, May 15). *Tim Gurner believes our housing crisis will be resolved when young Aussies inherit the 'incredible wealth' from the Baby Boomers.* [Tweet]. Twitter. https://twitter.com/60mins/status/864065346516377600?lang=en

Smith, C, Silverstone, Y., Whittall, N., Shaw, D., & McMillan, K. (2021, April 30). *The future of work: A hybrid model.* Accenture. https://www.accenture.com/us-en/insights/consulting/future-work

Stein, J. (2013, May 20). *Millennials: The me me me generation.* Time. https://time.com/247/millennials-the-me-me-me-generation/

Terlep, S. (2016, December 16). *Millennials are fine without fabric softener; P&G looks to fix that.* The Wall Street Journal. https://www.wsj.com/amp/articles/fabric-softener-sales-are-losing-their-bounce-1481889602

The Associated Press – NORC Center for Public Affairs. (2016, May). *Working longer: The disappearing divide between work life and retirement.* https://apnorc.org/wp-content/uploads/2020/02/AP-NORC-2016_Working-Longer-Poll_Report1.pdf

The Economist, T. [@TheEconomist]. (2016, June 30). *Why aren't millennials buying diamonds?* [Tweet]. Twitter. https://twitter.com/theeconomist/status/748670361840009216?lang=en

The Wall Street Journal. (2017, December 4). Vol. 30, no. 11: Millennials. *Style and Substance Blog.* https://www.wsj.com/articles/vol-30-no-11-millennials-01557858336

Thompson, D. (2016, November 2). *Why do millennials hate groceries?* The Atlantic. https://www.theatlantic.com/business/archive/2016/11/millennials-groceries/506180/

Time. [@TIME]. (2017, May 15). *Millionaire to millennials: Stop buying avocado toast if you want to buy a home.* [Tweet]. Twitter. https://twitter.com/time/status/864166012689817600?lang=en

Tracy, M. (2013, May 9). *Millennials in our time: What the magazine mangled in its controversial cover story.* The New Republic. https://newrepublic.com/article/113164/time-magazine-cover-story-millennials-misses-mark

Urick, M.J., Hollensbe, E.C., Masterson, S.S., & Lyons, S.T. (2017). Understanding and managing intergenerational conflict: An examination of influences and strategies. *Work Aging and Retirement, 3*(2), 188–185.

Van Fleet, J. [@HorrorFilms101]. (2016, July 3). *Why isn't a debt-addled generation in an era of obscene wealth inequality buying cheap gems acquired in shitty conditions?* [Tweet]. Twitter. https://twitter.com/HorrorFilms101/status/749663928544694273

XpertHR. (2021, June 9). *Employee benefits 2021: XpertHR Survey report.* https://www.xperthr.com/benchmarking-and-surveys/employee-benefits-2021-xperthr-survey-report/49981/

U.S Bureau of Labor Statistics. (2020, September 20). *Employee tenure summary.* https:///www.bls.gov/news.release/tenure.nr0.htm

U.S Bureau of Labor Statistics. (2021, June 8). *Job Openings and Labor Turnover Survey news release.* https://www.bls.gov/news.release/archives/jolts_06082021.htm

U.S. Bureau of Labor Statistics. (2022, January 4). *Number of quits at an all-time high in November 2021.* https://www.bls.gov/opub/ted/2022/number-of-quits-at-all-time-high-in-november-2021.htm

Chapter 5

Gender and Conflict Styles

Gender in the Workplace

Gender colors everything in society, from the way we dress to the way we interact with our peers, and workplace interactions are no exception. In this chapter, we will look at what our interview and focus group participants told us about gender in the workplace and look at gender differences in conflict styles. The general perception, supported by research, is that men tend to be more competitive than women on average (Brewer et al., 2002; Holt & DeVore, 2005; Thomas et al., 2008), especially when it comes to negotiating salaries. This is what Mary, the Generation X archivist, told us in a focus group:

> I think when it comes to negotiating, I think women maybe are not as comfortable with a hard-boiled negotiation. It may have changed by now. I know that was something that I had not been comfortable with. I mean, I could argue a point, but as far as saying 'I should get this much instead of that,' I'd be a lot less comfortable with that... I don't know that there's a difference so much across generations, but I did see that gender divide and think perhaps that a lot of the wage gap could be attributed to that. Women are a lot less likely to speak up and say I want more money.

Research supports the idea that men are more competitive. In a study by Neil Brewer and his colleagues at Flinders University of South Australia, they found that women scored higher in Rahim's avoiding style, while men scored higher in the dominating style (Brewer et al., 2002). Similarly, Kenneth Thomas with the Naval Postgraduate School, along with his colleagues, conducted a study utilizing data from the Thomas-Kilmann Conflict Mode Instrument of 200 men and 200 women across six different organizational levels (Thomas et al., 2008). They found that men were more competitive across all organizational levels, consistent with the findings in the study conducted by Jennifer Holt with Holt Enterprises

DOI: 10.4324/9781003246824-5

Consulting Services and Cynthia Devore with Inver Hills Community College, that men are more competitive (Holt & Devore, 2005).

But are we seeing a change in younger generations with a trend toward females becoming more assertive? As Millennials were raised with Title IX promoting gender equality, this may have shaped their views. In our interviews, we heard that Millennial women may be more ready to stand up for themselves in negotiations. While a majority of Millennials in our interviews replied that Millennial males are more assertive than Millennial females, a third viewed women as more assertive and men as more passive. In addition, almost 40% of non-Millennials reported that Millennial men were more passive and Millennial females more assertive. Conversely, only 8% of non-Millennials reported that Millennial men were more assertive and Millennial women were more passive. In particular, it was mentioned that men have withdrawn and become more passive since the MeToo movement, while women have become more assertive and competitive.

In our interviews, we asked three distinct questions: "Do you think gender identity impacts GENERATIONAL COHORTS' negotiation style and approach?" with a "How?" follow-up question. Millennials', Generation Xers', and Baby Boomers' were inserted in the question for generational cohort, creating three separate questions on gender impact. Any mention of assertive or passive behavior was introduced by the participants.

George, the Baby Boomer executive, said the Millennial women he works with are extremely assertive. He said:

> They are fearless. They absolutely know their value; they know their worth. They've been assured by their mother, the generation prior, Title IX, the list goes on, that they're fearless. They walk in, and there's a total ownership of whatever they're doing. They look to you as a manager, like, 'I'm here and I have a purpose, and here's what I need, this is what I've got going.' And they're like, there's no sense of difference between sexes, genders. It's like, here's where we're going.

George said Millennial women in negotiations make up for their lack of experience with assertiveness. He shared:

> Millennial women typically don't have the historical reference, so they're going to deal with the facts and more of what they have right in front of them, and they are more aggressive in that respect, and good for them. They're fearless because they feel that they're backed up with what they know, but they don't have that historical experience or relationship. So, they've got to go with what's in front of them versus what I knew ten years ago. It's just the nature of the beast, but I don't see them as wilting flowers. They're not like that.

Frank, the Baby Boomer lawyer, agrees and adds that the Millennial males he has dealt with tend to be less assertive. He told us:

> I think that the female Millennials are doing better, and they will negotiate a little bit more. The male Millennials that I have dealt with seem less willing to negotiate or take a stand or to argue their views. They'll present something and if you don't agree with them, they're quite willing to just let it go versus, I think the female Millennials will try to push their position a little bit more.

Hala, the Millennial manager, said she has seen this tendency in women of her own generation. She states:

> I think that people who identify as female from the Millennial generation are significantly more outspoken than female Baby Boomers, and I see that more in the sense of Baby Boomer males' expectations. The big boss where I work right now is a 74-year-old white guy, whose theory of the job is from old white politicians, and it is very macho, very boisterous in the sense of a big personality, and I think that he, he has just made some comments in the past that he just kind of prides himself on being a progressive male because he hired me when I was pregnant, and he has kind of bragged about that at times whereas all this insinuates to me is that females of his generation wouldn't be quite so bold as to try to get a new job when they're pregnant or to try to speak out about something.

Luke, a Baby Boomer running his own consulting firm agreed that Millennial women tend to be more aggressive, while the men are more passive. He shares:

> Women tend to be less emotional - Millennial women tend to be less emotional or dramatic in their approach. They tend to be very matter of fact, very straightforward. Millennial men tend to be non-confrontational. They don't want to get into a big back and forth. They tend to withdraw quickly.

Juliana Horowitz and her colleagues at Pew Research found that Millennial women are more likely than older generations to say men have it easier (Horowitz et al., 2017). Their survey of 4,573 adults, looking at how far the United States has come on gender equality, found that roughly half (52%) of Millennial women say men have it easier compared with 37% or fewer among older generations as shown in Figure 5.1.

The same Pew researchers found that Millennial males and females also have differing opinions on changing gender roles, with more women in

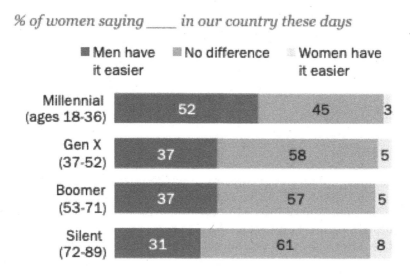

% of women saying _____ in our country these days

Figure 5.1 Among Women, Millennials Most Likely to See Advantages for Men.

Note. From *Wide Partisan Gaps in U.S. Over How Far the Country Has Come on Gender Equality*, by J. Horowitz, K. Parker, and R. Stepler, 2017. Pew Research Center, Washington, D.C. (https://www.pewsocialtrends.org/2017/10/18/wide-partisan-gaps-in-u-s-over-how-far-the-country-has-come-on-gender-equality/).

the workplace and more men taking on childcare (Horowitz et al., 2017). They found that only 48% of Millennial women feel these changes have improved their lives compared to 61% of Millennial men who view these gender role changes as beneficial to women. Comparatively, responses from older generations did not show similar gender differences.

Another recent issue impacting gender in the workplace is the increase in the number of sexual discrimination lawsuits, which we'll discuss in more detail in Chapter 7. This can result in male executives avoiding one-on-one time or travel with female employees, creating advantages for males who can spend more time with the boss. In 2018, Gillian Tan and Katia Porzecanski conducted interviews with 30 senior executives (Tan &

Porzecanski, 2018). Writing for Bloomberg, they report gender unease on Wall Street results in apprehension on the part of males to mentor or even work with females. The two write:

> In fact, as a wealth adviser put it, just hiring a woman these days is 'an unknown risk.' What if she took something he said the wrong way? Across Wall Street, men are adopting controversial strategies for the #MeToo era, and in the process, making life even harder for women (para. 2).

Tan and Porzecanski (2018) mention the "Pence effect," after former Vice President Pence stated that he avoids dining alone with any women other than his wife. Stephen Zweig, an employment lawyer with FordHarrison, is quoted by Tan and Porzecanski as saying "If men avoid working or traveling with women alone or stop mentoring women for fear of being accused of sexual harassment, those men are going to back out of a sexual-harassment case and right into a sexual-discrimination complaint" (para. 10).

These recent developments raise the question of how gender manifests in the workplace and the impact of gender on conflict style. In 2020, M. Afzalur Rahim, the scholar who created the Rahim Organizational Conflict Inventory-II, teamed up with fellow Western Kentucky University professor Jeffrey P. Katz to analyze 40 years of questionnaire data to examine whether conflict management approaches in the workplace are impacted by gender (Rahim & Katz, 2020). They found "that female employees consistently use more noncompeting strategies (integrating, obliging, avoiding and compromising) than male employees and male employees consistently use more competing strategy (dominating) than female employees" (Rahim & Katz, 2020, p. 1).

While research supports males having a more assertive style, the results of our interviews and focus groups found evidence of assertiveness among Millennial females and passivity among Millennial males. Considering that Millennial females are less likely to view gender role changes benefiting them and are more likely than older females to say that men have it easier these days, coupled with Millennials being raised with Title IX, do these contribute to more assertive conflict styles in Millennial females? And, have Millennial males raised in this same environment adopted more passive conflict styles? While the research presented here did not examine whether there is a correlation between these views of gender roles and conflict styles, these are interesting questions for future research. What this research does compare are male-to-female and same-gender conflict styles within and across generations. So, we will see how Millennial males and females compare to same-gender Generation Xers and Baby Boomers. But before we get to that, let's take a brief look at the female versus male pay gap in the United States.

While the male-to-female wage differential is a complex subject, a brief overview will provide perspective on the work environment of our study participants. Looking at part-time and full-time employees in the United States aged 16 and older, Amanda Barroso and Anna Brown with Pew Research Center report that women's wages in 2020 were 84% compared to men's wages (Barroso & Brown, 2021). This is consistent with numbers from the U.S. Census Bureau looking at full-time workers over the age of 15 (not including part-time employees), showing females earned 83% compared to their male colleagues (U.S. Census Bureau, 2022). However, looking specifically at younger workers aged 25 to 34-years-old, the Pew Center researchers found that the wages of women relative to men improved but still have not reached parity, with women earning 93% compared to men as shown in Figure 5.2 (Barroso & Brown, 2022). This narrower gap in younger workers is consistent with what we have seen in the past.

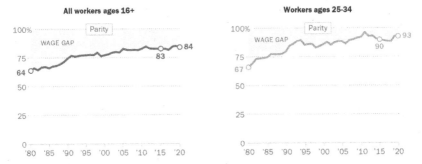

Median hourly earnings of U.S. women as percentage of men's median among ...

Note: Estimates are for civilian, non-institutionalized, full- or part-time employed workers with positive earnings. Self-employed workers are excluded.
Source: Pew Research Center analysis of Current Population Survey data.

PEW RESEARCH CENTER

Figure 5.2 **The Gender Pay Gap in U.S. Has Remained Stable in Recent Years, But Is Narrower among Young Workers.**
Note. Pew Research Center, Washington, D.C. defines Millennial birth years as 1981 to 1996 versus the definition in this study of 1982 to 2000. From *Gender Pay Gap in U.S. Held Steady in 2020*, by A. Barroso and A. Brown, 2021. Pew Research Center, Washington, D.C. (https://www.pewresearch.org/fact-tank/2021/05/25/gender-pay-gap-facts/).

Looking at the narrower pay gap between younger males and females, marriage and parenting decisions may be a contributing factor. As noted by Pew researchers Kristen Bialik and Richard Fry, Millennials are marrying later in life (Bialik & Fry, 2019). Looking at individuals aged 25–37, Bialik and Fry found that 46% of Millennials were married versus 57% of Gen Xers, 62% of late Boomers, 67% of early Boomers, and 83% of Silents. Bialik and Fry further noted that in 2016, 48% of 20 to 35-year-old Millennial females had become parents. At the same age, 57% of Generation X females and 58% of Baby Boomers were already mothers. Therefore, while the narrowing wage gap is encouraging, increased pay discrepancies may manifest later than age 25 to 34 if women devote more time to parenting responsibilities at a later age and spend less time in the workforce at that point. The fact that Millennials are marrying later and delaying childhood supports the possibility that this wage gap may increase over the lifetime of Millennial women. However, this may be tempered by more progressive workplace policies and an increase of females in higher paying jobs predominantly occupied by males in the past.

Looking at the gender representation in our data from the Thomas-Kilmann Conflict Mode Instrument, there is a fairly even distribution of males versus females across the three generational cohorts. For the 3,412 Baby Boomers, 46% are female and 54% are male. Comparatively, for the 4,254 Generation Xers, 48% are male and 52% are female. Lastly, our 3,245 Millennials are 50% male and 50% female. The lower percent of Baby Boomer females, compared to Generation X and Millennial females, is consistent with the increase in female employment participation rates since 1979. In total, the percent of males in this study is 52% and the percent of females is 48%, reflecting the differing labor force participation rates of males versus females.

Let's begin our investigation of how gender impacts conflict styles, a sub-question of our main research question looking at the dominant conflict styles of Millennials, Generation Xers, and Baby Boomers. We will begin by looking at male-to-female and same-gender comparisons of conflict styles across the aggregated 13 years of data. In addition, the conflict styles of Millennials, Generation Xers, and Baby Boomers will be examined at the three different data points of 2006, 2012, and 2018. Lastly, we'll look at gender differences in conflict styles for same-age Millennials and Generation Xers, including male-to-female and same-gender.

Male-to-Female Conflict Styles: Aggregated 13-Year Comparison

We'll begin by looking at male-to-female comparisons within each generational cohort by using aggregated data for the 13-year time frame. We'll use our two-proportion z-tests again to see if there are male-to-female differences for the five conflict styles of competing, avoiding, collaborating, accommodating, and compromising. So, we'll look at Millennial males to females, Generation X males to females, and Baby Boomer males to females.

The commonly held belief that men are likely to be more competitive than women holds true for all three cohorts in this study. Remember, our competing style is assertive and uncooperative. Looking at our Millennials, 16% of the males have a competing style versus 11% of the females.

However, the gap is a little larger for Gen Xers and Baby Boomers. For Generation X, 17% of the males have a competing style versus 10% of the females, and 14% of Baby Boomer males have a competing style versus only 7% of Baby Boomer females. The percent difference between males and females with competing styles is 5% for Millennials versus 7% for Gen Xers and Baby Boomers. So, we see a narrower gap between the percent of Millennial males and females with a competing style which is interesting given the qualitative findings that Millennial males are more passive and Millennial females are more assertive. However, we should point out that males across all three cohorts are still *more* likely than females to compete as corroborated by our statistical analysis.

Our avoiding style is uncooperative and unassertive. When it comes to avoiding, 22% of Millennial females, 21% of Generation X females, and 23% of Baby Boomer females employ this style compared with 21% of Millennial males, 19% of Generation X males, and 18% of Baby Boomer males. The only significant finding in our analysis is that Baby Boomer females are *more* likely than males to have an avoiding conflict style, but we do not see this difference between Millennial or Generation X males and females.

The collaborative style is assertive and cooperative. It is employed by 15% of Millennial males versus 14% of Millennial females. For Gen X, it's 17% for males compared with 16% of Gen X females, and for Baby Boomers, it's 24% for males versus 21% for females. As with the avoiding style, the result for Baby Boomers is statistically significant – Baby Boomer males are *more* likely to collaborate than females, but this difference was not found with Millennial or Generation X males and females.

Turning to an accommodating conflict style, individuals with this style are cooperative and unassertive. The percent of females with this style is 15% for Millennials, 14% for Generation Xers, and 13% for Baby Boomers. For males, it is 13% for Millennials, 11% for Generation Xers, and 9% for Baby Boomers. Our statistics tell us that Generation X and Baby Boomer females are *more* likely than males from their cohorts to accommodate. However, there is no significant difference between Millennial males and females. When looking at an accommodating style, once again our Millennials do not show a gender difference.

The compromising conflict style is mid-level assertive and mid-level cooperative. It is used by 39% of Millennial females, 40% of Generation X females, and 37% of Baby Boomer females. Looking at males, 37% of Millennials, 36% of Generation Xers, and 36% of Baby Boomers use the compromising style. We see a gender difference with Millennials and Generation Xers, with females *more* likely to employ a compromising style compared to their male cohort members. However, when we look at Baby Boomer females versus males, the compromising results are not statistically significant.

A summary of the results of our male-to-female analysis across Millennials, Generation Xers, and Baby Boomers is shown in Figure 5.3, showing conflict styles by gender and generational cohort.

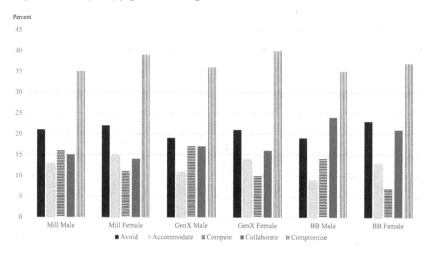

Figure 5.3 Percent of Conflict Style by Gender and Generational Cohort.
Note. Based on the five Thomas-Kilmann conflict styles, with styles for each generation and gender adding to 100%.

As an observation, it is interesting to note the gender consistency in the percentages of conflict styles. Millennial, Generation X, and Baby Boomer females all have a higher percent of avoiding, accommodating, and compromising styles compared to males in their cohorts. And males across the three generations all have a higher percent of competing and collaborative styles compared to females from the same generations. Looking at the five conflict styles, we observe that Millennials have two significant findings for gender differences in conflict styles. This compares with three findings for Generation Xers and four findings for Baby Boomers, showing a narrowing of gender differences in conflict styles for younger generations. The results are summarized in Table 5.1 showing the conflict style percentages and whether these results are statistically significant. A blank cell in the results row means the result was not statistically significant.

Same-Gender Conflict Styles: Aggregated 13-Year Comparison

Next, to help us isolate changes that occur within the same gender, we'll look at how men and women stack up to their same-gender members across the different generations. For example, are Millennial women more

Table 5.1 Male-to-Female Conflict Styles by Generational Cohort

	Avoid	Accommodate	Compete	Collaborate	Compromise
Millennials					
Females	22%	14%	11%	14%	39%
Males	21%	13%	16%	15%	37%
Results	Females more likely to avoid	Females more likely to accommodate	Males more likely to compete		Females more likely to compromise
Gen Xers					
Females	21%	14%	10%	16%	40%
Males	19%	11%	17%	17%	36%
Results		Females more likely to accommodate	Males more likely to compete		Females more likely to compromise
Baby Boomers					
Females	23%	13%	7%	21%	37%
Males	18%	9%	14%	24%	36%
Results	Females more likely to avoid	Females more likely to accommodate	Males more likely to compete	Males more likely to collaborate	

Note. If a participant has two equally weighted conflict styles, both are reported.

competitive compared to Generation X or Baby Boomer females? And are Millennial men more passive than males from previous generations?

For the competitive style, both assertive and uncooperative, younger generations have a higher percent of this style compared to older generations. For females, 11% of Millennial females and 10% of Generation X females employing this strategy compared with 7% of Baby Boomer females. Our analysis confirms that Millennial and Generation X females are *more* likely to compete than Baby Boomer females. For males, 16% of Millennials and 17% Generation Xers have competing styles compared with 14% for Baby Boomer males. Again, our results show that Millennial and Generation X males are *more* likely to compete compared to Baby Boomer males. These findings are consistent with the results of the studies mentioned in Chapter 3. Thomas Ng with the University of Hong Kong and the Daniel Feldman with the University of Georgia found higher levels of organizational citizenship among older workers, signifying a greater cooperation (Ng & Feldman, 2008). Similarly, Julien Birkinshaw with London School of Business and his colleagues found greater older workers are more focused on working collaboratively (Birkinshaw et al., 2019).

Turning to the avoiding conflict style, we find a higher percent of this style with older females compared to younger females, with Baby Boomer females *more* likely to have an avoidant conflict style compared to Generation X females. The percentage of Millennial females with an avoiding style is 22% versus 21% for Generation X females and 23% for Baby Boomer females. For males, the opposite is true – we find a lower percent of this style for Baby Boomer males compared to non-Baby Boomer males. Looking at males, 21% of Millennial males have an avoiding style versus 19% for Generation X males and 18% for Baby Boomer males. Our results are significant that Millennial males are *more* likely to avoid than Gen X and Baby Boomer males.

The significant finding of an avoiding style for Millennial males reflects the higher percent of Millennial males in the 2006 to 2018 workforce with an avoiding behavior compared to males from the other two cohorts. This is consistent with our interview responses indicating that Millennial men withdraw from conflict. Stay tuned as we further explore these results when we look at the avoiding style over time and examine same-age Millennials versus Generation Xers further on in this chapter.

When we look at the accommodating conflict style, we see the percentages of women with an accommodating style slightly increasing for each subsequent generation. For Baby Boomers, Generation Xers, and Millennials, they are 13%, 14% and 15%, respectively. The only significant finding in the female-to-female comparison is that Millennial females are *more* likely to accommodate compared to Baby Boomer females. For males, the percent of an accommodating style also increases for each succeeding cohort with 9% for Baby Boomers, 11% for Generation Xers, increasing to

13% for Millennials. We find that Millennial males are *more* likely to accommodate compared to both Generation X and Baby Boomer males, and Generation X males are *more* likely to accommodate than Baby Boomer males. With cooperative and unassertive elements, this finding, consistent with the finding for the avoiding style, is consistent with what we heard in our interviews with Millennial males having more passive conflict styles.

There is a wider difference in the percent of the collaborating style across generations than in the other conflict styles, both in female-to-female and male-to-male comparisons. For females, 14% of Millennials, 16% of Generation Xers, and 21% of Baby Boomers have a collaborative style. Our results show that Generation X females are *more* likely to collaborate compared to Millennial females. In addition, Baby Boomer females are *more* likely to collaborate compared to both Millennials and Generation X females. For males, the percent with a collaborative style is 15% for Millennials, 17% for Generation Xers, and 24% for Baby Boomers, and the analysis results find that Generation X males are *more* likely than Millennial males to collaborate, and Baby Boomer males are *more* likely to collaborate than Millennial and Generation X males.

Lastly, the compromising conflict style has the least variation when looking at the same-gender comparison. The percentage of this style among Millennial, Generation X, and Baby Boomer females is 39%, 40%, and 37%, respectively. Turning to males, 35% of Millennials and Baby Boomers have a compromising style compared to 36% of Generation Xers. The only significant finding is that Generation X females are *more* likely than Baby Boomer females to use a compromising style.

A summary of the same-gender conflict styles are provided in Table 5.2 with results showing generational cohorts more likely to employ a specific conflict style. A blank cell means there are no statistically significant results.

Changes over Time

We just looked at conflict styles by gender for each generation using accumulated data for the 2006-to-2018-time frame. Now, we examine conflict styles by gender over the three distinct database years of 2006, 2012, and 2018. This will show how the conflict styles change over the time periods.

We're starting off with a bang with the avoiding conflict style – there is a considerable 156% increase in the percent of this style for Millennial males between 2006 and 2018, going from 9% to 23%. As previously noted, since Millennials in the 2006 database are 21/22 years of age, the 9% avoiding style at that age versus 23% at age 33/34 may be an age effect. This finding of Millennial males becoming more avoiding and passive is consistent with the findings in the interview results, where the average

Table 5.2 Same-Gender Comparisons of Conflict Styles

Conflict Style	1. Females			Males		
	Millennial vs. Gen X	Millennial vs. Baby Boomer	Gen X vs. Baby Boomer	Millennial vs. Gen X	Millennial vs. Baby Boomer	Gen X vs. Baby Boomer
Compete		Millennials more likely	Gen X more likely		Millennials more likely	Gen X more likely
Avoid			Baby Boomer more likely	Millennial more likely	Millennial more likely	
Accommodate		Millennial more likely		Millennial more likely	Millennial more likely	Gen X more likely
Collaborate	Gen X more likely	Baby Boomer more likely	Baby Boomer more likely	Gen X more likely	Baby Boomer more likely	Baby Boomer more likely
Compromise			Gen X more likely		Baby Boomer more likely	

Note. Based on the conflict styles by gender in the Thomas-Kilmann Conflict Mode Instrument data.

age of the Millennial participants is 30.4 and the mean age is 31. It's interesting to note that even with the low percent of an avoiding style at age 21/22, Millennial males were still *more* likely to avoid than Baby Boomer and Gen X males when we looked over the 13-year time frame in the previous section. Looking at Baby Boomer males over the 13-year span, the avoiding style increased 31% (from 16% to 21%), while the percent for Generation X males remained stable (18% to 18%).

Millennial females also increased their avoiding style, though not nearly as much – there is a 29% increase in avoiding behavior for Millennial women, increasing from 17% to 22%. As such, the increase in avoiding style for Millennials overall across the 13-year time frame is largely driven by the 156% increase in Millennial males with avoiding conflict styles. Looking at Gen X females, they have a 5% increase (from 20% to 21%) in avoiding style, while Baby Boomer females have a 20% increase (from 20% to 24%).

Figure 5.4 shows the results of our gender analysis of an avoiding conflict style over the three time periods. With an avoiding style, we see the greatest change over time in the Millennial group consistent with research showing the greatest changes occur in the 20–40 age range. However, we see change in the other generations, as well. Turning to our statistics toolbox, we find Millennial females in the 2006 data when they are 21 and 22-year olds are *more* likely than Millennial males to avoid conflict; Baby Boomer females are *more* likely to avoid compared to Baby Boomer males in 2006 and 2012 compared to their male counterparts. While not statistically significant, it's interesting to note that Millennial females in 2018

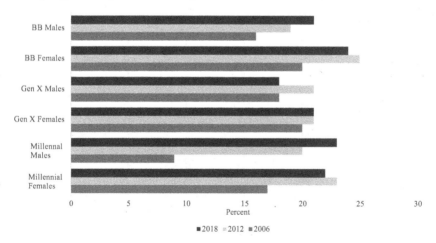

Figure 5.4 Avoiding Conflict Style by Generation and Gender: 2018, 2012, 2006.

Note. Based on the avoiding conflict styles by gender in the Thomas-Kilmann Conflict Mode Instrument data.

are the only cohort that has a lower percent of avoiding style compared to their male cohort members, at 22% versus 23%.

What do our results look like for when we switch to same-gender comparisons? The only significant female-to-female result is that Baby Boomer females are *more* likely than Generation X females to use an avoiding style in 2012. However, there were more findings in the male-to-male comparisons. In 2006, Generation X and Baby Boomer males are *more* likely to use an avoiding style compared to Millennial males. This is not unexpected given the low percent of avoiding style for age 21 and 22 Millennial males. However, by 2018, when Millennials are 33 and 34 years old, they are *more* likely to have an avoiding conflict style compared to Generation X males. The results of the male-to-female and same-gender analyses for an avoiding conflict style are shown in Table 5.3.

Table 5.3 Male-to-Female and Same-Gender Avoiding Conflict Style over Time: Significant Findings

2006	
Male to female	Millennial and Baby Boomer females more likely than their male cohort members to avoid
Male to male	Gen X and Baby Boomer more likely than Millennial to avoid
2012	
Male to female	Baby Boomer females more likely than Baby Boomer males to avoid
Female to female	Baby Boomer more likely than Gen X to avoid
2018	
Male to male	Millennial more likely than Gen X to avoid

Note. Based on the avoiding conflict styles by gender in the Thomas-Kilmann Conflict Mode Instrument data.

As with the avoiding conflict style, Millennials show the largest change in an accommodating conflict style over the three time periods. The percent of Millennial females with an accommodating style decreases 42% (from 25% to 14%) between 2006 and 2018, and at the same time, Millennial males show a massive 200% increase (from 5% to 15%) in this unassertive and cooperative conflict style. For Generation Xers, males experienced a 10% increase (from 10% to 11%) in the accommodating style, while the percent for females stayed the same (at 14%). Lastly, Baby Boomer females experienced an 8% decrease (from 13% to 12%), while males had a 13% increase (from 8% to 9%) in the percent of accommodating style.

What did we see in our analysis? In 2006, 21- and 22-year-old Millennial females were *more* likely than Millennial males to use an accommodating style. But, in both 2012 and 2018 when they were older, there were no significant differences between Millennial males and females. As one of the elements of an accommodating style is unassertive behavior, it is possible that the finding of no significant difference in accommodating conflict styles between Millennial males and females may be due to an increase in unassertive behavior in Millennial males. To find out, we will compare Millennial males to other males to see if they are more likely to employ styles that include an unassertive element like accommodating and avoiding – stand by for those results. Looking at Generation X females, they are *more* likely than Generation X males to employ an accommodating style in 2006, 2012, and 2018. Similarly, Baby Boomer females are *more* likely than the male members of their cohort to use an accommodating style in 2006 and 2012. Figure 5.5 shows the results of our male-to-female comparisons over time.

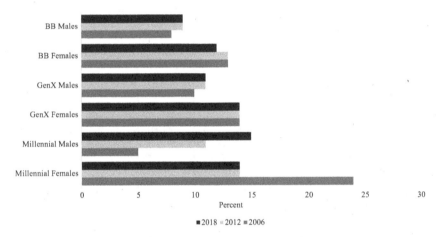

Figure 5.5 Accommodating Conflict Style by Generation and Gender: 2018, 2012, 2006.

Note. Based on the accommodating conflict styles by gender in the Thomas-Kilmann Conflict Mode Instrument data.

Turning to a same-gender comparison of an accommodating style over time, in 2006, 21- and 22-year-old Millennial females are *more* likely than Generation X and Baby Boomer females to accommodate. Looking at Millennial males, they are *more* likely to use this unassertive and cooperative conflict style compared to Gen X and Baby Boomer males in 2018 when they are 34/35 and Generation X and Baby Boomers were 39/40 and 56/57, respectively. While the ages of the three generational cohorts are different in 2018, this finding provides support for the more passive conflict styles for Millennial males in the workplace, as shown in the interviews. The only other significant result for an accommodating style is that Generation X males in 2006 are *more* likely than Baby Boomer males to use an accommodating style. The results of the male-to-female and same-gender analyses for the accommodating conflict style are shown in Table 5.4.

Table 5.4 Male-to-Female and Same-Gender Accommodating Conflict Style over Time: Significant Findings

2006	
Male to female	Millennial, Gen X, and Baby Boomers females more likely than their male cohort members to accommodate
Male to male	Gen X males more likely than Baby Boomer males to accommodate
Female to female	Millennial females more likely than Gen X and Baby Boomer females to accommodate

2012	
Male to female	Gen X and Baby Boomer females more likely than their male cohort members to accommodate
Female to female	Baby Boomer females more likely than Gen X females to accommodate

2018	
Male to female	Gen X females more likely than Gen X males to accommodate
Male to male	Millennial males more likely than Gen X and Baby Boomer males to accommodate

Note. Based on the competing conflict styles by gender in the Thomas-Kilmann Conflict Mode Instrument data.

Millennials experience the largest percent change in the competing style over the study period compared to the Generation X and Baby Boomers with a 59% decrease for Millennial males (from 34% to 14%) and 43% increase (from 7% to 10%) for Millennial females. In contrast to the increase in the competitive style of female Millennials, Generation X females had a 45% decrease (from 11% to 6%) in competing style during the same time frame and there was a 17% decrease (from 18% to 15%) in the competing style for Generation X males. While the ages of these cohorts are different, they still have some overlap with Gen X ranging in age from 27 to 40 versus Millennials ranging in age from 21 to 34. For Baby Boomers, females show a 17% increase (from 6% to 7%) in competing style, while Baby Boomer males show a 20% decrease (from 15% to 12%). The competing style over time is shown in Figure 5.6.

What did we find when we looked for statistical significance? In the comparison of males-to-females and a competing conflict style over time, males are *more* likely in all three generational cohorts and across all three time frames to be more likely to employ a competing conflict style versus

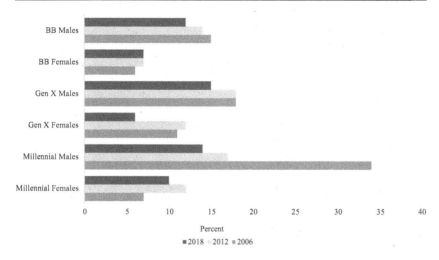

Figure 5.6 Competing Conflict Style by Generation and Gender: 2018, 2012, 2006.

their female cohort members. Turning to the same-gender comparison of a competing conflict style, in 2018, Millennial females are *more* likely than Generation X and Baby Boomer females to have a competitive conflict style. In addition, Millennial females are *more* likely than Baby Boomer females to have a competitive style in 2012. Further, Generation X females are *more* likely to have a competitive style in 2006 and 2012 compared to Baby Boomers. Turning to males, in 2006 in their early 20s, Millennial males are *more* likely to be competitive compared to Generation X and Baby Boomer males. Further, Millennial males are *more* likely to use a competitive style compared to Baby Boomer males in 2012 but there is no significant finding for Millennial males and a competitive style in 2018. Lastly, Generation X males are *more* likely to employ a competitive style versus Baby Boomer males in 2012 and 2018. The results of the male-to-female and same-gender analyses for the competing style are shown in Table 5.5.

Turning to the collaborative style, over the 13-year period from 2006 to 2018, both female and male Millennials saw a decrease in the collaborating style, dropping by 7% (from 15% to 14%) and 12% (from 17% to 15%), respectively. Similarly, Generation X females experienced an 11% decrease (from 18% to 16%) as did Generation X males (from 19% to 17%). Lastly, the collaborative style for Baby Boomers decreased by 17% (from 23% to 19%) for females and 12% (from 26% to 23%) for males. These results are shown in Figure 5.7.

Looking at male-to-female comparisons of the collaborative style, the only statistically significant result is that Baby Boomer males are *more* likely to collaborate than Baby Boomer females in the 2018 database. When it comes to same-gender comparisons for the collaborative style,

Table 5.5 Male-to-Female and Same-Gender Competing Conflict Style over Time: Significant Findings

2006

Male to female	Males more likely to compete across all three cohorts
Female to female	Generation X more likely to compete than Baby Boomers
Male to male	Millennials more likely to compete than Gen X and Baby Boomers

2012

Male to female	Males more likely to compete across all three cohorts
Female to female	Millennial and Gen X more likely to compete than Baby Boomers
Male to male	Millennials and Gen X more likely to compete than Baby Boomers

2018

Male to female	Males more likely to compete across all three cohorts
Female to female	Millennials more likely to compete than Gen X and Baby Boomers
Male to male	Gen X more likely to compete than Baby Boomer

Note. Based on the competing conflict styles by gender in the Thomas-Kilmann Conflict Mode Instrument data.

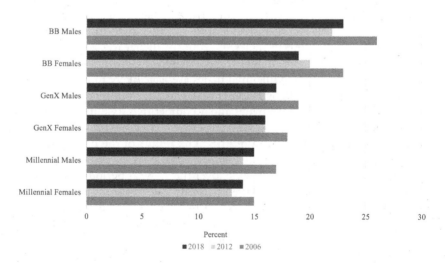

Figure 5.7 Collaborating Conflict Style by Gender: 2018, 2012, 2006.
Note. Based on the collaborating conflict styles by gender in the Thomas-Kilmann Conflict Mode Instrument data.

female Baby Boomers are *more* likely to collaborate than Millennials and Gen Xers across all time periods. We see the same result with males – Baby Boomer males across all three time periods are *more* likely than Millennial and Gen X males to collaborate. The results for the male-to-female and same-gender analyses for the collaborative style are shown in Table 5.6.

Table 5.6 Male-to-Female and Same-Gender Collaborating Conflict Style over Time: Significant Findings

2006	
Female to female	Baby Boomers more likely than Millennials and Gen X to collaborate
Male to male	Baby Boomers more likely than Millennials and Gen X to collaborate
2012	
Female to female	Baby Boomers more likely than Millennials and Gen X to collaborate
Male to male	Baby Boomers more likely than Millennials and Gen X to collaborate
2018	
Male to female	Baby Boomer males more likely to collaborate than Baby Boomer females
Female to female	Baby Boomers more likely than Millennials and Gen X to collaborate
Male to male	Baby Boomers more likely than Millennials and Gen X to collaborate

Note. Based on the collaborating conflict styles by gender in the Thomas-Kilmann Conflict Mode Instrument data.

Looking at the final conflict style of compromising, Millennials swapped over the time frame, with females seeing a 5% increase (from 38% to 40%) in compromising style from 2006 to 2018, while Millennial males had a 6% decrease (from 35% to 33%). For Generation Xers, females and males had an increase in compromising style of 16% (from 37% to 43%) and 9% (from 35% to 38%), respectively, and for Baby Boomers, the percent of compromising style remained stable over the 13-year time frame with females at 38% and males at 35%. These are shown in Figure 5.8.

In the analysis of males to females and a compromising style, the only statistically significant results come from the 2018 time period, with Millennial and Generation X females *more* likely to compromise compared to males in their cohorts. Looking at same-gender comparisons of a compromising conflict style, there are only two significant findings, also from 2018. In that year, Generation X females were *more* likely than Baby Boomer females to use a compromising style, and Generation X males

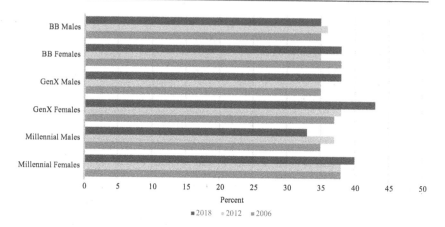

Figure 5.8 Compromising Conflict Style by Gender: 2018, 2012, 2006.
Note. Based on the compromising conflict styles by gender in the Thomas-Kilmann Conflict Mode Instrument data.

were *more* likely than Millennial males to use a compromising style. These gender analyses results for the compromising style are shown in Table 5.7.

Table 5.7 Male-to-Female and Same-Gender Compromising Conflict Style over Time: Significant Findings

2018	
Male to female	Millennial and Generation X females more likely than Gen X males to compromise
Female to female	Gen X more likely to compromise than Baby Boomer females
Male to male	Gen X more likely to compromise than Millennial

Note. Based on the compromising conflict styles by gender in the Thomas-Kilmann Conflict Mode Instrument data.

Same-Age Gender Analysis: Millennials and Generation Xers

We continue our gender analysis by looking at same-age Millennials and Generation Xers to remove age from the equation. This analysis calculates the percent of avoiding, accommodating, competing, collaborating, and compromising conflict styles for male and female Millennials and Generation Xers at age 27/28 and 33/34. (You may recall that we use the two combined age groups of ages 27 and 28, and 33 and 34.) Then, we run our two-proportion z-tests to look for statistical significance.

Looking at an avoiding conflict style, with uncooperative and unassertive elements, we find that Millennial males have a higher percent of avoiding style compared to Generation X males in both age brackets. At ages 27/28, the percent of Millennial males with an avoiding style is approximately 3% higher than that of Generation X males, and that shrinks to approximately 2% higher by age 33 and 34. But despite those percent differences, both results are not significant from a statistical standpoint. Also, the percent of Millennial females with an avoiding style is higher than the percent of Generation X females with this style, but again, the results are not statistically significant. The avoid conflict style for same-age Millennials is shown in Figure 5.9.

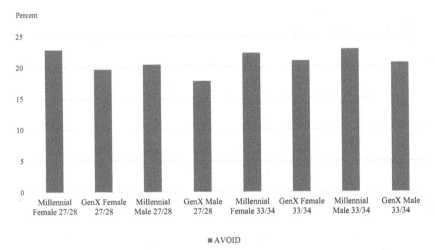

Figure 5.9 Avoid Conflict Style of Same-Age Millennials versus Generation Xers by Gender.
Note. Based on avoiding conflict styles by gender in the Thomas-Kilmann Conflict Mode Instrument data.

Turning to an accommodating conflict style, at ages 27/28, Millennial males have an approximately 1% higher occurrence of the accommodating style compared to Gen X males, but by the time they reach 33 and 34, the percent of Millennial males with an accommodating style is more than 4% higher than for Gen X males. Remember, this style is cooperative and unassertive. Looking at our statistics, while not significant at age 27/28, at the age 33/34 comparison, Millennial males are *more* likely to use an accommodating conflict style compared to Generation X males. What about females? Looking at a comparison of Millennial females to Generation X females, the percent differences across both time periods are minimal with no statistical differences. The comparison of an accommodating conflict style is shown in Figure 5.10.

For the competing style, the percentage of Millennial females with this style at age 27 and 28 is about 1% higher than for Generation X females, but by age 33 and 34, the percentage of Gen X females with a competing style is almost 2% higher than the percent for Millennial females. However, the

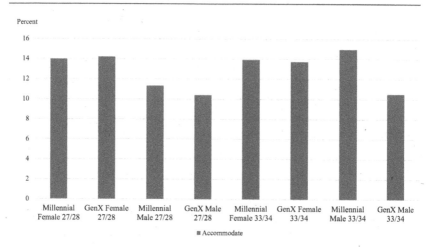

Figure 5.10 Accommodate Conflict Style of Same-Age Millennials versus Generation Xers by Gender.

Note. Based on accommodating conflict styles by gender in the Thomas-Kilmann Conflict Mode Instrument data.

results are not statistically significant over either age comparison. Looking at males for comparison, Generation X males had a slightly higher percentage of competing style at age 27 and 28 than Millennial males, but by less than 0.5%. By age 33 and 34, however, the percent of Millennial males with a competing style decreased by more than 3%, while the percentage of competing style for Generation X males remained essentially the same. So, the percent of Millennial males with a competing style at age 33 and 34 is approximately 4% lower than that of Gen X males, consistent with what we heard in the interviews that Millennial men may exhibit more passive behavior. While the results are not statistically significant at age 27/28, at age 33/34, the results are significant that Generation X males are *more* likely to compete compared to Millennial males. These results are shown in Figure 5.11.

Turning to a collaborative conflict style, at ages 27 and 28, the percent of Generation X females with a collaborative conflict style is 5% higher than for Millennial females and our statistical analysis finds that Generation X females are *more* likely to collaborate. But by ages 33 and 34, the difference between Millennial females and Generation X females drops to approximately 2%, mostly due to a decrease in female Generation Xers with a collaborative style. At this age comparison, while Generation X females continue to have a higher percent of collaborative style, the results are not statistically significant. Turning to males, at age 27 and 28, the percent of Generation X males with a collaborative conflict style is 4% higher than for Millennial males, and our statistical analysis finds that Generation X males are *more* likely to collaborate. But, by ages 33 and 34, the percent

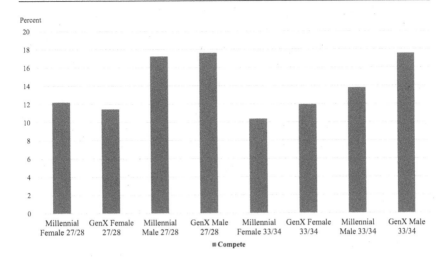

Figure 5.11 Compete Conflict Style of Same-Age Millennials versus Generation Xers by Gender.

Note. Based on competing conflict styles by gender in the Thomas-Kilmann Conflict Mode Instrument data.

of Generation X males with a collaborative style drops to approximately 1% higher than for Millennial males. The statistical toolbox results are not significant at the age 33/34 comparison. The same-age collaborative conflicts styles are shown in Figure 5.12.

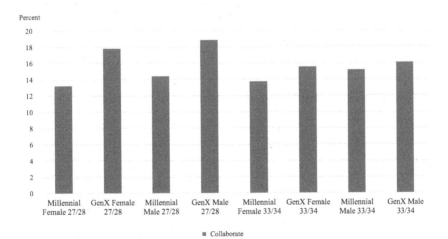

Figure 5.12 Collaborate Conflict Style of Same-Age Millennials versus Generation Xers by Gender.

Note. Based on collaborative conflict styles by gender in the Thomas-Kilmann Conflict Mode Instrument data.

The last conflict style examined for same-age Millennials and Generation Xers is the compromising style. At ages 27 and 28, the percent of compromising conflict styles for Millennial females and males is approximately 1% higher than for Generation X females and males, respectively. By ages 33 and 34, the percent of Millennial females with a compromising style is 2% greater than for Gen X females, but the numbers run opposite for males, with the compromising style for Millennial males 2% less compared to Generation X males. However, our statistics find no significance at either time period for males or females. See Figure 5.13 for the percent comparison of the compromising conflict style.

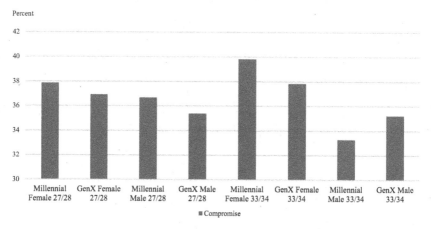

Figure 5.13 Compromise Conflict Style of Same-Age Millennials and Generation Xers by Gender.

Note. Based on collaborative conflict styles by gender in the Thomas-Kilmann Conflict Mode Instrument data.

What We Learned about Gender Differences

The most consistent result looking at male-to-female results is that males across all generations are significantly *more* likely to use a competing style compared to females. Second, female Baby Boomers are *more* likely than their male counterparts to use avoiding and accommodating styles. We also find that younger Millennial females are *more* likely to use an avoiding style compared to Millennial males but this changes as Millennial's age. By 2018, Millennial females have a lower percent of avoiding style compared to their male cohort members, the only cohort in any time period where we see males at a lower percent than females for this conflict style. In addition, Generation X females are *more* likely than males to use the accommodating conflict style. For the compromising style, Millennial and Generation X females are *more* likely to compromise than their male cohorts. Lastly, Baby Boomer males are *more* likely than their female cohort members to use the collaborative style.

Summarizing the notable same-gender comparisons in our aggregated 13-year analysis, Millennial and Generation X females are *more* likely than Baby Boomer females to compete, consistent with our interview findings of more assertiveness in younger females. For males, the findings are consistent with our findings for females – Millennial and Generation X males are *more* likely than Baby Boomer males to compete. Further, Millennial males are *more* likely to avoid and accommodate compared to Gen X and Baby Boomer males, while Millennial females are *more* likely than Baby Boomer females to accommodate. For both the female-to-female and male-to-male comparisons of a collaborating style, Baby Boomers are *more* likely to employ this style versus the other two generations. Lastly, in both the male-to-male and female-to-female comparisons, Generation Xers are *more* likely than Millennials to collaborate.

For our Millennial to Generation X same-age gender comparison, our analysis finds that while the percent of Millennial males at age 27/28 with an avoiding conflict style is approximately 3% higher than for Gen Xers, the result was not statistically significant. However, we did find that Millennial males are *more* likely than Generation X males to have an unassertive and cooperative, or accommodating, style at ages 33/34. The unassertive element may be the "passive" behavior we heard about in our interviews. And Generation X males are *more* likely to employ a competing conflict style compared to Millennial males at ages 33/34. Lastly, the results are significant that age 27/28 Generation X males are *more* collaborative than Millennial males, again with an assertive element. The fact that both the competitive and collaborative styles include a high assertiveness level and Generation X males are more likely to employ these styles compared to Millennial males is consistent with Millennial males being viewed as passive in our interviews.

Looking at same-age gender analysis for females, despite the belief expressed by some of our participants that Millennial women are more competitive than previous generations, the results did not show significant differences between Millennial and Generation X women at age 27/28 or age 33/34. However, back in Chapter 3, we learned that Millennial and Generation X females are more competitive than Baby Boomer females. So, Millennial women being more competitive than previous generations holds true when comparing them to Baby Boomer females. And while ages 27/28 Generation X females are *more* likely to collaborate than Millennial females, this is not true at the age 33/34 comparison.

In Chapter 3, we looked at generational conflict styles, how these change over time, and the conflict styles of same-age Millennials and Generation Xers. Then in Chapter 4, we heard what our participants told us about what Millennials want and value in the workplace. In this chapter, we gained insight on the impact of gender on conflict styles. Next, in Chapter 6, we'll look at the technology skills of Millennials, their use of online support groups, and how they can leverage social media to drive movements of interest.

References

Barroso, A., & Brown, A. (2021, May 25). *Gender pay gap in the U.S. held steady in 2020*. Pew Research Center. https://www.pewresearch.org/fact-tank/2021/05/25/gender-pay-gap-facts/

Bialik, K., & Fry, R. (2019). *Millennial life: How young adulthood today compares with prior generations*. Pew Research Center. https://www.pewsocialtrends.org/essay/millennial-life-how-young-adulthood-today-compares-with-prior-generations/

Birkinshaw, J., Manktelow, J., D'Amato, V., Tosca, E., & Macchi, F. (2019). Older and wiser? How management style varies with age. *MIT Sloan Management Review, 60*(4), 75–81.

Brewer, N., Mitchell, P., & Weber, N. (2002). Gender role, organizational status, and conflict management styles. *The International Journal of Conflict Management, 13*(1), 78–94.

Holt, J.L., & Devore, C.J. (2005). Culture, gender, organizational role, and styles of conflict resolution: A meta-analysis. *International Journal of Intercultural Relations, 29*(2), 165–196. https://doi.org/10.1016/j.ijintrel.2005.06.002

Graf, E., Brown, A., & Patten, E. (2019, March 22). *The narrowing, but persistent, gender gap in pay*. Pew Research Center. https://www.pewresearch.org/fact-tank/2019/03/22/gender-pay-gap-facts/

Horowitz, J., Parker, K., Stepler, R. (2017). *Wide partisan gaps in U.S. over how far the country has come on gender equality*. Pew Research Center. https://www.pewsocialtrends.org/2017/10/18/wide-partisan-gaps-in-u-s-over-how-far-the-country-has-come-on-gender-equality/

Ng, T. W. H., & Feldman, D. (2008). The relationship of age to ten dimensions of job performance. *Journal of Applied Psychology, 93*(2), 392–423. https://doi.org/10.1037/0021-9010.93.2.392

Ng, E.S.W., Schweitzer, L., & Lyons, S.T. (2010). New generation, great expectations: A field study of the Millennial generation. *Journal of Business and Psychology, 25*(2), 281–292.

Rahim, M.A., & Katz, J.P. (2020) Forty years of conflict: The effects of gender and generation on conflict-management strategies. *International Journal of Conflict Management, 31*(2), 1–16.

Sincavage, J. (2004, June). The labor force and unemployment: Three generations of change. *Monthly Labor Review*. https://www.bls.gov/opub/mlr/2004/06/art-2full.pdf

Tan, G., & Porzecanski, K. (2018, December 3). *Wall Street rule for the #MeToo era: Avoid women at all cost*. Bloomberg. https://www.bloomberg.com/news/articles/2018-12-03/a-wall-street-rule-for-the-metoo-era-avoid-women-at-all-cost

Thomas, K., Thomas, G., & Schaubhut, N. (2008). Conflict styles of men and women at six organizational levels. *International Journal of Conflict Management, 19*(2), 148–166.

U.S. Department of Labor. (2020). *Women in the labor force.* https://www.dol.gov/agencies/wb/data/facts-over-time/women-in-the-labor-force#civilian-labor-force-by-sex

U.S. Department of Labor. (2020). *Civilian labor force by sex.* https://www.dol.gov/agencies/wb/data/facts-over-time/women-in-the-labor-force#civilian-labor-force-by-sex

United States Census Bureau. (2022 March 15). *Equal pay day: March 15, 2022.* Release number CB22-SFS.33. https://www.census.gov/newsroom/stories/equal-pay-day.html

Chapter 6

Support Networks
Millennials and Social Media

Technological Skills Surpass Interpersonal Skills

The stereotype of Millennials continually connected to their phones or other devices is well-known. Drexel, the Baby Boomer business executive, said in one focus group that he sees it all the time when he conducts training seminars. During a focus group he said:

> When they come in the room, and almost every one of them is a Millennial, they come in and set their phones down. And I have to say, 'OK guys, I get it, if you need to do some work on your phone, that's fine, we're going to continue with the course.' Because it's like, I'm not going to win the fight.

"But that's a lack of respect!" cried Saddie, a Baby Boomer in the education field. Drexel continued:

> I've learned and realize it's just going to be part of the culture and life and they're going to absorb what I do – and I've got some things I do to make sure of that. You can't fight it. It's going to be a part of their lot – and they grew up with it and they understand it. It is the way they do EVERYTHING (emphasis added), right? They don't even bring in paper for notes. It's all right here.

He pointed at his phone and continued:

> Do you need paper?' And they say 'Nope, I've got it covered.' And they're doing it on their phones or on a laptop. So, it's like it's part of their DNA. So, you either have to learn to accept it and work with it or if you reject it, they're like 'Whatever,' and now they're real pissed and they can't get over the fact they can't look at their phone.

For some Millennials, on the other hand, hearing old people gripe about phones can be quite annoying as well. Jamie, the Millennial government sector employee, shares:

DOI: 10.4324/9781003246824-6

I've had that experience where I was attending a classical music concert. And my husband and I were having actually a really lovely day together. But my mom needed me to respond to an email so before the concert began, I was emailing her. And, since I was emailing my mom, my husband was on his phone as well. We were just having a really lovely day - it was just really special for us to be at the concert together and then another concert member thought it was okay to turn around and 'You know, you young people should talk to each other.' And I was like, 'I wonder why young people don't come to the arts - you know!' So, I mean, I know that every lens has its own experience so I'm sure that older people have felt like younger people disrespected them. But in that moment, I just felt like 'You really have no idea of what's going on here and I'm not really sure why you felt that it was okay to try to, like, shame us.' I mean, I was emailing my mom.

We heard in our interviews that Millennials are more likely to avoid conflict, but the way they avoid conflict is often different from older generations because many of them grew up more likely to text or instant message their friends than knock on their doors and ask if they can play. As a result, Millennials' technological proficiencies tend to surpass their oral and interpersonal competencies. Linda, a Baby Boomer manager in the financial sector in the Southeast United States, comments:

Millennials seem very, very comfortable and familiar with using computer software, technology. They have a very good grasp of all of that, and they are able to also manipulate and use whatever appears in print or on the media, or I guess whatever computer stuff is out there. They're able to use it to their benefit. I would say that the Baby Boomers seem to have better communication or social ability skills. That may arise from the fact that they didn't have as many games or computers or things to do when they were growing up. They did more interpersonal relationships.

Some researchers agree. "After having studied Millennials and having worked with them closely during the past several years, we believe there is a gap between where these students are and where they need to be in terms of effective interpersonal communication skills" (Hartman & McCambridge, 2011, p. 23), writes Jackie Hartman of Kansas State University and Jim McCambridge of Colorado State University. Hartman and McCambridge cite CEOs from 5,000 U.S. companies who report in a 2008 survey that being an effective communicator is an important skill for career success and advancement. Yet Millennials, while overly adept at digital skills, are not focused on developing the type of interpersonal communication skills that are traditionally perceived to help career advancement. While we see greater digital communication in a post-pandemic world, interpersonal skills still play a role on video communication platforms such as Zoom where you are speaking to each other via video.

More than a decade after the research by Hartman and McCambridge, Millennials continue to have the reputation as a digitally connected generation. In the interviews leading up to this book, 85% of non-Millennials made numerous references to the technological proficiency of Millennials. Similarly, over 60% of Millennials made mention of their technological expertise. This is consistent with the findings of other researchers regarding the technological superiority of Millennials. Regarding their verbal and people skills, in our interviews, almost 40% of non-Millennials mentioned that Millennials lack these skills, and almost 25% of Millennials mentioned the lack of verbal/people skills in their generation.

The differences are even seen between older and younger Millennials, with older Millennials feeling they are behind their younger cohort members from a technology standpoint. Matteo, the Millennial working for a not-for-profit organization, said:

> I still have a flip phone. I met new people this week that were in their twenties, and they use a whole different platform, and my flip phone doesn't have the capacity to do that, so some of them go out of their way to let me know what's going on because I couldn't keep up.

Holly, the Millennial working in the public sector who supervises a group of younger employees, agreed. She said:

> I mean, I barely use Facebook anymore and they're already on these other things that I don't even ever want to sign up to. And they really just thought I had no idea what was going on in the world because I didn't follow them on whatever. So, yeah - it's not about conflict but clearly communication, and they did know a lot more than me about what was happening around them. Because of that and I didn't, so I'm missing out... And I think it's just also about how they communicate with each other. There's a whole conversation I'm missing because I'm not a part of that.

Jamie, the Millennial government sector employee, said the annoyance can go both ways.

> There is sort of an expectation that more junior members will help more senior members navigate certain aspects of new software that we're using, or people will kind of choose to opt out and just like 'I can't learn this,' in ways that I don't think would be okay for a junior person on the team to say. Like 'I don't feel like learning that.' But at

the same time, I've had supervisors who are older than I was who are very engaged in learning technologies so I wouldn't say that it was across the board everyone older than me.

We did hear from our non-Millennial interviewees that they appreciate Millennials' technological proficiencies, and they described situations in which these skills came in extremely handy. As an example, one interviewee, a Baby Boomer male executive in the Southeast United States, talked about bids for an internal company website that reached $1 million. However, Millennial employees were able to come up with a plan to build the website for $250,000, saving the company $750,000. That's a significant contribution!

Online Support Group

Given what we know about Millennials avoiding conflict and using technology to communicate more skillfully than other generations, it should not come as a surprise that when challenges arise, Millennials are more likely than other generations to withdraw and seek outside support on social media rather than face-to-face, which calls into question whether technology impacts how Millennials resolve disputes. In the interviews and focus groups we conducted, 54% of non-Millennial participants and 24% of Millennial participants mentioned that Millennials turn to online sources when they need help or advice especially when a conflict occurs. The online support group provides suggestions and feedback when a conflict occurs.

Carrie, the Generation X manager for a large retail store, said she has seen firsthand how Millennials use technology and their online network to help with problems at work:

> The younger kids are more inclined to start the conversation and all the crap that's gonna come with that online. We'll find out about a conflict involving a Millennial from somebody's Facebook account.... And it's like a discussion board and they'll post, you know, if they're having a problem with their department, if they see something good, if they hear scuttlebutt coming down there's going to be this change. They're all on it. Everybody.

Janelle, the Generation X attorney, said in one focus group she finds it strange how open Millennials on her timeline can be, sometimes putting out even unflattering news about themselves. She said:

> It's things like 'I just flunked this test' or 'I just got fired.' Or something like that. I'm not going to broadcast negative things about myself

right, but they do. They do and they don't process at the same rate we do. I'm wondering, is it that they put it out there and they don't have to process it themselves? Their followers are processing it for them.

"They do it so quickly," agreed Catherine, the Baby Boomer educator. "They don't stop and think before they post anything!"

George, the Baby Boomer executive, adds "That's how they communicate. We picked up the phone, which doesn't happen anymore."

"Or you go visit someone face-to-face." adds Catherine.

Don, the Baby Boomer engineer, tells us:

Well, a lot of it depends on what kind of feedback they're looking for too. Someone may just want a shoulder to cry on - I just flunked my test. And other ones may be bragging about stuff. I'm great. You know I've got all this stuff. So, there's a lot of bragging and there's a lot of consoling. But they put it out so fast and they don't think about it. Andrew Weiner - think about it.

Don was referencing Anthony Weiner, a Baby Boomer Democratic Congressman from New York who resigned in disgrace after an explicit photo he sent to a woman on Twitter was made public. Then, in 2017, he was sentenced for sending obscene photos to an underage girl.

These comments on Millennials' online interactions are quite interesting, especially Janelle's question on how Millennials may use their online support group to help them process. George, the Baby Boomer executive, has some interesting insights on how Millennials use their online support group, referencing the use of social media in the aftermath of the Marjory Stoneman Douglas High School shooting on February 14, 2018, in Parkland, Florida. He shares:

They'll go online and seek out help and advice through chat rooms or other areas where they have companions like them that they can talk it through, and they'll come back with a solution - very happy, very proud that I threw this out there to my group. In the Parkland shooting, to be able to get massive amounts of information collected at the same time, creating entire causes overnight. Like Me Too. Those are created overnight because of the technology, right? So, they've learned, technology can help them further their cause so much faster.

Millennials exhibiting an avoiding behavior and then turning to their online support group for help and advice may be engaging in an information gathering process that allows them to be better prepared for the interaction. While non-Millennial interviewees described talking with peers and direct approaches to resolving conflict, it is fascinating to see the

Millennials' use of technology to provide workplace support. Millennials' preference for less interpersonal and face-to-face communication and a greater use of technological interaction may bring a new aspect to the traditional conflict resolution process.

Part of Millennials' preference for digital over face-to-face communication may stem from the helicopter parent phenomenon we have already discussed. Perhaps their parents assumed more of the face-to-face discussions for their Millennial children. However, it is interesting to note that while the findings from the interviews and focus groups in this study support that Millennials withdraw when they face conflict, our interviews and surveys also found that Millennials will be direct in advocating for themselves and for what they want. Almost 50% of non-Millennials reported this Millennial advocacy. Therefore, it is important to point out the nuanced difference involved in Millennials withdrawing from conflict yet being assertive in advocating for themselves. And, while other generations may view the behavior as avoiding, perhaps Millennials are simply relying on their digital skills rather than face-to-face communication.

Another consideration is that avoidance may be a useful tactic in certain situations. Sometimes it is more effective to circumvent conflict when it's clear that engaging will not result in a desirable outcome, especially when there are power asymmetries or if you are not prepared for the interaction. In those situations, the wiser approach may be to back off and not fight a losing battle. As such, Millennials' avoidance in some situations may be more effective than a competitive or more confrontational conflict style. And yet, too much reliance on avoiding conflict can lead to its own set of issues including failure to have your voice heard.

Social Media Use

In 2021, a trove of leaked Facebook documents sparked new questions about the effect of social media networks on society, including sacrificing mental health in favor of more clicks and ad revenue. Frances Haugen, the whistleblower, discussed how Facebook's algorithms can result in showing users content that may be less favorable and perhaps even harmful (Feiner, 2021). A second whistleblower claiming Facebook spreads misinformation came forth later in 2021. While social media was not included as a topic of research in the study presented in this book, we did want to mention what some of our interviewees shared about the effects of social media and how Millennials use it. Matteo, the Millennial working for a not-for-profit, mentioned that people can look to social media for validation and confirmation. He said:

> A generalization is we're superficial, that we think more about the way we look, and we rely on that confirmation from society that we're

good looking or whatever. And then we take the selfie stuff. I saw a video recently and they were at Coachella, and they were too focused on taking selfies and they weren't even enjoying the event they were at because they were so much more worried about giving everyone else knowledge about what they were doing and what they were able to do and accomplish and it's just kind of sad. Because I think we come across as confident, but my personal perception is, if you're really confident, you don't need to make sure everyone knows what you're doing all the time. You know what I'm saying?

Makenzie, a Millennial working for a manufacturer in the Southeast, shares:

Millennials are great at social media - we use it all the time. But it's really overwhelming, and everyone posts these photoshopped pictures and about how great they are. All their accomplishments. And it's really hard to keep up with.

For some, social media use can lead to darker mental health outcomes. Jenny Marie blogs for the National Alliance on Mental Illness (NAMI) saying:

Millennials are often referred to as the "anxious generation." They were the first to grow up with the constant overflow of the Internet and social media. The Internet can make life better, but it can also make life complicated, as Millennials often compare their personal and professional achievements to everyone else's. This can result in low self-esteem and insecurity. (Marie, 2019, para 7)

NAMI finds that while social media can have a negative impact on one's mental health, it also provides a forum to discuss topics of concern (Harris, 2021). This allows participants to hear from others, realize they are not alone, and find support for the issues they are facing. This is consistent with what we heard in our interviews and focus groups, with Millennials more open to sharing things on social media compared to older generations. It's clear that the non-Millennials in our focus group are baffled by how Millennials air things on social media. But, as NAMI noted above, these social media platforms provide a place where people can be heard and receive input. In fact, Millennials appear to be leading the charge on being more open about mental health issues.

In 2015, journalism students at American University distributed a survey to receive input from Millennials on stress and mental health, with respondents self-selecting if they wanted to participate (Lorusso & Barnes, n.d.). Their 20-question "Matters of the Mind" survey found that while mental health is still stigmatized, their Millennial respondents are more open to talking about their mental health issues than older generations.

In discussing the results of the survey on The Millennial Minds website, Marissa Lorusso and Sophia Barnes note that survey found "Nearly three in four respondents agree that Millennials are 'much more open to addressing mental health topics than older people'" (Lorusso & Barnes, n.d., para. 33).

This sentiment was captured in a 2019 tweet from social media director Jordan Chamberlain, @jordylancaster, which has since garnered more than 52,000 retweets and 218,000 likes (Chamberlain, 2019). Here's what the tweet says:

> Boomers: I heard she went to *looks around nervously* *whispers* Therapy
>
> Millennials/Gen Z: LMAOOOO YALL GUESS WHAT MY THERAPIST TOLD ME TODAY

While older generations may view needing assistance with mental health as a stigma, many younger adults appear more open about seeking support.

Memes and the Media

Memes, often humorous depictions of behaviors or cultural phenomena, spread rapidly across digital platforms. One popular meme aimed at Millennials and Generation Zs shared across Facebook has spawned several variations. The meme shows one of several focal points of engaged young activists, including David Hogg, climate activist Greta Thunberg, or an anonymous pink-haired protester that declares, "My generation is going to start a revolution!" (My Generation, n.d.) to which icons of older generations' grit like cowboy actor Sam Elliott, a World War II soldier, or *Full Metal Jacket* actor and Marine Corps drill instructor R. Lee Ermey reply, "Your generation can't start a lawnmower" (Your Generation, n.d.).

In addition to memes, numerous satirical videos pit Millennials against Baby Boomers, especially on online platforms like YouTube, but also on traditional broadcast television. On her self-titled talk show, Ellen DeGeneres (2016, 2019), a Baby Boomer, challenges Millennials and fellow Boomers to identify objects unique to the others' generation, highlighting differences between the two. A segment may see a Millennial tasked with dialing a rotary phone or a Boomer with deciphering the meaning of an emoji. In an April 2022 sketch appearing on the Late Show with Stephen Colbert, Colbert talks about a Pew Research study by Stella Sechopoulos (2022) finding younger people have it harder than older generations before engaging in a scripted interview segment with Late Show writer Eliana Kwartler, a Millennial, in which they exaggerate generational stereotypes. Kwartler cracks jokes about the difficulty young people have finding their first home, and Colbert, born in 1964 at the late end of the Boomer range, jokingly offers some sage wisdom.

"Here's what you do, friendly advice," the host says. "You are really good at your job. You deserve a raise. You need to go to your boss and ask for more money."

"Can I have more money?" Kwartler asks.

"No," Colbert says. "Eliana Kwartler, everybody" (The Late Show with Stephen Colbert, 2022)!

Millennials are keenly aware of the traits that are often generalized to their cohort. They've fought back with their own memes, including the dismissive "OK Boomer," a catch-all retort for when Baby Boomers get under Millennials skins. More venomously, some younger people dubbed COVID-19 "Boomer remover" when it was discovered in the early days of the pandemic that the disease was much more lethal among elderly populations. The term Millennial itself is sometimes used to disparage younger Americans as described by the Wall Street Journal in a 2017 post:

> 'Millennials' has become a sort of snide shorthand in the pages of The Wall Street Journal. We have blamed them for the housing shortage, their fickle shopping habits or for fleeing New Jersey. We have had a laugh at their expense over behaviors such as a fear of doorbells or their discovery of the TV antenna. And at other times we have treated them like an alien species (Wall Street Journal, 2017, para. 1).

The blog post goes on to say "What we usually mean is young people, so we probably should just say that. Many of the habits and attributes of Millennials are common for people in their 20s, with or without a snotty term" (Wall Street Journal, 2017, para. 1). Millennials say they are often blamed for things that are simply not their fault. Some stereotypes may represent broader economic or societal changes across all cohorts, some may be youth-related, while others result from the environment in which Millennials were raised. But an important piece of this discussion is that the technology of today allows messaging to be widely disseminated, immediately reaching Millennials' screens. So, the way this messaging is communicated – that technology – is key.

The Medium Is the Massage

In 1967, Marshall McLuhan and Quentin Fiore published the book "The Medium is the Massage: An Inventory of Effects" discussing the profound impact of different mediums and technologies (McLuhan & Fiore, 1967). In that discussion, McLuhan and Fiore address how the medium itself, whether it be print, online, video, artistic, etc., can massage our senses since the form the message takes impacts how that message is received. In fact, the intended title of the book was the medium is the message. However, when a printing error resulted in changing the word message to massage, McLuhan insisted on keeping it since it illuminated the importance of the medium.

It's interesting that McLuhan died in 1980, before platforms like Facebook and Twitter were launched. But, as McLuhan prophesied, the impact of these digital technologies, and the different mechanisms used to communicate, impact our world. With global reach, digital natives like Millennials grew up interfacing digitally with phones and laptops rather than communicating face-to-face. They are connected to what's happening now. While their parents may have walked to the library, used the old hardcopy card cataloging drawers to find a book, and then asked the librarian to help them find it, Millennials have this information at their fingertips. Are we surprised that this generation interacts differently? And much more efficiently?

Thomas Cooper, who worked as a graduate assistant to McLuhan for seven years during the 1970s, described in a 2020 article the ways in which social media has changed traditional culture Cooper, 2020). "They exist within a culture in which children now spend twice as much time with machines as with their parents and in which media are increasingly a substitute for marriage and associated with divorce" (Cooper, p.50), he wrote. He further describes the impact our current media can have on marital happiness if partners prefer spending time with their media of choice, whether that be news, sports, podcasts, etc., rather than spending time with their spouse.

Perhaps this constant stimulation of media at one's fingertips, and always being connected, has led to movements like cottagecore. Cottagecore is a social media movement that focuses on a simpler, pastoral lifestyle, reflected with floral prints, home-baked food, harmony with nature, and unplugging from a hectic world. As noted by Deutsch L.A. brand strategist Amelia Hall (2020), this type of lifestyle may appeal to younger generations who have never experienced life unplugged or off-the-grid. Another recent and related trend is called Grandmillennial, describing an increasing popular aesthetic among some Millennials with Victorian furniture, chintz, pleated lampshades, floral wallpaper, and other vintage items. The word Grandmillennial comes from combining grandma and Millennial, but like the portmanteau suggests, the design blends the old with the new, creating a nostalgic alternative to mid-century modern and minimalist design trends.

#Vanlife is another trend among younger generations desiring a more basic and nomadic lifestyle. Jump in a van with a bed, if you can find one given today's demand, and enter what is billed as a simpler lifestyle. You can travel and catch jobs at various stops along the way or work remotely from your van. Since the pandemic began, RV manufacturers have reported record-breaking sales as well as younger faces on the customers in a business that previously catered mainly to retirees.

Cottagecore and #vanlife feature outdoor living and a more basic lifestyle, yet ironically both rely on technology for their existence. They both grew in popularity during the pandemic when quarantine claustrophobia set in for many, and millions no longer found themselves tied to an office desk in order to get their paycheck. According to Google Trends, the search terms "cottagecore" (Google Trends, n.d.a) and "vanlife" (Google Trends, n.d.b) peaked in late 2021.

Of course, some Millennials say they cannot afford an apartment, much less a tricked-out camper van or pastoral estate, and some would likely rather keep their high-speed internet connections and running water than run off to live in the woods. But it is worth noting that, for some young adults raised in a world of rapid technological change, the ultimate act of rebellion is to embrace rural life, if only online.

Technology and Activism

Consistent with the logic underlying McLuhan and Fiore's book in the 1960s, the technological savviness of Millennials and the use of social media in their messaging are influencing the political and economic environment in the United States in new and unique ways. Key to that messaging is having the means to communicate. According to Emily Vogels with Pew Research, as of 2019, 93% of Millennials owned smartphones (Vogels, 2019). This compares with 90% of Generation Xers, 68% of Baby Boomers, and 40% of Silents. Vogel further reports that 86% of Millennials use social media, compared with 76% of Generation Xers, and 9% of Baby Boomers.

Ruth Milkman of the City University of New York talks about how Millennials are driving social movements spanning issues of immigration, racial injustice, corporate responsibility, and sexual discrimination (Milkman, 2017). And the technological and social media savviness of Millennials is driving the success of these movements. An example of the intersection of politics, social issues, and social media is found in the actions of Millennials' following the 2018 Marjory Stoneman Douglas High School shooting. After that event, the students united as advocates of gun control, and their efforts were widely heard around the country. David Hogg, a student present at the time of the shooting, spoke out strongly against gun violence. Following Hogg's activism, Fox News commentator Laura Ingraham opined in a tweet that Hogg was "whining" about not getting into his top college choices.

"David Hogg Rejected By Four Colleges To Which He Applied and whines about it. (Dinged by UCLA with a 4.1 GPA...totally predictable given acceptance rates.)" (Ingraham, 2018a), she tweeted with a link to a story by the conservative Daily Wire.

In response, Hogg called on his estimated over 900,000 Twitter followers to boycott Fox News and reach out to advertisers on Ingraham's program (Hogg, 2018). As a result of the compound effect of his Twitter followers calling for a boycott, several large advertisers pulled ads from Fox News, including TripAdvisor, Hulu, Nestle, Wayfair, Nutrish, Expedia, and Johnson and Johnson.

Wayfair issued a statement saying "The decision of an adult to personally criticize a high school student who has lost his classmates in an unspeakable tragedy is not consistent with our values" (McMurry, 2018, p. 10), as reported by ABC News. In the wake of the advertising exodus, Ingraham left her show to guest hosts for a week and issued an apology. She tweeted:

> Any student should be proud of a 4.2 GPA —incl. @DavidHogg111. On reflection, in the spirit of Holy Week, I apologize for any upset or hurt my tweet caused him or any of the brave victims of Parkland. For the record, I believe my show was the first to feature David immediately after that horrific shooting and even noted how 'poised' he was given the tragedy. As always, he's welcome to return to the show anytime for a productive discussion. (Ingraham, 2018b)

While Ingraham remains a popular host, what began as a battle by one Millennial resulted in the loss of significant advertisers for a major corporation. Furthermore, #NeverAgain and other social media movements initiated by the Parkland shooting have been active in advocating for legislation aimed at preventing gun violence. This is just one example of the substantial power of the united efforts of Millennials, and their use of social media to effect change. This generation is driving social movements via Twitter and other technologies as shown with causes like #NeverAgain, #Dreamers, #OccupyWallSt, #MeToo, #TimesUp, and #BlackLivesMatter. Given the ability of Millennials to leverage Twitter, TikTok, Instagram, Snapchat, YouTube, WhatsApp, Telegram, and other platforms, organizations attuned to the social media use of Millennials will be better positioned to understand the needs and interest of this group of vital employees.

Some Millennial focus group participants brought up social media on their own when asked about the importance of social movements in their lives. Julia, the Millennial working in Human Resources, shared in a focus group that activism is very important. She said:

> I think the difference between Millennials and the other generations is that we've realized the power that comes from social media, how

quickly we can affect and change things. So, there's a lot of things to say within the United States that probably need to be changed and updated. We have a lot of archaic laws. A lot of archaic ways of thinking, and so, to be able to have that power to really bring a spotlight to movements and other causes, is important. I mean, you can't beat it.

Hala, the Millennial working for the fortune 500 company, added to the focus group discussion on social movements:

In past generations, I think there were only two ways to mobilize and be involved. It was either marching or protesting, or your power was in your vote. I think for Millennials, being able to engage using technology for some people is easier, it gives us a different platform as compared to, if marching is not your thing, cool. We can start a petition online. It allows a lot of people to work not only in their capacity but also in their comfort level. I don't want to march. I can completely start this petition and be just as engaged and feel like I'm doing something without being on the forefront.

Despite worries about the blinkering effects of social media – the idea that tech algorithms show us content we are predisposed to agree with, sheltering us further from opposing arguments – research suggests Millennials are open to exploring social media feeds that have opinions that are different from their own. According to a study from The Associated Press – NORC Center for Public Affairs & American Press Institute (2015), 70% of Millennials report that their social media feeds have an equal amount of similar and dissimilar opinions to their own. What is more, the study reports that 73% of Millennials say that they sometimes, often, or always explore opinions that diverge from their own, indicating an openness to differences. Millennials' ingrained tendency to seek out multiple sources and perspectives, along with their higher-than-average rate of educational attainment, likely contributes to the common observation about the generation that we explored in Chapter 4, their habit of questioning and wanting to know why.

Social media use has spread across the generations to the point where Facebook, originally created exclusively for college students, is now considered a Baby Boomer platform by many younger individuals. And although people of all generations now feel generally comfortable using the web to gather news and share their thoughts, it is important to remember that those who grew up in front of a screen view digital life fundamentally differently than those who moved to cyberspace to keep up in their workplaces or with their grandchildren. Think about learning to play an instrument or speak a foreign language. It's possible to learn to play an instrument well as an adult, but all things being equal, an adult learner will almost always struggle to keep up with a musician who has been practicing since she was barely out of the crib. The same goes for speaking a new language — as they are developing, children can learn new languages and master different sounds more efficiently than adults.

Millennials' brains were shaped not just by what they saw on their screens, but by the medium itself, as McLuhan likely would have said, and as the numbers from The Associated Press – NORC Center for Public Affairs & American Press Institute (2015) survey reveal, they are confident navigators of the digital space and seek out multiple viewpoints. However, even though Millennials are digitally savvy, they are not immune to fraud. According to a 2019 report from the Federal Trade Commission (FTC) looking at fraud reports filed between September 2017 and August 2019, individuals in their 20s and 30s are more likely than those over age 40 to lose money to fraud (Fletcher, 2019). A contributing factor may be Millennials' greater use of the mediums included in the FTC report including online shopping.

Millennials' use of digital platforms to seek input from their online group or advance their causes of interest makes sense given their immersion in this technology for most of their lives. Engaging with these platforms provides the benefit of extensive reach and often instantaneous feedback. It also comes with the stress of being continually on, comparison to others, and exposure to negativity. What is clear is that the digital world has reshaped how we communicate, and Millennials were at the forefront of the explosion of this movement. In the next chapter, we will hear how Millennials use this technology to engage in issues of importance to them.

References

Associated Press – NORC Center for Public Affairs & American Press Institute. (2015). *The Millennial insight project: How Millennials use and control social media*. Media Insight. https://www.americanpressinstitute.org/publications/reports/survey-research/millennials-social-media/

Chamberlain, J. [@jordylancaster]. (2019, July 24). *Boomers: I heard she went to *looks around nervously* *whispers* Therapy Millennials/Gen Z: LMAOOOO YALL GUESS WHAT MY THERAPIST TOLD ME TODAY*. [Tweet]. Twitter. https://twitter.com/jordylancaster/status/1154211439080542208?lang=en

Cooper, Thomas. (2020). McLuhan, social media and ethics. *New Explorations: Studies in Culture & Communication, 1*(2), 48–54. https://jps.library.utoronto.ca/index.php/nexj/article/download/35086/26862/

DeVaney, S.A. (2015). Understanding the millennial generation. *Journal of Financial Service Professionals, 69*(6), 11–14.

Feiner, L. (2021, October 5). *Facebook whistleblower: The company knows it's harming people and the buck stops with Zuckerberg*. CNBC. https://www.cnbc.com/2021/10/05/facebook-whistleblower-testifies-before-senate-committee.html

Fletcher, E. (2019, October 1). *Not what you think: Millennials and fraud*. Federal Trade Commission. https://www.ftc.gov/news-events/data-visualizations/data-spotlight/2019/10/not-what-you-think-millennials-fraud

Flood, B. (2022, April 19). *'The five' finishes as no. 1 cable news program, Laura Ingraham outdraws Rachel Maddow for top solo female*. Fox News. https://www.foxnews.com/media/the-five-finishes-as-no-1-cable-news-program-laura-ingraham-outdraws-rachel-maddow-for-top-solo-female

Google Trends. (n.d.a). Cottagecore. [Trend data]. https://trends.google.com/trends/explore?date=all&geo=US&q=cottagecore

Google Trends. (n.d.b). Vanlife. [Trend data]. https://trends.google.com/trends/explore?date=all&geo=US&q=vanlife

Hall, A. (2020, April 15). *Why is 'cottagecore' booming? Because being outside is now the ultimate taboo*. The Guardian. https://www.theguardian.com/commentisfree/2020/apr/15/why-is-cottagecore-booming-because-being-outside-is-now-the-ultimate-taboo

Harris, M. (2021). *How social media is changing the way we think about social media*. National Alliance on Mental Illness. https://www.nami.org/Blogs/NAMI-Blog/June-2021/How-Social-Media-Is-Changing-the-Way-We-Think-About-Mental-Illness

Hartman, J.L., & McCambridge, J. (2011). Optimizing Millennials' communication styles. *Business Communication Quarterly*, 74(1), 22–44.

Hogg, D. [@davidhogg111]. (2018, March 28). *Pick a number 1-12 contact the company next to that #*. [Tweet]. Twitter. https://twitter.com/davidhogg111/status/979168957180579840

Ingraham, L. [@IngrahamAngle]. (2018a, March 28). *David Hogg Rejected By Four Colleges To Which He Applied and whines about it. (Dinged by UCLA with a 4.1...* [Tweet]. Twitter. https://twitter.com/IngrahamAngle/status/979021639458459648

Ingraham, L. [@IngrahamAngle]. (2018b, March 29). *Any student should be proud of a 4.2 GPA—incl. @DavidHogg111. On reflection, in the spirit of Holy Week, I...* [Tweet]. Twitter. https://twitter.com/IngrahamAngle/status/979404377730486272

Lorusso, M., & Barnes, S. (2022). *Matters of the mind: A look at Millennials and mental health*. The Millennial Minds. http://www.themillennialminds.com/survey/

Marie, J. (2019, February 27). *Millennials and mental health*. National Alliance on Mental Illness. https://www.nami.org/Blogs/NAMI-Blog/February-2019/Millennials-and-Mental-Health

McLuhan, M., & Fiore, Q. (1967). *The medium is the massage: An inventory of effects*. Bantam Books.

McMurry, E. (2018, March 29). Laura Ingraham apologizes 'for any upset or hurt' caused by her comments on Parkland student David Hogg. But the Parkland student, as of yet, is not accepting the apology. ABC News. https://abcnews.go.com/US/laura-ingraham-apologizes-upset-hurt-caused-comments-parkland/story?id=54102676

Milkman, R. (2017). A new political generation: Millennials and the post-2008 wave of protest. *American Sociological Review, 82*(1), 1–31. https://doi.org/10.1177/0003122416681031

My generation is going to start a revolution. [Digital image]. (n.d.) https://knowyourmeme.com/photos/1625180-cursed-boomer-images

Peluchette, J.V., Kovanic, N., & Partridge, D. (2013). Helicopter parents hovering in the workplace: What should HR managers do? *Business Horizons, 56*(5), 601–609.

Pew Research Center. (2014, March). *Millennials in adulthood: Detached from institutions, networked with friends.* http://www.pewsocialtrends.org/2014/03/07/millennials-in-adulthood/

Pew Research Center. (2018, March 1). *The generation gap in American politics: wide and growing divides in views of racial discrimination.* http://www.people-press.org/2018/03/01/the-generation-gap-in-american-politics/

Rahim, M.A. (1983). A measure of styles of handling interpersonal conflict. *Academy of Management Journal, 26*(2), 368–376.

Raines, S. (2013). *Conflict management for managers: Resolving workplace, client, and policy disputes.* Jossey-Bass.

Sechopoulos, S. (2022, February 2022). *Most in the U.S. say young adults today face more challenges than their parents' generation in some key areas.* https://www.pewresearch.org/fact-tank/2022/02/28/most-in-the-u-s-say-young-adults-today-face-more-challenges-than-their-parents-generation-in-some-key-areas/

Somers, P., & Settle, J. (2010). The helicopter parent: Research toward a typology (Part I). *College and University, 86*, 18–27.

The Ellen DeGeneres Show. (2016, May 5). *Baby Boomers vs. Millennials.* [Video]. YouTube. https://www.youtube.com/watch?v=JADG4hXaqy4

The Ellen DeGeneres Show. (2019, April 10). *Baby Boomer vs Millennial: Analog vs. digital.* [Video]. YouTube. https://www.youtube.com/watch?v=TH5HXvF24lA

The Late Show with Stephen Colbert. (2022, April 14). *Generation fights: Housing edition with Stephen Colbert and Eliana Kwartler.* [Video]. YouTube. https://www.youtube.com/watch?v=4GXdfFrIMSE

The Wall Street Journal. (2017, December 4). Vol 30, No. 11: Millennials. *Style and Substance Blog.* https://www.wsj.com/articles/vol-30-no-11-millennials-01557858336

Vogels, E. (2019, September 9). *Millennials stand out for their technology use, but older generations also embrace digital life.* Pew Research Center. https://www.pewresearch.org/fact-tank/2019/09/09/us-generations-technology-use/

Your generation can't start a lawnmower. [Digital image]. (n.d.) https://knowyourmeme.com/photos/1362876-gunnery-sgt-hartman

Chapter 7

A Higher Purpose
Social, Political, and Economic Issues

What We Heard in Our Interviews and Focus Groups: Issues That Matter

Kelly, the Baby Boomer executive, believes a necessary component in hiring and retaining Millennials is knowing what drives them. She said:

> You have to understand their value systems. Their value systems are geared toward charitable, environmental issues. And how the community responds or is a participant in making the world a better place. So that's one of the things that companies have to sort of change their attitudes. You have to realize that as a manager.

As we discussed in Chapter 4, when Millennials were asked "what do you want from work and what do you value in a work environment?" 62% reported the desire to be contributing and adding value to a larger cause beyond themselves. Millennials want to be engaged in the workplace and feel that their job is part of a mission bigger than earning profits. Millennials were also more apt to identify and discuss social movements of interest to them compared to members of older generations. Nearly half of Millennials interviewed mentioned women's rights and sexual harassment as topics of great importance. Ellie, the Millennial advertising manager said:

> Particularly important to me is women's health and reproductive rights. And I am in the process of starting to volunteer at Planned Parenthood in my town as a patient advocacy volunteer. It's kinda two part; kind of outlining a political agenda in my state for patients just so they are aware of what's happening on a larger political level within the organization and what the priorities are, and the other piece of it is collecting patient stories so that they can be used in larger organizations and in advocacy work. I feel like Millennials are most engaged on this issue level. I think all of the generations care, but in terms of

DOI: 10.4324/9781003246824-7

doing tangible actions in your community now, I see Millennials doing it much more often.

The second most mentioned issues were LGBTQ+ (lesbian, gay, bisexual, transgender, queer or questioning, and others in the community) and
environmental issues, which were cited by approximately a third of Millennials. In contrast, while most non-Millennials did not name particular
social movements of interest, about 15% said they are engaged with movements focused on women's equality, stopping sexual harassment, building a wall on the border with Mexico, and the right to bear arms. It is
interesting to note that Millennials and non-Millennials alike mentioned
women's issues, though Millennials were more likely to do so. The more
recent attention on sexual harassment and differences in how different
generations view this issue will be discussed below.

Today we live in a world where it is not surprising to hear news stories
about powerful executives accused of sexually harassing female employees. Women are coming forward to tell their stories. Those accused include Andrew Cuomo, Governor of New York; Hollywood icon Harvey
Weinstein; self-help expert Tony Robbins; Les Moonves, executive at
CBS; R&B star R. Kelly; and Today show host Matt Lauer, to name
a few. In this environment, we have seen emerging movements like
#Metoo and #TimesUp, and the Women's March on Washington on
January 21, 2017, with sister marches in various locations throughout
the world. While estimates vary, approximately 470,000 people were
reported to have participated in the march in Washington with between
3,267,134 and 5,246,670 people participating throughout the United
States per Erica Chenworth and Jeremy Pressman (Chenworth & Pressman, 2017).

In a study led by Ksenia Keplinger at Leeds School of Business at the
University of Colorado, the researchers surveyed 500 women at two time
periods, 2016 and 2018, to assess the impact of the women's movement and
ask if anything has changed regarding sexual harassment (Keplinger et al.,
2019). Looking at a cross-sectional survey of 500 women, one finding is
that the study participants "feel better supported and empowered and are
not ashamed to speak up against sexual harassment" (p. 1). The researchers also found a reduction in some of the more blatant forms of sexual
harassment such as unwanted sexual advances but an increase in gender
harassment which can include teasing, name calling, or bullying based on
one's gender.

Consistent with the findings by Keplinger and her colleagues, another
study by James Campbell Quick and M. Ann McFadyen looks at the question of whether we have made progress addressing sexual harassment,
and the results are mixed (Quick & McFadyen, 2017). While they report
that sexual harassment complaints are down, the issue continues to be

problematic and has "morphed" with greater research needed on harassment of lesbian, gay, transgender, and others.

And how do the generations differ in their views of sexual harassment and its importance? Pew Researcher J. Baxter Oliphant reports that 81% of 18-to-29-year-olds report that sexual harassment is a very important issue versus 75% of those 30-to-49-years-old, 68% of 50-to 64-year-olds, and 70% of those over 65 (Oliphant, 2017). This is consistent with what we heard in our interviews and focus groups, with Millennials involved with #MeToo, #TimesUp, and other movements to address sexual harassment. In another Pew study reported by Nikki Graf in 2018, only 42% of age 18 to 29-year-olds felt the increased focus on sexual harassment made it harder for men to know how to interact with women in the workplace while the numbers climbed to 47% for 30 to 49-year-olds; 52% for 50 to 64-year-olds, and 66% for those age 65+ (Graf, 2018).

Another important issue identified by Millennials is LGBTQ+ rights. Millennials grew up witnessing a sea change in gender, sexuality, and LGBTQ+ rights. As children, they watched politicians argue over whether to allow gay people to serve in the military and whether they should be allowed to legally marry. Don't Ask Don't Tell (DADT) and the Defense of Marriage Act (DOMA) were signed by President Bill Clinton in 1993 and 1996, respectively. DADT, in effect from 1993 until 2011, barred openly gay, lesbian, or bisexual individuals from serving in the U.S. military. DOMA, defining marriage as the union of one man and one woman, denied same-sex couple numerous benefits including coverage under a spouse's health care plan or the right to jointly file taxes. DOMA's definition of marriage was ultimately struck down by the Supreme Court as was the provision allowing states not to recognize same-sex marriage.

In 2012, Democratic President Barrack Obama announced his support for same-sex marriage, previously supporting civil unions but reserving the word marriage for straight couples. By 2021, Justin McCarthy with Gallup reports that a record 70% of Americans support gay marriage – the highest number recorded (McCarthy, 2021). McCarthy does highlight the notable differences by age. For individuals 18-to-34-years-old, 84% support gay marriage while the numbers for 35-to-54-year-olds and those 55 and older are 72% and 60%, respectively.

The portion of Americans identifying as LGBT increased dramatically in the 2010s according to Gallup polls, and it's mainly attributed to Millennials (Newport, 2018). In their polling, Gallup found the expansion in the number of Americans who identify as LGBT was driven primarily by those born between 1980 and 1999. Frank Newport at Gallup reports that the percentage of Millennials who identify as LGBT expanded from 7.3% to 8.1% from 2016 to 2017, up from 5.8% in 2012 (Newport, 2018). The almost 1% increase in LGBT identification among Millennials from 2016 to 2017 was the biggest year-to-year increase among any age group since tracking began in 2012, Newport reported. By contrast, Gallup found that the LGBT percentage in Generation X rose only 0.2% from 2016 to 2017. They found no change in LGBT percentage among Baby Boomers and Traditionalists.

By 2021, Jeffrey Jones at Gallup reports that the number of adults in the United States who identify as lesbian, bisexual, gay, or transgender increased to a record high of 7.1%, doubling the percent in 2012 when Gallup began tracking this statistic (Jones, 2022). In addition, Jones reports that while 86% of respondents reported that they were heterosexual, an additional 7% of respondents did not provide their sexual orientation. For Millennials, 10.5% identified as LGBT versus the 8.1% recorded in 2017. Generation Z will also be impacting the number of individuals identifying as LGBT as 21% of Generation Z adults identified as LGBT in 2021.

This change is reflected in the media. Over time, popular media consumed by Millennials went from portraying LGBT people in minor roles to the stars of the show, reflecting a shift in attitudes. A major milestone came in 1997 when actor and comedian Ellen DeGeneres announced she was gay in a 1997 episode of her self-titled sitcom. Her coming out led to a conservative backlash and a parental advisory on the episode, as well as the start of a decline in ratings that led to the cancelation of the show the next year, but the tide would soon turn. DeGeneres came back to successfully host her show for a remarkable 19 seasons, slated to end in 2022.

In 2021, the Gay and Lesbian Alliance Against Defamation, or GLAAD, reported an increase in LGBTQ characters on primetime television in recent years, although it dropped from 10% to 9% in the 2020 report which they chalked up to the COVID-19 pandemic halting production on several shows (Robb, 2021). But, in 2019, LGBT representation on primetime broadcast TV was at its highest proportion since it began tracking the statistic. Looking at films, David Robb with GLAAD reports that 22.7% of the 44 films released by the major studios in 2020 had LGBTQ actors versus 18.6% in 2019 (Robb, 2021).

Another topic of interest to Millennials reported in our interviews is the environment and especially the changing climate. This is corroborated by a Pew Research poll conducted in 2021 by Alec Tyson and his fellow researchers that found Millennials are more likely than other generational cohorts to say climate should be the government's top priority to ensure a sustainable planet for future generations, – 71% of them, compared with 67% for Generation Z, 63% for Gen Xers, and 57% for Baby Boomers and older (Tyson et al., 2021). In addition, there are differences in views of the importance of climate change by political alignment (Tyson et al., 2021). Eighty-five percent of Democratic Millennials say addressing the climate should be a top priority versus 48% of Republican Millennials, with Millennials more likely to be Democratic than Republican which we'll discuss further on in this chapter. These results are shown in Figure 7.1.

Younger Republicans more likely than older to prioritize reducing effects of climate change now

% of U.S. adults who say ...

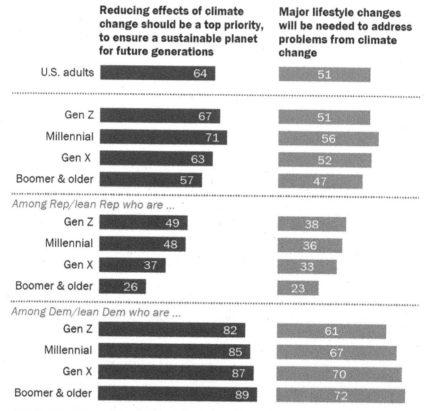

Note: Respondents who gave other responses or did not give an answer are not shown.
Source: Survey conducted April 20-29, 2021.
"Gen Z, Millennials Stand Out for Climate Change Activism, Social Media Engagement With Issue"

PEW RESEARCH CENTER

Figure 7.1 Younger Americans More Likely to Say Reducing Effects of Climate Change Should Be a Top Priority.

Note. from *Gen Z, Millennials Stand Out for Climate Change Activism, Social Media Engagement with Issue*, by A. Tyson, B. Kennedy, and C. Funk, May 26, 2021, Pew Research Center, Washington, D.C. (https://www.pewresearch.org/science/2021/05/26/climate-energy-and-environmental-policy/)

We know that younger adults are at the forefront of climate change protests. Their engagement is driven by the prospect of inheriting a dying world and passing that world on to their children. This further creates stress which impacts the mental health of young adults. Caroline Hickman from University of Bath and her colleagues conducted a survey of 10,000 people aged 16 to 25 – Generation Zs and the youngest Millennials – and found 45% said climate anxiety and distress is affecting their daily lives (Hickman et al., 2021). Three-quarters of the respondents agreed with the statement "the future is frightening" (p. e863), and 59% said governmental responses to climate change are "betraying me and/or future generations" (p. e869).

According to Alicia Adamczyk with CNBC, "around 76% of older Millennials, ages 33 to 40, think climate change poses a serious threat to society" (Adamczyk, 2018, para. 8), per a survey conducted by The Harris Poll for CNBC. As a result, Adamczyk reports that Millennials are focusing on minimizing their carbon footprints and changing the way they invest to better align with their views on sustainability. While mental health effects are experienced by survivors of natural disasters such as wildfires and hurricanes, a 2017 American Psychological Association report by Susan Clayton and her colleagues finds that high levels of stress can also result from thinking about the long-term impact of climate change on earth (Clayton et al., 2017). The researchers found that anxiety over actual or potential impacts of climate change can lead to increased stress, which can cause serious problems like substance abuse, anxiety disorders, and depression.

We've explored three issues of importance to Millennials reported in our interviews and focus groups – women's rights and sexual harassment; LGBTQ+; and the environment and climate change. To better understand what a Millennial-led future will look like, we'll examine their political behavior and the resulting impact on elections, diversity and Millennials' desire for inclusion, and views on racial injustice. Taken together, these issues will shape how Civic Millennials will focus their advocacy in the future and the outcomes will manifest in a Millennial-led workplace. These topics were selected because represent unique and noteworthy Millennial characteristics discovered through our research.

A Millennial-Led Future: Politics, Diversity, Inclusion, and Racial Justice

You may have noticed that the positions and issues of interest to Millennials discussed earlier in this chapter seem more aligned with the Democratic Party than the Republicans. In fact, the majority of Millennials identify as Democrats rather than Republicans as shown in Figure 7.2.

Thirty-five percent of Millennials are affiliated with the Democratic Party and another 24% of Millennials lean Democratic, for an overall 59% preference for the Democratic Party, according to Pew Research (2018). Millennials' preference for the Democratic Party is the largest Democratic representation of any recent generational cohort, Pew finds. Compared to the 59% democratic preference of Millennials, Generation Xers and Baby Boomers have a 48% preference for the Democratic Party while Silents have a 43% democratic preference.

Generational differences in midterm preferences wider in early 2018 than in recent midterm years

Congressional vote preference, by generation, based on registered voters...

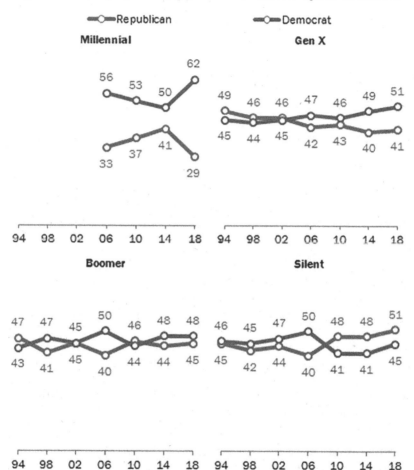

Note: Based on registered voters. Other/Don't know responses not shown. Previous years include all pre-election Pew Research Center surveys conducted in the calendar year of the election. 2018 data from January survey.

Source: Survey of U.S. adults conducted Jan. 10-15, 2018.

PEW RESEARCH CENTER

Figure 7.2 Millennials Are the Most Democratic Generation, Silents the Most Republican.

Note. From *The Generation Gap in American Politics: Wide and Growing Divides in Views of Racial Discrimination,* by Pew Research Center, Washington, D.C. 2018 (http://www.people-press.org/2018/03/01/the-generation-gap-in-american-politics/).

While political affiliation may vary over time, the political orientation one adopts in early adulthood typically continues to be influential over one's lifetime, as observed in a Pew Research Center report (2015). As an example, Pew notes the Greatest generation, born between 1901 and 1927 and experiencing the 1929 Great Depression and policies of Democratic President Franklin D. Roosevelt, have been more likely to support democrats. Turning to Millennials, with 59% of Millennials identifying as Democratic in 2018 versus only 32% of Millennials identifying as Republican (Pew Research, 2018), even if adjustments to party affiliation occur over time, Millennials can be expected to remain more Democratic than Republican given this significant spread.

While younger individuals are known to be less likely to vote, this changed in the 2004 Presidential election when young voter turnout increased by 12% compared to the 2000 election as reported by Pew Research (2007). This 12% increase was the largest increase in any age group and coincides with Millennials born between 1983 and 1986 turning 18 and becoming eligible to vote for the first time. The research group further notes that this increase in young voters was led by females and African Americans. And in 2008, while only 41% of Millennials were eligible to vote in the 2008 Presidential election due to their age, Millennials were influential supporters of Barack Obama as reported by Morley Winograd with the University of Southern California Marshall School of Business and business executive and researcher Michael Hais, helping Obama become the first Black president of the United States (Winograd & Hais, 2014). Further, Tom Rosentiel and his colleagues with Pew Research reported that 66% of voters under 30 cast a ballot for Obama in 2008 (Rosentiel et al., 2009).

So, how did Democratic leaning Millennials impact the 2018 midterm elections? At the time of these elections, essentially 100% of Millennials were eligible to vote, excluding only individuals born between November 2, 2000 and December 31, 2000 who were still under the age of 18 for the 2018 midterms. As per the Center for Information and Research on Civic Learning and Engagement at Tufts University, or CIRCLE, 28.2% of youth voters, defined as individuals between the ages of 18 and 29, voted in the 2018 midterm elections (CIRCLE, 2019). This compares to approximately 13% of youth voters who are estimated to have voted in the 2014 midterm elections. Further, CIRCLE found that the youth vote in 2018 increased in each of the 42 surveyed states compared to the 2014 elections. Jason Linkins, writing for Think Progress, reported that Millennial turnout was high in key states including Florida, Georgia, Wisconsin, Ohio, and Nevada, and the youth vote was a decisive factor in the Democrats taking control of the House of Representatives (Linkins, 2018). Looking specifically at Millennials versus the age 18 to 29 youth voters referenced by CIRCLE, Cilluffo and Fry (2019b) report that participation for Millennial voters from 2014 to 2018 doubled from 22% to 42%.

Looking at congressional vote preference in 2018, Pew Research reports that Millennials were 62% Democratic and 29% Republican (Pew Research, 2018). For the same year, Pew reports congressional voter preference for Generation Xers was 51% Democratic versus 41% Republican, 48% Democrat versus 45% Republican for Baby Boomers, and 51% Republican versus 45% Democratic for Silents. It is important to note that younger cohorts are not always more democratic. In fact, looking at Generation X, this cohort was more Republican than Democratic from 1994 through approximately 2004 (Pew Research, 2018).

Turning to the 2020 Presidential election, voter turnout was at an all-time high of 66% (Igielnik et al., 2021). In the midst of a global pandemic and resulting economic instability, racially diverse Millennials and Generation Zs accounted for 30% of voters, 22% for Millennials and 8% for Generation Zs (Igielnik et al., 2021). Meanwhile, Generation X, Baby Boomers, and Silents accounted for 25%, 36%, and 8% of voters, respectively. Looking at eligible voters (voters and non-voters), the researchers report that Baby Boomers and Silents in 2020 accounted for 44% of eligible voters, losing their majority to the younger generations.

In the 2020 Presidential election, the first in which 100% of Millennials were old enough to vote, Millennial voters supported President Joe Biden, a Democrat, against Republican incumbent Donald Trump by a margin of 19% (Igielnik et al., 2021). Looking at Millennials and Generation Z combined, the margin of support for Biden over Trump was 20%. Meanwhile, Gen Xers narrowly chose Biden by a 3% margin while Baby Boomers and members of the Silent Generation preferred Trump by margins of 3% and 16%, respectively. Democrats are likely happy to hold such a commanding lead among young voters, who will presumably be casting ballots for generations to come, but there is a warning in the numbers as well.

Although Millennial turnout increased, Biden actually narrowed his margin over Trump among Millennials compared with previous Democratic candidate Hillary Clinton, who in 2016 beat Trump by a 25 point margin among Millennial voters (Igielnik, 2021). This could be evidence of a split among Democratic voters with younger Democrats preferring candidates they perceive as more progressive, such as Sens. Bernie Sanders and Elizabeth Warren in the Democratic primaries, and older Democrats favoring more centrist candidates.

Regardless of the whether Millennials prefer more centrist or progressive candidates, the overall Democratic tendencies of Millennials support a future Democratic agenda impacting the political, social, and economic environment of the United States. Fifty-seven percent of Millennials prefer a bigger role for government, versus 50% for Generation Xers, 43% for

Baby Boomers, and 30% for the Silent Generation, according to a Pew Research poll (Pew Research, 2018). As part of this larger government role, two-thirds of surveyed Millennials believe that the United States government should provide healthcare for all of its citizens, and 56% of Millennials think more should be done to help the needy. As the voices of Millennials are heard in upcoming elections, these issues will be front and center. A future legislative agenda focused on these issues has the potential to additionally impact employment laws and transform the work environment, but the path to such progressive legislation is far from clear, despite Millennials' preferences.

As an example, Ernst and Young Global Vice Chair of Diversity and Inclusiveness Karyn Twaronite wrote in 2015 that Millennials around the world are more likely to say it is important to receive paid parental leave – 74% of Millennials say so, versus 71% of Gen Xers and 58% of Boomers – as well as onsite or subsidized childcare, again, 62%, 57%, and 47%, respectively (Twaronite, 2019). At the time of this writing, the fate of some initiatives originally included in President Biden's signature economic package remains uncertain. Millennials could be more disappointed than other generations by what they may perceive as broken campaign promises, and time will tell how this impacts their turnout in future elections.

Looking at the diversity of Millennials, this cohort is more diverse than the generations that preceded them. They are 21% Hispanic, 13% African American, 7% Asian, and 3% non-White, for a total of 44% non-White Millennials, according to Pew Research (2018). Only Generation Z, who follow Millennials, are more diverse consistent with the increasing diversity in younger generations in the United States. Perhaps influenced by that diversity, the same study finds that 80% of Millennials view openness to different people from around the world as "essential to who we are as a nation" (p. 22). This compares to 68% of Generation Xers, 61% of Baby Boomers, and 54% of Silents who hold this view as shown in Figure 7.3.

It is interesting to note that this openness is consistent across Millennials from different races and ethnicities. For instance, 79% of White Millennials told Pew Research (2018) that they favor openness compared to 80% of all Millennials who support openness. Specifically asked whether immigrants strengthen America, while this view has generally increased for all generational cohorts over the past few decades, 79% of Millennials report that immigrants strengthen the United States compared with 66% of Generation Xers, 56% of Baby Boomers, and 45% of the Silent generation (Pew Research, 2018).

While support for openness is more prevalent among Democrats in general, more Millennial Democrats express this view compared to Democrats from other generations per the Pew study. Ninety-one percent of Millennial Democrats view America's openness as essential to who we are as a nation versus 87% of Gen Xer Democrats, 78% of Boomer Democrats,

Across generations, majorities see U.S. 'openness' as 'essential' to its identity

% who say ...

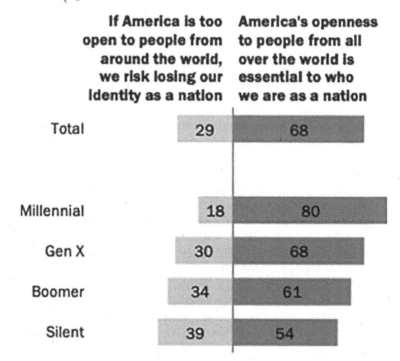

Note: Don't know responses not shown.
Source: Survey of U.S. adults conducted June 27-July 9, 2017.

PEW RESEARCH CENTER

Figure 7.3 Across Generations, Majorities see U.S. "Openness" as "Essential" to Its Identity.

Note. From *The Generation Gap in American Politics: Wide and Growing Divides in Views of Racial Discrimination*, by Pew Research Center, Washington, D.C. 2018 (http://www.people-press.org/2018/03/01/the-generation-gap-in-american-politics/).

and 68% of Silent Democrats. Similarly, among Republicans, Millennials were the only cohort with a majority reporting that America's openness is essential to its national character. Surveying Republicans, Pew found that 61% of Millennials said so compared with 46% of Gen Xers, 42% of Baby Boomers, and 38% of Silent Republicans.

Like Baby Boomers, the diverse Millennial cohort came of age during a push for expanded civil rights. Young Millennials watched the Rodney King riots break out in 1992 and the Million Man March three years later. As they entered adulthood, Millennials formed the nucleus of the Black Lives Matter movement, and it is their generation that is most likely to participate in protests focused on racial equality. Pew Researchers found that 41% of the participants in the 2020 racial justice protests were between 18 and 29, while that age bracket makes up only 19% of the nation's population (Barroso & Minkin, 2020). And those in the 50 to 64 age bracket make up 26% of the U.S. adult population, but only 15% of them were involved in the protests.

Writing in the wake of the 2020 Black Lives Matter protests, the Brookings Institute's William Frey notes that the difference between activism in the past, such as the Civil Rights movement in the 1960s, and today's protests is that current movements are occurring at the same time the country is experiencing demographic transformation (Frey, 2020). According to the Brookings data, by 2030, just over half of those under 50 will be non-White, while the 65 and older population will be more than 71% White. And Brookings estimates that the under-age 50 population in 2030 will be approximately 25% Latino or Hispanic, 14% Black, and 7% Asian American. With the diverse Millennial group assuming a majority role in society and the workforce, addressing racial issues will be a priority. "Diversity is not just their future—it is the nation's future," Frey writes (para. 7).

Thirty-three percent of Millennials and 40% of Generation Zs told Morning Consult pollsters in 2020 that they view companies that support current protests on social media more favorably as reported by Alyssa Meyers (Meyers, 2020). For Baby Boomers and Gen Xers, those numbers are 18% and 21%, respectively. In response to Black Lives Matter and other protests, several companies are publicly supporting these movements. Further, companies and sports teams are changing product names and branding to eliminate racist implications.

In a Pew Research study led by Horowitz (2021), they found that the 57% of all adults age 18+ say *not* seeing racial discrimination where it *does* exist is a bigger problem than people seeing racism where it does *not* exist, which was reported by 42% of the respondents. Looking at White respondents, 52% reported that the bigger problem for the country is seeing racial discrimination where it does *not* exist, with 48% reporting the bigger problem is *not* seeing racial discrimination where it *does* exist. Comparing this to Blacks, only 14% reported that the bigger problem for the country is seeing racial discrimination where it does *not* exist, with 84% reporting the bigger problem is *not* seeing racial discrimination where it *does* exist. Breaking this down by age, 61% of White individuals between the ages 18–29 see the bigger problem as people *not* seeing racial discrimination where it *does* exist while a majority of older White individuals see the bigger problem as people seeing racial discrimination where it really does *not* exist. These different views of younger versus older adults are shown in Figure 7.4.

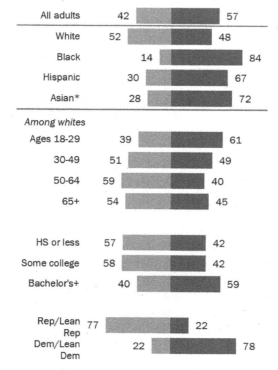

Nonwhites are more likely to say discrimination is overlooked

% saying, when it comes to racial discrimination, the bigger problem for the country is ...

■ People seeing racial discrimination where it really does NOT exist

■ People NOT seeing racial discrimination where it really DOES exist

All adults	42	57
White	52	48
Black	14	84
Hispanic	30	67
Asian*	28	72

Among whites

Ages 18-29	39	61
30-49	51	49
50-64	59	40
65+	54	45
HS or less	57	42
Some college	58	42
Bachelor's+	40	59
Rep/Lean Rep	77	22
Dem/Lean Dem	22	78

*Asians were interviewed in English only.
Note: Share of respondents who didn't offer an answer not shown. Whites, blacks and Asians include those who report being only one race and are non-Hispanic. Hispanics are of any race. "Some college" includes those with an associate degree and those who attended college but did not obtain a degree.
Source: Survey of U.S. adults conducted Jan. 22-Feb. 5, 2019. "Race in America 2019"

PEW RESEARCH CENTER

Figure 7.4 Non-Whites Are More Likely to Say Discrimination Is Overlooked.
Note. From *How Americans See the State of Race Relations*, by J. Horowitz, A. Brown, and K. Cox, 2021. Pew Research Center, Washington, D.C. (https://www.pewresearch.org/social-trends/2019/04/09/how-americans-see-the-state-of-race-relations/).

A 2018 Case Foundation study of Millennials conducted by Jean Case and Sean Tennerson examined the top three issues among White/Caucasians, Spanish/Hispanic/Latinos, Black/African Americans, and Asian. All four groups of Millennials listed civil rights and racial discrimination as one of their top three issues of importance (Case & Tennerson, 2018). In a Pew Research Study asking about efforts to give Black people equal rights to Whites in the United States, 68% of Millennials responded that more change is needed (Pew Research, 2018). This is reflected in the civic mindedness of Millennials, which has manifested in participation in recent protests.

Comparatively, when asked the same question, 62% of Generation Xers, 57% of Baby Boomers, and 54% of Silents responded that more needs to be done to give Black people equal rights (Pew Research, 2018). In addition, 52% of Millennials report that discrimination is the main reason why Black people cannot get ahead. Only 40% of Generation Xers, 36% Baby Boomers, and 28% of Silents reported that discrimination is the reason why Black people cannot get ahead.

Recall Howe and Strauss, who categorized Millennials as the Civic or Hero generation. In 2000, they predicted Millennials would be a very engaged group with the collective power to effect momentous change. Certainly, the large size of this generation provides the needed numbers to impact causes of interest. The prediction by Howe and Strauss is particularly resonant today given the large number of diverse youth involved in protests that have emerged throughout the country. Millennials are described by Howe and Strauss as the "powerhouse generation, full of technology planners, community shapers, institution builders, and world leaders" (Howe & Strauss, 2000, p. 5). In fact, Howe and Strauss state that Millennials may become known as one of the most important generations in history due to the positive change brought about by this generation.

Conflict between Rich and Poor

Another issue that will impact a Millennial-led future is how Millennial's view class conflict. To explore this, we'll look at how younger individuals in the United States view conflict between rich and poor compared with older individuals. Specifically, given the challenging economic environment experienced by the Millennial cohort when they were growing up, how do income levels and earnings satisfaction impact Millennials' views of conflict between rich and poor? The goal of these questions is to add another layer to this research on Millennials.

Pew Research Center conducted a Youth and Economy Survey that collected demographic and social data (Pew Research 2011). One of the findings of the study is that 66% of surveyed individuals in America believe that there are either strong or very strong conflicts between rich and poor people (Morin, 2012). This represents a 19% increase from the results of the previous Pew Research survey conducted two years prior that asked the same question about conflict between rich and poor.

Of specific interest to our discussion of Millennials, the survey found that individuals in the younger age group, specifically age 18 to 34, are more likely to report this conflict than the older age groups (Morin, 2012). A total of 71% of younger individuals reported strong or very strong conflict between rich and poor, the highest of any of the age groups surveyed, compared with 64% for individuals ages 35–49, 67% for those 50-to-64-years-old, and 55% for individuals age 65 and older that report this class conflict.

We know that Millennials are more technologically connected. As such, Millennials may be more aware of conflict between rich and poor given their access to information on digital platforms, and more likely to report such conflict. Furthermore, research on Millennials shows that they were significantly impacted by the recession and are the first generation in modern history to start out doing less well than its parents. As such, conflict between rich and poor reported by Millennials may be the result of the tough economic conditions experienced by this cohort. Given the size and impact of the Millennial generation, understanding their perceptions of conflict between social classes will provide insight on social dynamics in the future. And while the Pew research was conducted during the height of the Occupy Wall Street movement, when anger at perceived corporate greed in the United States financial system was at a high point, more current research finds young people still hold negative feelings toward the capitalistic economic system (Saad, 2021).

Based on a 2019 survey, Lydia Saad at Gallup reports that Millennials and Generation Zs views toward socialism remained at about 50% positive between 2010 and 2019, but their views of capitalism plummeted from 66% to 51% by 2019, putting the two economic systems at roughly equal popularity in the eyes of the youngest American generations (Saad, 2021). Looking at Generation Xers and Baby Boomers, who are old enough to have memories of the Cold War and anti-Soviet media, Saad reports they have much different views, with Generation Xers preferring capitalism over socialism 61% to 39% in 2019, and for Boomers and Traditionalists, the split was 68% to 32%.

As a result of the economic challenges faced by Millennials during their upbringing, the question is whether this experience results in a cohort effect impacting Millennials' views of conflict between rich and poor, with age being a less important factor. Remember way back in Chapter 3 when we ran binary regression analyses on the conflict styles for the different generations? We are about to do that again with the responses from the

Pew study to examine whether higher levels of perceived class conflict are correlated with having enough income to live the kind of life one wants and one's current income.

The two specific questions analyzed from the 2011 Pew study are "Do you now earn enough money to lead the kind of life you want, or not" (Pew Research, 2011, p. 10)? and "Last year, that is in 2010, what was your total family income from all sources, before taxes" (Pew Research, 2011, p. 18)? With these answers, we are going to look at two hypotheses: that people reporting that they cannot live the life they want with their current earnings are more likely to report conflict between rich and poor, and that people with lower earnings are more likely to report conflict between rich and poor.

The original Pew Research survey was conducted via telephone, surveying 2,048 adults 18 and up, including 808 between 18 and 34 years old. The specific question that was asked regarding conflict between rich and poor is

> In all countries, there are differences or conflicts between different social groups. In your opinion, in America, how much conflict is there between rich people and poor people: very strong conflicts, strong conflicts, not very strong conflicts, there are not conflicts. (Pew Research, 2011, p. 6)

In addition, "can't choose" and "don't know/refused" were included as additional response categories.

You may recall that a binary logistic regression requires two sets of data. For this one, we will put those who said there is "very strong" and "strong" conflict in one group and "some conflict" and "no conflict" in the other. As expected, based on the results of the Pew Research Center study, the regression analysis finds that age is significant, with non-Millennials less likely to view conflict than Millennials. Our analysis shows that non-Millennials are found to be 8% *less* likely to view conflict compared to Millennials. But let's dig deeper and look at the two hypotheses.

The first hypothesis, that individuals reporting they cannot live the life they want with their current earnings are more likely to report conflict between rich and poor, is confirmed by our analysis. The results show that people who earn enough to live the life they want are much *less* likely to view conflict. This confirms that satisfaction with one's earnings impacts one's view of conflict. Individuals satisfied with their incomes are 9% less likely to view conflict. This has implications whereby income *satisfaction* is correlated with Millennials being less likely to view conflict between rich and poor.

The second hypothesis examines whether individuals with lower earnings are more likely to report conflict between rich and poor, but the results find that people with *higher* incomes are *more* likely to view conflict. The findings show that individuals who earn more are 4% more likely to view conflict between rich and poor. The results of this research highlight the difference in views of conflict looking at an individual's satisfaction with income versus actual income. While satisfaction with one's earnings corresponds to lower perceived levels of conflict, higher income earners are *more* likely to report conflict between rich and poor. As this survey was conducted in 2011, Millennials would have been right in the thick of the tough employment environment in the United States following the Great Recession. As a result, dissatisfaction with their earnings may have impacted the larger number of younger individuals reporting conflict between rich and poor.

In addition to income level and having sufficient income to lead the life you want, additional independent variables included in the regression analysis include gender, age, education, and race including Hispanic/Latino/Spanish, Black, or Asian. Regarding gender, females are 18% *more* likely than males to report conflict between rich and poor. Looking at race, Blacks are 20% *more* likely to view conflict than non-Blacks, and Asians are 17% *more* likely than non-Asians to view class conflict. These findings may be due to minority groups being more aware of conflict than non-minorities; however, looking at the results for Hispanic, Latino, or Spanish individuals, this group is 9% *less* likely to view conflict between rich and poor. Lastly, while education was included in the analysis, it was not found to be significant.

As we have discussed, Millennials are a diverse cohort, engaged in social issues spanning women's rights, sexual harassment, LGBTQ+, and the environment. In order to have their voices heard, as we discussed in Chapter 6, Millennials leverage their technological expertise and social media skills, with the ability to reach numerous individuals at the click of a button. Leveraging another forum to have their voices heard, Millennial participation at the polls has increased with Millennials engaging in the political process to vote for representation in line with their beliefs. A majority of Millennials are either Democratic or lean Democratic and are known to favor a larger role for government including universal healthcare and programs to help the needy. In addition, this diverse cohort supports immigration and doing more to ensure equal rights for all individuals. Taken together, these issues spanning diversity, social issues, and political engagement shed light on how Millennials will impact society and the workplace of the future. Paid parental leave, addressing sexual discrimination and harassment, ensuring equal rights, and making the workplace more flexible and accommodating will be on the Millennial agenda.

References

Adamczyk, A. (2021, May 28). *76% of older millennials are worried about climate change-and it's impacting how they spend their money.* CNBC. https://www.cnbc.com/2021/05/28/how-climate-change-is-impacting-millennials-money-decisions.html

Bell, J., Poushter, M.F., Fagan, M., & Hunag, C. (2021, September 14). *In response to climate change, citizens in advanced economies are willing to alter how they live and work. Many doubt success of international efforts to reduce global warming.* Pew Research Center. https://www.pewresearch.org/global/2021/09/14/in-response-to-climate-change-citizens-in-advanced-economies-are-willing-to-alter-how-they-live-and-work/

Barroso, A., & Minkin, R. (2020, June 24). *Recent protest attendees are more racially and ethnically diverse, younger than Americans overall.* Pew Research Center. https://www.pewresearch.org/fact-tank/2020/06/24/recent-protest-attendees-are-more-racially-and-ethnically-diverse-younger-than-americans-overall/

Brown, G. (2017). The Millennials (Generation Y): Segregation, integration and racism. ABNF Journal, 28(1), 5–8.

Case, J., & Tennerson, S. (2018, March 16). *Don't put Millennials in a box.* The Case Foundation. https://casefoundation.org/blog/dont-put-millennials-in-a-box/?gclid=CjwKCAjwpeXeBRA6EiwAyoJPKmqwckCXHqPpxdJ_d4yO-dXmJKanAVxMTvy1Xbjek78aK3CneRMVswRoCcHEQAvD_BwE

Center for Information and Research on Civic Learning and Engagement. (2019, May 30). *28% of young people voted in 2018.* Tufts Tisch College. https://circle.tufts.edu/latest-research/28-young-people-voted-2018

Center for Information and Research on Civic Learning and Engagement. (2020, November 18). *Election week 2020: Youth voter turnout 52%-55%.* Tufts Tisch College. https://circle.tufts.edu/latest-research/election-week-2020#vote-choice-by-age-and-by-race/ethnicity

Cilluffo, A., & Fry, R. (2019a, January 30). *An early look at the 2020 electorate.* Pew Research Center. https://www.pewsocialtrends.org/essay/an-early-look-at-the-2020-electorate/

Cilluffo, A., & Fry, R. (2019b, May 29). *GenZ, Millennials, and GenX outvoted older generations in 2018 midterms.* Pew Research Center. https://www.pewresearch.org/fact-tank/2019/05/29/gen-z-millennials-and-gen-x-outvoted-older-generations-in-2018-midterms/

Clayton, S., Manning, C., Krygsman, K., & Speiser, M. (2017, March). *Mental health and our changing climate: Impacts, implications and guidance.* American Psychology Association. https://www.apa.org/news/press/releases/2017/03/-mental-health-climate.pdf

Chenworth E, & Pressman, J. (2017, February 7). *This is what we learned by counting the women's marches.* The Washington Post. https://www.washingtonpost.com/news/monkey-cage/wp/2017/02/07/this-is-what-we-learned-by-counting-the-womens-marches/

Da Silva, C. (2018, September 18). *Has Occupy Wall Street changed America?* Newsweek. https://www.newsweek.com/has-occupy-wall-street-changed-america-seven-years-birth-political-movement-1126364

Doherty, C., Kiley, J., & O'Hea, O. (2018, March 1). *The generation gap in American politics: wide and growing divides in views of racial discrimination.* Pew Research Center. http://www.people-press.org/2018/03/01/the-generation-gap-in-american-politics/

Frey, W. (2020, June 9). *The nation's racial justice protests are a pivotal moment for Millennials and Generation Z.* Brookings. https://www.brookings.edu/blog/-the-avenue/2020/06/08/the-nations-racial-justice-protests-are-a-pivotal-moment-for-millennials-and-gen-z/

Funk, C., & Kennedy, B. (2020, April 21). *How Americans see climate change and the environment in 7 charts.* Pew Research Center. https://www.pewresearch.org/fact-tank/2020/04/21/how-americans-see-climate-change-and-the-environment-in-7-charts/ft_2020-04-21_earthday_05/

Graff, N. (2018, April 4). *Sexual harassment at work in the era of #metoo. Many see new difficulties for men in workplace interactions and little effect on women's career opportunities.* Pew Research. https://www.pewresearch.org/social-trends/2018/04/04/sexual-harassment-at-work-in-the-era-of-metoo/

Hickman, C., Marks, E., Pihkala, P., Clayton, S., Lewandowski, E., Mayall, E., Wray, B., Mellor, C., & van Susteren, L. (2021). Climate anxiety in children and young people and their beliefs about government responses to climate change: A global survey. *The Lancet.* https://www.thelancet.com/journals/lanplh/article/PIIS2542-5196(21)00278-3/fulltext

Horowitz, J.M., Brown, A., & Cox, K. (2021, September 22). *How Americans see the state of race relations.* Pew Research Center's Social & Demographic Trends Project. https://www.pewresearch.org/social-trends/2019/04/09/how-americans-see-the-state-of-race-relations/

Howe, N., & Strauss, W. (2000). *Millennials rising: The next great generation.* Vintage Books.

Igielnik, R., Keeter, S., & Hartig, H. (2021, September 30). *Behind Biden's 2020 victory.* Pew Research Center – U.S. Politics & Policy. https://www.pewresearch.org/politics/2021/06/30/behind-bidens-2020-victory/

Jones, J. (2022, February 17). *LGBT identification in U.S. ticks up to 7.1%.* Gallup. https://news.gallup.com/poll/389792/lgbt-identification-ticks-up.aspx

Keplinger, K., Johnson, S., Kirk, J., & Barnes, L. (2019, July 17). Women at work: Changes in sexual harassment between September 2016 and September 2018. *Plos One.* https://doi.org/10.1371/journal.pone.0218313

Linkins, J. (2018, November 9). *In 2018, the youth vote turned out, and voted for Democrats, in droves. The young were a decisive factor in the Democratic wave. And they may be a generation lost to Republicans.* Think Progress. https://thinkprogress.org/in-2018-the-young-turned-out-went-democrat-22e194bc1255/

Marks, E., Hickman, C., Pihkala, P., Clayton, S., Lewandowski, E.R., Mayall, E.E., Wray, B., Mellor, C., & van Susteren, L. (2021, September 7). *Young People's voices on climate anxiety, government betrayal and moral injury: A global phenomenon.* SSRN. https://papers.ssrn.com/sol3/papers.cfm?abstract_id=3918955

McCarthy, J. (2021, June 8) *Record-high 70% in U.S. support same-sex marriage.* Gallup. https://news.gallup.com/poll/350486/record-high-support-same-sex-marriage.aspx

Meyers, A. (2020, June 2). *Brands are speaking out on Black Lives Matter. How are consumers going to respond?* Morning Consult. https://morningconsult. com/2020/06/02/brands-black-lives-matter-response-poll/

Morin, Rich. (2012, January 11). *Rising share of Americans see conflict between rich and poor.* Pew Research Center. http://www.pewsocialtrends.org/2012/01/11/-rising-share-of-americans-see-conflict-between-rich-and-poor/

Newport, F. (2018, May 22). *In U.S., estimate of LGBT population rises to 4.5%.* Gallup. https://news.gallup.com/poll/234863/estimate-lgbt-population-rises.aspx

Oliphant, Baxter. (2017, December 7). *Women and men in both parties say sexual harassment allegations reflect 'widespread problems in society'.* Pew Research. https://www.pewresearch.org/fact-tank/2017/12/07/americans-views-of-sexual-harassment-allegations

Parker, K., & Igielnik, R. (2021, July 14). *What we know about Gen Z so far.* Pew Research. https://www.pewresearch.org/social-trends/2020/05/14/on-the-cusp-of-adulthood-and-facing-an-uncertain-future-what-we-know-about-gen-z-so-far-2/

Pew Research Center. (2007, January 7). *How young people view their lives, futures and roles: A portrait of "generation next."* http://www.pewresearch.org/wp-content/uploads/sites/3/2010/10/300.pdf

Pew Research Center. (2011, December 6). *December 2011 youth and economy survey final questionnaire.* http://www.pewsocialtrends.org/2013/02/22/youth-economy/

Pew Research Center. (2015, April 30). *A different look at generations and partisanship.* https://www.pewresearch.org/politics/2015/04/30/a-different-look-at-generations-and-partisanship/

Pew Research Center. (2018, March 1). *The generation gap in American politics: Wide and growing divides in views of racial discrimination.* http://www.people-press. org/2018/03/01/the-generation-gap-in-american-politics/

Pew Research Center. (2020, May 30). *Views of scope of government, trust in Government, economic inequality.* Pew Research Center. https://www.pewresearch. org/politics/2018/03/01/2

Quick, J.C., & McFadyen, M.A. (2017) Sexual harassment: Have we made any progress? *Journal of Occupational Health Psychology, 22*(3), 286–298. https://doi. apa.org/doiLanding?doi=10.1037%2Focp0000054

Risman. (2004, August). *Gender as a social structure: Theory wrestling with activism.* Sage Publications. https://www.jstor.org/stable/4149444

Risman, B.J. (2018). *Where the millennials will take us: A new generation wrestles with the gender structure.* Oxford Scholarship Online. https://oxford.universitypressscholarship.com/view/10.1093/oso/9780199324385.001.0001/oso-9780199324385

Robb, D. (2021, July 15). *GLAAD film report: No transgender characters in major studio releases again last year, but more diversity & screen time for LGBTQ roles.* Deadline. https://deadline.com/2021/07/glaad-film-report-no-transgender-characters-in-hollywood-movies-2020-1234791678/

Rosenthiel, T. (2008, November 13). *Young voters in the 2008 election.* Pew Research Center. https://www.pewresearch.org/2008/11/13/young-voters-in-the-2008-election/

Saad, L. (2021, August 13). *Socialism as popular as capitalism among young adults in U.S.* Gallup. https://news.gallup.com/poll/268766/socialism-popular-capitalism-among-young-adults.aspx

Townsend, M. (2021, January 14). *Where we are on TV report - 2020.* GLAAD Media Institute. https://www.glaad.org/whereweareontv20

Townsend, M., & Deerwater, R. (n.d.). *Where we are on TV: 2020–2021.* GLAAD Media Institute. https://www.glaad.org/sites/default/files/GLAAD%20-%20 202021%20WHERE%20WE%20ARE%20ON%20TV.pdf

Twaronite, K. (2019). *Global generations: A global study in work-life challenges across generations.* Ernst and Young. https://www.ey.com/Publication/vwLUAssets/ Global_generations_study/$FILE/EY-global-generations-a-global-study-on-work-life-challenges-across-generations.pdf

Tyson, A., Kennedy, B., & Funk, C. (2021, August 6). *Climate, energy and environmental policy.* Pew Research Center Science & Society. https://www.pewresearch.org/science/2021/05/26/climate-energy-and-environmental-policy

Winograd, M., & Hais, M.D. (2014). *How Millennials could upend wall street and corporate America.* Brookings Institute. https://www.brookings.edu/research/-how-millennials-could-upend-wall-street-and-corporate-america/

Chapter 8

What We Learned about Millennials

The Research: Interviews, Focus Groups, and Conflict Styles Analysis

To shed light on Millennials in the workplace, the research started by conducting interviews and focus groups to ask the question "How do Millennials manage conflict in the workplace?" These sessions consisted primarily of open-ended questions to hear first-hand from Millennials and non-Millennials regarding their experiences in the workplace and covered the topics of conflict resolution, technology, gender identity, expectations, and team orientation. What we heard is that Millennials withdraw from and avoid conflict, but we also found they are apt to use an online support group to help resolve workplace conflicts. It was very interesting to gain insight into how this digital connection is used to help with workplace conflict, and this will be interesting to probe in future research.

Another important finding from the interviews and focus groups is that Millennials enjoy a creative and innovative environment that promotes learning and training. As Millennials are highly educated, it follows that they have an appreciation for an environment that promotes learning. Companies that embrace this and provide an environment that includes value-added training may be more able to satisfy their Millennial workers. Regarding training, Millennials did share that sitting in a classroom hearing lectures about corporate policy and procedures is not appealing, so the type of training, topic, and delivery mode are key. More hands-on and participatory training are preferred. Supplemental to training, giving Millennial's responsibilities that challenge them can address their desire to learn and grow.

Along this same theme, Millennials want to know the "why" behind things when they are assigned tasks in the workplace. Some interviewees described this as creating conflict and making Millennials in the workplace difficult to manage. However, we suggest that if managers take the time to explain the reason behind tasks, this could help minimize conflict. If time does not allow for an immediate explanation due to an impending

DOI: 10.4324/9781003246824-8

deadline or urgent need, offer to meet with the employee as soon as possible after the task is completed to discuss the process in place. Rather than simply explaining the process, listening to suggestions made by Millennials could result in better and more efficient ways of doing things. This curious and well-educated cohort may have innovative ideas for improving workplace efficiencies. Offering a forum for suggestions will not only meet Millennials' desire for input but may result in improved workplace efficiencies. There needs to be balance in this process – Millennials need to understand that some of their suggestions may not be implemented but telling them *why* they will not be implemented will go a long way.

Exploring the expectations of Millennials, they were consistently described as entitled with high expectations, especially regarding pay and promotions. And both Millennials and non-Millennials stated that Millennials will simply leave or quit if they are not satisfied. You may recall from Chapter 4 when we asked more probing questions when our interviewees described Millennials as "entitled," we often heard they have high expectations. It's possible that an employee with high expectations will exert additional effort to attain their goals and positively impact the workplace. A word of caution though as some research shows that high expectations can result in stress, especially if these expectations are unattainable. Continually striving for a high bar can create anxiety.

Beyond the internal anxiety that can result from high expectations, we did hear in our interviews that the high expectations of Millennials can create conflict in the workplace, especially with older workers who feel they had to work their way up the ladder and see Millennials wanting faster advancement opportunities. So, how can you satisfy and retain Millennials seeking to advance quickly within your organization? While promotions may not be possible after a short tenure, providing additional responsibilities may meet Millennials' need for advancement. It may be possible to satisfy Millennials without the official promotion. Potential ideas include assigning a Millennial to head up a task force or to work on a special project. This does not mean adding extra work without the pay but finding key areas within the scope of one's existing job to provide a leadership role or projects of special interest, depending on the interests of the employee. Seeking suggestions directly from the employee on ways to grow their job will ensure the proposed responsibilities or tasks will be viewed positively rather than seen as piling on more work. And employees may simply have suggestions on creative ways to do their job that may satisfy them until they advance.

Another suggestion to create an environment that appeals to Millennials and improves the retention of this talented cohort is to provide clear direction regarding what you expect. This is a basic management principle but more important than ever for Millennials – clearly tell them *what* you want accomplished and *why* it is important. This second step of telling the "why" is critical. So, employees are not just completing steps 1, 2, and 3, but understanding what it is they are accomplishing and how it fits in the big picture. Companies are often good at defining processes and procedures for *how* to do something but can ignore communicating the results and how they fit within the big picture.

Millennials will appreciate employers who listen to ideas on revising and adapting the "how" to do things and provide a forum for input. However, this does not mean companies should open the door to spontaneous trials of different ways to accomplish work tasks. And the traditional suggestion box is not recommended even if you put it online. To maintain quality and ensure proper outcomes, use work groups or other mechanisms to allow employees to provide suggestions in a way that allows review and evaluation. One idea is to have a work group with a broad representation of employees who review suggestions and provide feedback. The goal is for this multi-generational work group to fully assess the pros and cons of the suggestions, allowing employees to better understand the implications.

Another element of an attractive work environment for Millennials is flexibility. This desire for flexibility in the workplace was specifically mentioned by 77% of Millennials interviewed. Certainly, the current pandemic has resulted in numerous organizations embracing virtual work and becoming more comfortable with this type of arrangement. A company that can accommodate a more flexible schedule will be more attractive to Millennials. While this is more challenging for retail and service industries, flex schedules with several consecutive days off is an option. For example, employees can work three days on, four days off, switching the following week to four days on, three days off.

Another consideration for Millennial workers is flexibility in when they work – Millennials in our interviews expressed a desire to determine their own work hours. While we are seeing more virtual work post-pandemic, younger workers are still looking for more flexibility in *when* they work, not just where. It's interesting that we did see coincidental evidence in our interviews of Millennials following more fluid schedules than non-Millennials with over 55% of Millennials in this study arriving late for scheduled interviews by an average of 35 minutes. Conversely, only one non-Millennial was late for their interview by approximately eight minutes and apologized profusely for being late. In contrast, while over half of Millennials were late for their interviews, only one apologized for the lateness, perhaps suggesting a greater acceptance of time fluidity.

An additional theme that resonated in this study was the desire by Millennials to receive frequent and timely feedback. Providing this feedback in the workplace may enhance the experience of Millennials, but it is important to have practices in place to ensure that this happens. Have regularly scheduled bi-weekly touch base meetings and a process to provide timely feedback after the completion of tasks. Managers who build these interactions into their schedules may better satisfy those seeking regular feedback compared to the annual review used by many organizations today. And as mentioned in Chapter 4, when you meet, don't simply review a list of current tasks or assignments, rather take this opportunity to tell your employees how they are doing and solicit their input and feedback.

As one example of providing more frequent feedback in line with the preference of Millennials, General Electric (GE) is implementing a performance app that provides more frequent feedback (Nisen, 2015). GE's former annual performance review that ranked employees was an essential component of GE's culture for many years. That is now being replaced with a system that appeals to Millennials. The new system works off preset employee goals, whereby the employee can request feedback at any time rather than waiting to hear. Other companies are also moving away from annual formalized reviews including Microsoft, Accenture, and Adobe (Nisen, 2015).

We heard in our interviews and focus groups that Millennials are defensive and feel judged as a generation, so it will be helpful to include positive feedback along with suggestions for improvement. While correcting negative behavior may take precedence over praising positive behavior, it is especially important to provide the positives. Older generations in the workplace will also appreciate this positive feedback. So, Millennials may be paving the way for change that benefits all generations at work.

Looking at teams, research shows that Millennials prefer working as a group (DeVaney, 2015; Hartman & McCambridge, 2011). This was corroborated in our interviews and focus groups with both Millennials and non-Millennials expressing a preference for teamwork. However, almost half of Millennials also mentioned a preference for individual work depending on the situation. In deconstructing the interviews, Millennials say they prefer teams for the social aspect, not necessarily the work aspect. In the workplace, they often want individual responsibilities where they are not dependent on others. Furthermore, Millennials view teams as egalitarian with equal members, but the lack of authority can result in confusion and stalemate. Non-Millennials seem to prefer teams for practical reasons, as they provide efficiency and the ability to produce a better end product given numerous sources of knowledge. In addition, non-Millennials view teams as having an authoritarian structure with a team leader or leaders. The concept of teams is complex and requires a more in-depth analysis in future research.

Another surprising finding stems from the question regarding the impact of gender on the conflict styles of Millennials. While the majority of Millennials describe males as more assertive than females, 30% describe women as more assertive, and 25% say males and females negotiate the same. In addition, almost 40% of non-Millennials reported that Millennial men were more passive and females more assertive. The MeToo movement was cited as a factor in males withdrawing and becoming more passive. Regarding other social movements, nearly half of Millennials interviewed mentioned women's rights and sexual harassment as a topic of great importance, with LGBTQ+ and environmental issues mentioned, as well.

Consistent with the finding that almost half of non-Millennials describe Millennials as self-focused, it was interesting to see that Millennials in interviews were more likely to talk about themselves. This is consistent with findings in the research that Millennials are more narcissistic compared to other generations. Asked the same questions, non-Millennials were less likely to talk about themselves compared to Millennials.

Another coincidental finding in this research is the movement to redesign office space to make it more Millennial centric. The significant importance of this generation is recognized with this move to make office space more desirable to Millennials. A word of caution here as initial feedback from some companies implementing this open concept is that it is distracting, and employees may be less productive. Also, the COVID-19 pandemic is changing views of shared spaces, with some workers preferring individual work areas. Again, this is an area for future research.

In addition to the interviews and focus groups, rigorous quantitative analyses were performed as part of this research using results from 11,000 test-takers of the Thomas-Kilmann Conflict Mode Instrument. These conflict styles, defined by level of cooperation and level of assertiveness, are avoiding (unassertive and uncooperative), accommodating (unassertive and cooperative), competing (assertive and uncooperative), collaborating (assertive and cooperative), and compromising (mid-assertive and mid-cooperative).

While the focus of this research is on the conflict styles of Millennials, insight on how these styles differ by generation provides insight on intergenerational workplace dynamics. To figure it all out, we performed a longitudinal cohort study looking at the conflict styles of Millennials, Generation Xers, and Baby Boomers present in the workplace over a 13-year period to answer the question "What are the dominant conflict styles for Millennials, Generation Xers, and Baby Boomers?" From this analysis, we not only learned the dominant conflict styles of these generational cohorts, but the styles each of these cohorts is *less* likely to employ We then extended the analysis to look at how these styles change over time as well as how gender impacts conflict styles. Lastly, we conducted an analysis of same-age Millennials and Generation Xers to tease age from cohort effect. The research question asked in this part of the study is "How do the conflict styles of Millennials compare to the conflict styles of Generation Xers?"

Let's start by looking at what we learned in our analysis of the dominant conflict styles for Millennials, Generation Xers, and Baby Boomers. For the accommodating conflict style, there are two key findings. First,

Millennials are *more* likely to accommodate than Generation Xers and Baby Boomers, employing an unassertive and cooperative conflict style. As heard in our interviews, Millennials are more likely to have an unassertive approach to conflict. However, the unassertive element is paired with the cooperative element in the accommodating style rather than the less cooperative element in the avoiding conflict style. The second finding is that Baby Boomers are *less* likely to accommodate.

Looking at an avoiding style, while we heard in the interviews and focus groups that Millennials are likely to avoid, the results of our analysis were not significant for Millennials having this unassertive and uncooperative style. However, it is important to point out the different ages of the Millennial participants included in the quantitative and qualitative studies. In the quantitative study, there are three distinct age groups for Millennials in the three databases including 21 and 22-year-olds in the 2006 database, 27 and 28-year-olds in the 2012 database, and 33 and 34-year-olds in the 2018 database. Looking at those databases, the percentage of Millennials with an avoiding style is 13.57%, 21.44%, and 22.43%, respectively, considerably different for the 21 and 22-year-olds versus the older Millennials.

While the percent of the avoiding conflict style for Generation Xers is fairly stable over the 13-year study period and the percent for Baby Boomers increases 26%, the percent for Millennials changes significantly, increasing 65% from age 21/22 to 33/34. As such, the 21 and 22-year-olds in the statistical analysis with a comparatively low percent of avoiding style could account for the lack of confirmation of an avoiding style for Millennials as found in our interviews. Furthermore, the mean age for Millennials in the interviews and focus groups is 31 and does not include any participants as young as 21/22-years-old. To further examine this and see if the lack of consensus between the two studies is impacted by the 21 and 22-year-old Millennials in the statistical analysis, we investigate same-age Millennials and Generation Xers at ages 27/28 and 33/34 to isolate age. This will tell us if either of these cohorts is more or less likely to avoid at these same-age comparisons. These results will be discussed further on in this chapter.

While an avoiding style was not confirmed for Millennials in the quantitative analysis, interesting results were found for the other two generations. Generation X was found *less* likely to utilize an avoiding style, and, while Baby Boomers are often described as direct and non-avoiding, this generational cohort was found *more* likely to employ an avoiding style.

Turning to a competing conflict style, with assertive and uncooperative elements, the results defy our stereotypes. First, we find our younger cohorts, Millennials and Generation Xers, are *more* likely to employ a competitive conflict style and despite descriptions in the literature that Baby Boomers are competitive, this generational cohort is found *less* likely to employ a competing style.

Regarding a collaborative conflict style, we once again have three findings. Baby Boomers were the only generation found *more* likely to employ this conflict style which incorporates high assertiveness and high cooperation. So, we do see assertiveness within this generational cohort but with a cooperative element rather than the uncooperative element in the competing style. In contrast to Baby Boomers, both Millennials and Generation Xers are found *less* likely to collaborate.

Turning to a compromising style, which is mid-level assertive and mid-level cooperative, Generation X was found *more* likely to employ this conflict style compared to non–Generation Xers. However, Baby Boomers are found *less* likely to compromise versus non–Baby Boomers.

Regarding the significance of the higher education and higher work levels control variables, these were found to be significant, either positively (more likely to employ a specific style) or negatively (less likely to employ a specific style), with the exception that higher education levels were not found to be significant for competing or accommodating styles. Furthermore, the education and work level results across the five conflict styles were the same for all three generations, including the direction of the finding (either positive or negative) showing the consistency in conflict style by education and work level.

Looking at work rank, higher level employees across all three cohorts are *more* likely to compete, collaborate, and compromise, and *less* likely to avoid and accommodate, which have unassertive elements. This suggests the assertive element in the competing and collaborative styles may be an asset when climbing the corporate ladder. Looking at education level, more highly educated individuals are *less* likely to avoid, *less* likely to collaborate, and *more* likely to compromise. What these results tell us that it is important to pay attention to work levels and education levels when examining conflict styles.

In summarizing the findings, Millennials are *more* likely to use accommodating and competing conflict styles and *less* likely to use a collaborating style. Turning to Generation Xers, as with Millennials, this cohort is *more* likely to use a competing style. Generation Xers are also *more* likely to use a compromising style. However, they are *less* likely to use avoiding or collaborating styles. Looking at Baby Boomers, they are *more* likely to employ collaborative and avoiding styles, and *less* likely to use competing, compromising, or accommodating styles. These results are shown in Table 8.1.

These conflicting conflict styles within an organization, for example, Millennials and Generation Xers who are *more* likely to employ a competitive style working alongside Baby Boomers who are *less* likely to use a competitive style, may escalate the level of conflict.

When we looked at our data spanning 13 years to examine dominant conflict styles, we also looked at how these styles change over time.

Table 8.1 Conflict Styles of Millennials, Generation Xers, and Baby Boomers

	Avoiding Unassertive & Uncooperative	Accommodating Unassertive & Cooperative	Competing Assertive & Uncooperative	Collaborating Assertive & Cooperative	Compromising Mid-Assertive & Mid-Cooperative
Generation more likely to use style	Baby Boomers	Millennials	Millennials and Generation Xers	Baby Boomers	Generation Xers
Generation less likely to use style	Generation Xers	Baby Boomers	Baby Boomers	Generation Xers and Millennials	Baby Boomers

Note. Based on analysis of the Thomas-Kilmann Conflict Mode Instrument data.

Looking at our consolidated snapshot of the percent of conflict styles for all three generational cohorts from 2006 to 2018, the avoiding style increases, the competing style decreases, the collaborating style decreases, the compromising style increases (Generation Xers) or remains fairly stable (non-Generation Xers), and the accommodating conflict style either decreases (Millennials) or stays essentially the same (non-Millennials). So, regardless of age, three of the predominant conflict styles moved in the same direction for all three generations. This snapshot shows us a 2006 to 2018 workplace with more avoiding, less competitive, and less collaborative conflict styles. Some of our interview participants suggest that heightened human resource management along with an increased concern about the legal ramifications of certain workplace behaviors has resulted in more avoidance at work.

When we drill down on each individual time periods of 2006, 2012, and 2018, we find some results that are consistent across all three time periods studied. First, Millennials are more likely than Baby Boomers across all three time periods studied to employ a more competitive conflict style while Generation Xers are more likely than Baby Boomers to employ a competing style in two of the three time periods. Similarly consistent, Baby Boomers are more likely than Millennials and Generation Xers to use a collaborative style over all three time periods. Lastly, Millennials and Generation Xers are more likely than Baby Boomers to use an accommodating style over two of the three periods. As such, these findings are not impacted by large differences in the data in one or two time periods but represent consistent findings over the 13-year period.

Another topic examined in our review of dominant conflict styles is how gender impacts these styles. The results show consistent findings for females and males across all five conflict styles. Female Millennials, Generation Xers, and Baby Boomers have a higher percent of accommodating, avoiding, and compromising styles compared to males in their generational cohorts. Furthermore, males across all three generations have a higher percent of competing and collaborative styles compared to their female cohort members. Consistent with other research findings that men are more competitive than women (Holt & DeVore, 2005; Thomas et al., 2008), this study finds that males across all generations are more likely to use a competing style compared to females, across all three time periods studied.

Looking at an avoiding conflict style, Baby Boomer females are *more* likely to avoid compared to males in their cohort; however, it is interesting to note that there is no significant male-to-female difference in avoiding behavior for Millennials and Generation Xers. For the accommodating conflict style, Gen X and Baby Boomer females are *more* likely to use this style compared to their male cohort member but, again, there is no significant finding for male-to-female differences with Millennials. For the collaborating style, Baby Boomer males were *more* likely than Baby Boomer females to collaborate while Generation X and Millennial females are *more* likely to compromise than Millennial males.

It is interesting to observe that the male-to-female comparisons over the five conflict styles shows four significant results for Baby Boomers, three significant results for Generation Xers, and only two significant results for Millennials. As such, the difference in male-to-female conflict styles narrows over each successive generation, with the least difference in male-to-female conflict styles observed in the Millennial generation.

While we often look at male-to-female comparisons, to shed further light on the impact of gender and conflict styles, we also looked at same-gender comparisons to see if there are female-to-female or male-to-male differences. Some of the major findings include that Millennial and Generation X females are *more* likely than Baby Boomer females to compete. Furthermore, Baby Boomer females are *more* likely than females from the other two generations to collaborate. For male-to-male findings, consistent with the female-to-female result, Millennials and Generation Xers are *more* likely than Baby Boomers to compete. Millennial males are also *more* likely than males from the other two cohorts to accommodate and avoid. Lastly, Baby Boomers are *more* likely than Millennials and Gen X to collaborate.

The final question we address in the research for this book is "How do the conflict styles of Millennials compare to the conflict styles of Generation Xers?" While the previous analysis provides meaningful insight on generational differences in conflict styles in the workplace over time, this investigation allows us to look at same-age Millennials and Generation Xers to eliminate the possible impact of age on our results. Given what our interview subjects had to say, we assume Millennials would be more likely to have an accommodating or avoiding conflict style compared to Generation Xers, but the results are not so simple. And while we did hear Millennials in general avoid conflict, this was more often mentioned in reference to males with some interviewees describing Millennial females as more assertive.

Looking at an accommodating conflict style, at age 33/34, Millennials are *more* likely to employ this unassertive and cooperative conflict style compared to same-age Generation Xers. At age 27/28, we have the same finding for an avoiding conflict style with Millennials *more* likely to use this conflict style, with unassertive and uncooperative elements, compared to same-age Generation Xers, consistent with the interview reports that Millennials avoid conflict. It is important to point out that Millennials show unassertive conflict styles at both same-age comparisons with the difference being unassertive and uncooperative (avoiding) at age 27/28 and an unassertive and cooperative (accommodating) style at age 33/34.

Another significant finding from the statistical analysis of the Thomas-Kilmann conflict styles is that age 27/28 Generation Xers are *more* likely than Millennials to collaborate, with assertive and cooperative elements. In addition, Generation Xers are *more* likely than Millennials to compete, with assertive and uncooperative elements, at age 33 and 34. Millennials have a 3% decrease in the percent of competing style between ages 27/28 and 33/34, while Generation Xers have a 0.5% increase in competing behavior over the same-age timeline. Consistent with our finding that Millennials are *more* likely to have either avoiding and accommodating styles with unassertive elements at both age comparisons, Generation Xers are *more* likely to have assertive conflict styles compared to Millennials at both same-age comparisons, with the difference being whether the style is assertive and cooperative (collaborating) or assertive and uncooperative (competing). These results are summarized in Table 8.2.

Table 8.2 Conflict Styles of Same-Age Millennials and Generation Xers

	Age 27/28	Age 33/34
Millennials are...	More likely than Gen X to have a more unassertive and uncooperative (avoiding) conflict style	More likely than Gen X to have a more unassertive and cooperative (accommodating) conflict style
Generation Xers are...	More likely than Millennials to have a more assertive and cooperative (collaborative) conflict style	More likely than Millennials to have a more assertive and uncooperative (competing) conflict style

Note. Based on analysis of the Thomas-Kilmann Conflict Mode Instrument data.

Adding gender into the mix, we asked whether Millennial males are more likely than Generation X males to have an avoiding conflict style, but the results did not show a significant difference. The second gender-related question we asked is whether Millennial males are more likely than Generation X males to have an accommodating conflict style. The result is significant at age 33/34, with Millennial males *more* accommodating compared to Generation X males, consistent with what the interviewees had to say. The third gender question is whether Millennial females are more likely than Generation X females to have a competitive conflict style. This was not significant over either age comparison. However, looking at males, the result for age 33/34 is significant with Generation X males *more* likely to compete compared to Millennial males. As the competitive style has an assertive element, this finding is consistent with the qualitative findings that Millennial males are less assertive.

The last gender question we asked is whether Millennial females are more likely than Generation X females to have a collaborative conflict style, but it turns out the opposite is true. Generation X females have a higher *percent* of collaborative style across both age comparisons, but our statistics show that Generation X females are *more* likely than Millennial females to collaborate at ages 27/28; however, the result is not significant at ages 33/34. Similarly, Generation X males are *more* likely than Millennial males to collaborate at age 27/28, with no significant difference at age 33/34. The results are shown in Table 8.3.

Table 8.3 Same-Age Gender Comparison of Generation X and Millennials Conflict Styles

	Age 27/28	Age 33/34
Millennial Males are…		More likely to be unassertive and cooperative (accommodating) compared to Gen X males
Generation X Males are…	More likely to be assertive and cooperative (collaborating) compared to Millennial males	More likely to be assertive and uncooperative (competing) compared to Millennial males
Generation X Females are…	More likely to be assertive and cooperative (collaborating) compared to Millennial females	

Note. Based on analysis of the Thomas-Kilmann Conflict Mode Instrument data.

Consolidated Research Findings

So, let's pull together our findings and see where we find consistency. Starting with the interviews and focus groups, our participants reported that Millennials are likely to avoid conflict and that Millennial males are less assertive. Looking at our statistical analysis, we find that Millennials are *more* likely to accommodate compared to Generation Xers and Baby Boomers over the 13-year study period. Furthermore, in our same-age comparison, Millennials are *more* likely to use the accommodating style compared to Generation Xers at ages 33/34 and *more* likely to use an avoiding style compared to Generation Xers at ages 27/28. While avoiding and accommodating are different styles in the Thomas-Kilmann Conflict

Mode Instrument, they both include an unassertive element consistent with passivity; the only difference is that avoiding has an uncooperative element while accommodating has a cooperative element. As such, our findings suggest that Millennials are more likely to employ unassertive conflict styles. Consistent with these findings, Generation Xers are *more* likely than same-age Millennials to use a competing style (assertive and uncooperative) at ages 33/34 and a collaborating style (assertive and cooperative) at ages 27/28, with both styles having an assertive element.

Looking further at our same-age comparison by gender, Millennial males are *more* likely than Generation X males to use an accommodating style (unassertive and cooperative) at ages 33/34. Comparatively, Generation X males are *more* likely to use a competing style (assertive and uncooperative) at ages 33/34 and collaborative style (assertive and cooperative) at ages 27/28 compared to same-age Millennial males. Turning to females, Generation Xers are more likely to employ a collaborative (assertive and cooperative) than Millennial at ages 27/28. Again, these findings show more assertive conflict styles with Generation Xers compared to Millennials.

Regarding what we heard in the interviews about Millennial females being more assertive, the findings are more nuanced. We did find that Millennial and Generation X females are more likely to use the competing style compared to Baby Boomer females, so there is a higher likelihood of the competitive conflict style with the assertive element in the younger female cohorts. Furthermore, when we drill down on individual time frames, we learn that that Millennial females in 2018 were more likely than Generation X females to employ a competing conflict style. However, there was no significant finding in the competing style comparison of same-age Millennial versus Generation X females.

Although not inclusive of every result given the breadth of this study, Table 8.4 provides the consolidated results of the predominant findings on the conflict styles of Millennials over the different studies in this research.

Politics, Diversity, and Social Media Use

Change is coming – Baby Boomers and Silents in the 2020 election no longer held a majority block with Millennials and Generation Xers making up 47% of the voters and Gen Z accounting for 8% of the voters per a 2021 Pew Research report (Igielnik et al., 2018). Breaking down the 47%, Millennial voters made up 22% of the vote and Generation Xer 25%. However, Generation Z, who made up only 8% of the 2020 vote, will continue to have a stronger voice in elections as they reach voting age. And we know that Generation Z and Millennials are similarly aligned on social and political issues (Parker et al., 2019). We also know that the majority of Millennials are Democratic or lean Democratic and favor a larger

Table 8.4 Consolidated Findings: Conflict Styles of Millennials versus
Other Generational Cohorts

Interviews and Focus Groups	13-Year Consolidated Statistical Analysis of Conflict Styles of Millennials, Gen Xers, and Baby Boomers	Same-Age Statistical Analysis of Millennials and Gen Xers
Millennials avoid conflict	Millennials *more* likely than Gen X and Baby Boomers to accommodate (unassertive and cooperative) Millennials *less* likely than Gen X and Baby Boomers to collaborate (assertive and cooperative) Conversely, Millennials *more* likely than Baby Boomers and Gen X to compete (but includes age 21/22 Millennials)	Millennials *more* likely than Gen X to avoid (unassertive and uncooperative) at 27/28 Millennials *more* likely than Gen X to accommodate (unassertive and cooperative) at 33/34 Gen X *more* likely than Millennials to collaborate (assertive and cooperative) at 27/28 Gen X *more* likely than Millennials to compete (assertive and uncooperative) at 33/34
Millennial males less assertive	Millennial males *more* likely than Gen X and Baby Boomer males to avoid (unassertive and uncooperative) Millennial males *more* likely than Gen X and Baby Boomer males to and accommodate (unassertive and cooperative)	Millennial males age 33/34 *more* likely to accommodate (unassertive and cooperative) than Gen X males Gen X males age 27/28 *more* likely to collaborate (assertive and cooperative) than Millennial males Gen X males age 33/34 males *more* likely to compete
Millennial females more assertive	Millennial females more likely than Baby Boomer females to compete (assertive and uncooperative) Millennial females in 2018 more likely than Gen X females to compete (assertive and uncooperative)	No significant difference in Millennial to Gen X females in competing style analysis Gen X females age 27/28 more likely to collaborate (assertive and cooperative)

Note. Based on analysis of the Thomas-Kilmann Conflict Mode Instrument data.

role for government including doing more for the needy and providing health care for all its citizens (Pew Research, 2018).

A democratic legislative agenda with a focus on social consciousness and a larger role for government, as supported by Millennials, has the potential to impact employment laws and transform the work environment. Looking at the workplace, companies that offer paid time off for volunteer work and support socially conscious initiatives should prove appealing to this cohort. Several Millennials interviewed for this study acknowledged their appreciation of paid time off from work to pursue volunteer activities that are important to them. It is interesting that this was mentioned exclusively by Millennials, with non-Millennials not discussing this as an important benefit.

Another issue analyzed to enlighten a Millennial future is the diversity and inclusiveness of this generation. Rather than focusing on nationalism and building a wall, Millennial's view openness to different people from around the world as critical to our nation and identity. Given Millennials' diversity, views on immigration, and openness to different people, Millennials can be expected to be advocates for economic and political change that aligns with these views and characteristics. Given that 68% of Millennials say that more needs to be done to give Black Americans equal rights (Pew Research, 2018), it can be expected that a political and social agenda for Millennials will include addressing discrimination. In organizations, addressing discrimination and providing equal rights will be key, and incorporating social consciousness into the workplace will resonate with Millennials.

When both Millennials and non-Millennials in this study were asked the same question about involvement in social causes, 50% of Millennials talked about causes of interest versus only 15% of non-Millennials. Millennials have engaged in protests from gun control following the Marjory Douglas Stoneman High School shooting to the more recent Black Lives Matter demonstrations. In addition, Millennials have increased their presence at the polling box, with youth voters increasing their participation from the 2004 Presidential election through the 2020 Presidential election. While Strauss and Howe predict that the expected progressive Millennial agenda will represent a political, economic, and social shift that may result in strife and conflict (Strauss & Howe, 1997; Howe & Strauss, 2000), the causes embraced by Millennials portend a focus on addressing discrimination and economic inequality.

To further understand Millennials' social views, data from Pew Research was used to explore the 2011 Youth and Economy survey finding that younger individuals are more likely to report conflict between rich and poor (Morin, 2012). Looking beyond age, an analysis was conducted to examine income levels and earnings satisfaction to understand how these impact one's view of class conflict. (For those of you interested in the methodology, a binary logistic regression was employed.) The results show that individuals satisfied with their incomes are 9% *less* likely to view conflict between rich and poor. Furthermore, while individuals with lower earnings were expected to be more likely to report conflict between rich and poor, the opposite was true. People with higher incomes, not lower incomes, are 4% *more* likely to view conflict. The Pew Research Center Youth and Economy survey was conducted in 2011, on the heels of the 2007 to 2009 Great Recession, a very difficult economic time for Millennials entering or new to the workforce. As such, dissatisfaction with their earnings may have impacted the larger number of Millennials reporting conflict between rich and poor.

Lastly, the impact of Millennials' use of social media was examined. This generation is driving social movements via Twitter and other technologies as shown with popular hashtags such as #NeverAgain, #Dreamers, #OccupyWallSt, #MeToo, #TimesUp, and #BlackLivesMatter. Given the ability of Millennials to leverage Twitter, TikTok, Instagram, Snapchat, YouTube, Facebook, WhatsApp, Telegram, and other platforms, organizations attuned to the social media use of Millennials will be better positioned to understand the needs of this group of employees.

Final Thoughts

Understanding how Millennials resolve conflict and what issues are most important to them will help organizations recruit and retain Millennials. It is important to point out that the patterns that emerge from this research provide overall insights about the Millennial generation rather than absolutes. When we look at the analysis of conflict styles, we see interesting differences by cohort and gender. However, these differences emerge over time and are not universal. As an example, we found that younger females are more likely than Baby Boomer females to use a competing conflict style. However, while this is a statistically significant finding, it will not apply to all younger females. It's important to seek to understand each individual. Also, remember that conflict styles may change under different circumstances and when different level employees interact.

While the findings are not universal, significant insights are revealed about Millennials overall including their less assertive conflict style, a narrowing of gender differences in how male and female Millennial's approach conflict, and the reliance on an online support group to help resolve conflict. These are all pieces of information that help us better understand Millennials. Furthermore, the engagement of Millennials in social movements and the political process can be expected to impact the future, consistent with their goals for a more democratic and inclusive society.

I suggest rather than thinking of Millennials as entitled, understand that they have high expectations which can lead to better outcomes. And while Millennials may not be as loyal to companies as previous generations, they have a loyalty and commitment to social causes, and are determined to affect positive change in our world. Furthermore, it's not that Millennials don't like to follow instructions; they think critically and look for new and better ways to approach problems. Lastly, don't think of Millennials as lazy – they work hard but want better work-life balance. And let's face it – they have a better grip on work life balance than older generations.

Millennials embrace the notion of YOLO – you only live once. Good for them to want to experience life and carve out personal time, returning to work re-energized and ready to contribute. Yes – they may be more apt to leave a job if dissatisfied, but workplaces that provide an environment that appeals to Millennials and allows them to reach their potential will reap the benefits. Don't forget the company that saved $750,000 by having Millennials design their internal website.

Today, we are hearing more about the Japanese concept of ikigai or finding one's purpose in life. In Japanese, "iki" often translated as life comes from the word "ikiru" which means to live and "gai" means value or worth. So, ikigai captures one's purpose for living. It's what drives us to get up every day. Hector Garcia and Francesu Miralles write about ikigai in their book, describing the large number of centenarians in Okinawa who stay active and pursue activities throughout their lifetimes that bring them joy and purpose (Garcia & Miralles, 2016).

YOLO and ikigai are concepts we are hearing more about, and while all generations pursue a purpose-driven life, perhaps Millennials are more adept at integrating their work environment with their drive for purpose. As such, Millennials will feel connected to organizations that align with their purpose-driven desires. While many organizations are not in a field directly associated with social causes important to Millennials, companies can still be involved with initiatives significant to this cohort. For example, a company can adopt climate change as an initiative and provide numerous options for employees to get involved from participating in local or national committees to allowing days off from work to attend events aimed at addressing climate change. Or companies can allow employees to select their cause of interest and provide ways within the workplace to support employees in pursuing those interests.

As we look to the future, Millennials are a ray of light. They are diverse, concerned with social issues, engaged with efforts to protect the environment, curious, well-educated, and technologically savvy. Millennials expect a lot and will work hard to get what they want. And they accept diversity and are focused on addressing social injustice, economic inequities, global warming, and other environmental issues. They ask questions that help us look at the way we've always done things. We know that businesses must continually evolve to stay competitive, and this questioning behavior, if harnessed properly, can positively contribute to the bottom line. Millennials are well poised to make this world a better place from the workplace to society overall.

References

Campbell, S.M., Twenge, J.M., & Campbell, W.K. (2017). Fuzzy but useful constructs: Making sense of the differences between generations. *Work, Aging and Retirement, 3*(2), 130–139.

Cilluffo, A., & Fry, R. (2019, May 29). *GenZ, Millennials, and GenX outvoted older generations in 2018 midterms.* Pew Research Center. https://www.pewresearch.org/fact-tank/2019/05/29/gen-z-millennials-and-gen-x-outvoted-older-generations-in-2018-midterms/

DeVaney, S.A. (2015). Understanding the millennial generation. *Journal of Financial Service Professionals, 69*(6), 11–14.

Foster, J., Campbell, K., & Twenge, J. (2003). Individual differences in narcissism: Inflated self-views across the lifespan and around the world. *Journal of Research in Personality, 37*, 469–486. https://doi.org/10.1016/S0092–6566(03)00026-6

Garcia, H., & Miralles, F. (2016). *Ikigai: The Japanese secret to a long and happy life.* Penguin Books.

Ghitza, Y., & Robinson, J. (2021, November 5). *What happened in 2020 national analysis.* Catalist. https://catalist.us/wh-national/

Graf, N. (2017, May 16). *Today's young workers are more likely than ever to have a bachelor's degree.* Pew Research Center. https://www.pewresearch.org/fact-tank/2017/05/16/todays-young-workers-are-more-likely-than-ever-to-have-a-bachelors-degree/

Hartman, J. L., & McCambridge, J. (2011). Optimizing Millennials' communication styles. *Business Communication Quarterly, 74*(1), 22–44.

Holt, J. L., Devore, C. J. (2005). Culture, gender, organizational role, and styles of conflict resolution: A meta-analysis. *International Journal of Intercultural Relations, 29*(2), 165–196. https://doi.org/10.1016/j.ijintrel.2005.06.002

Howe, N., & Strauss, W. (2000). *Millennials rising: The next great generation.* Vintage Books.

Igielnik, R., Keeter, S., & Hartig, H. (2021, September 30). *Behind Biden's 2020 victory.* Pew Research Center – U.S. Politics & Policy. https://www.pewresearch.org/politics/2021/06/30/behind-bidens-2020-victory/

Kilmann, R., & Thomas, K. (1977). Developing a forced-choice measure of conflict handling behavior: The "mode" instrument. *Educational and Psychological Measurement, 37*(2), 309–325.

Kilmann, R.H., & Thomas, K.W. (2009). *Conflict mode instrument.* Mountain View.

Morin, Rich. (2012, January 11). *Rising share of Americans see conflict between rich and poor.* Pew Research Center. http://www.pewsocialtrends.org/2012/01/11/-rising-share-of-americans-see-conflict-between-rich-and-poor/

Nisen, M. (2015, August 18). *How Millennials forced GE to scrap performance reviews: Known for its "rank and yank" reviews, the company has switched to a performance app.* The Atlantic. https://www.theatlantic.com/politics/archive/2015/08/how-millennials-forced-ge-to-scrap-performance-reviews/432585/

Parker, K., Graf, N., & Igielnik, R. (2019, January 17). Generation Z looks a lot like Millennials on key social and political issues. Pew Research. https://www.pewresearch.org/social-trends/2019/01/17/generation-z-looks-a-lot-like-millennials-on-key-social-and-political-issues/

Pew Research Center. (2007, January 7). *How young people view their lives, futures and roles: A portrait of "generation next."* http://www.pewresearch.org/wp-content/uploads/sites/3/2010/10/300.pdf

Pew Research Center. (2011, December 6). *December 2011 youth and economy survey final questionnaire.* http://www.pewsocialtrends.org/2013/02/22/youth-economy/

Pew Research Center. (2018, March 1). *The generation gap in American politics: Wide and growing divides in views of racial discrimination.* http://www.people-press.org/2018/03/01/the-generation-gap-in-american-politics/

Rosenthiel, T. (2008, November 13). *Young voters in the 2008 election.* Pew Research Center. https://www.pewresearch.org/2008/11/13/young-voters-in-the-2008-election/

Sessa, V.I., Kabacoff, R.I., Deal, J., & Brown, H. (2007). Generational differences in leader values and leadership behaviors. The Psychologist-Manager Journal, 10(1), 47–74.

Strauss, W., & Howe, N. (1997). *The fourth turning: An American prophecy.* Broadway Books.

Thomas, K., Thomas, G., Schaubhut, N. (2008). Conflict styles of men and women at six organizational levels. *International Journal of Conflict Management*, 19(2), 148–166.

Twenge, J.M., Konrath, S., Foster, J.D., Campbell, W.K., & Bushman, B.J. (2008). Egos inflating over time: A crosstemporal meta-analysis of the Narcissistic Personality Inventory. *Journal of Personality, 76*(4), 875–901.

Index